Communities of Resistance

Communities of Resistance

Writings on Black Struggles for Socialism

A. SIVANANDAN

VERSO

London · New York

First published by Verso 1990
© A. Sivanandan 1990
All rights reserved

Verso
UK: 6 Meard Street, London W1V 3HR
USA: 29 West 35th Street, New York, NY 10001-2291

Verso is the imprint of New Left Books

British Library Cataloguing in Publication Data

Sivanandan, A. (Ambalavaner) *1923–*
    Communities of resistance : writings on black struggles
for socialism.
    1. Great Britain. Racism. Political aspects
    I. Title
    323.141

    ISBN 0-86091-296-5
    ISBN 0-86091-514-X pbk

US Library of Congress Cataloging-in-Publication Data

Sivanandan, Ambalavaner.
    Communities of resistance : writings on Black struggles for
socialism / A. Sivanandan.
        p.   cm.
    ISBN 0-86091-296-5. – ISBN 0-86091-514-X (pbk.)
    1. Blacks—Great Britain—Politics and government.   2. Blacks—
Great Britain—Social conditions.   3. Socialism—Developing
countries.   4. Socialism—Great Britain.   5. Racism—Great Britain.
I. Title.
DA125.A1S57   1990
305.8'96041—dc20

Typeset in Baskerville by Leaper & Gard Ltd, Bristol, England
Printed in Finland by Werner Söderström Oy

For Jabe – beyond owing

Contents

Acknowledgements   ix

1   The Heart Is Where the Battle Is: An Interview with
    the Author   1

RECLAIMING THE FIGHT   17

2   All that Melts into Air Is Solid: The Hokum
    of New Times   19

RECLAIMING THE FIGHT AGAINST RACISM   61

3   Challenging Racism: Strategies for the 1980s   63
4   RAT and the Degradation of Black Struggle   77
5   Blacks and the Black Sections   123

FOR SOCIALISM   129

6   Britain's Gulags   131

7 Race, Class and Brent   138
8 Left, Right and Burnage   145
9 Racism 1992   153

SOCIALISM AND IMPERIALISM   161

10 Warren and the Third World   163
11 New Circuits of Imperialism   169

RACE, CLASS AND STATE IN POST-COLONIAL
SOCIETIES   197

12 Sri Lanka: A Case Study   199

Acknowledgements

'All that Melts into Air Is Solid' was first published in *Race & Class*, vol. 31, no. 3 (1990); 'Challenging Racism' in *Race & Class*, vol. XXV, no. 2 (1983); 'RAT and the Degradation of Black Struggle' in *Race & Class*, vol. XXVI, no. 4 (1985); 'Blacks and the Black Sections' in *Searchlight* (October 1985); 'Britain's Gulags' in *New Socialist* (November 1985); 'Race, Class and Brent' in *Race & Class*, vol. 29, no. 1 (1987); 'Left, Right and Burnage' in *New Statesman* (27 May 1988); 'Racism 1992' in *New Statesman & Society* (4 November 1988); 'Warren and the Third World' in *Race & Class*, vol. XXIV, no. 2 (1982); 'New Circuits of Imperialism' in *Race & Class*, vol. 30, no. 3 (1989); 'Sri Lanka: A Case Study' in *Race & Class*, vol. XXVI, no.1 (1984).

===================== 1 =====================

The Heart Is Where the Battle Is

An Interview with the Author

A. Sivanandan

How did British politics and culture first impinge upon you?

They did not really impinge as such; British culture and politics were what I was born into. They were already there, they formed me. It was not so much British politics as British administration that pervaded everything – schools, professions, the running of the country, the post office, the railways. And it was in these areas of the British administration that a lot of the English-educated people like myself, and my father before me, came into contact with British culture. Of course we came into contact with British culture first via education – particularly the Tamils because we come from the North of Sri Lanka (Ceylon as it then was) and the North is arid country where nothing grows except children. There are no mountains or rivers, the water is saline, the farms are not large holdings but small plots.

My grandfather was one of the smallest of smallholders and his chief ambition was to send his sons to an 'English school' (where, that is, the medium of instruction was English) so that they could learn English and thereby find 'proper jobs' and some sort of economic and social mobility. That was the ambition of most people in the North and in all the Tamil areas.

1

My father finally made it from the Tamil-medium school to an English-medium school by the time he was thirteen or fourteen, just for a couple of years, and then entered the postal service as a clerk. And his ambition, in turn, was to send his children to the foremost English schools and give them a better chance of entering the professions or leading a better social life. Because he was in the postal service, the British Raj transferred him from one malarial station to another. These civil servants (both Tamils and Sinhalese, but mainly Tamils) were the pioneers who opened up the country, the jungles and uninhabited areas, for British colonisation.

The best schools were in the metropolis, Colombo, in the Sinhala South, and were often run by Catholic or Anglican religious orders. And because my education was disrupted by my father being transferred from place to place, I was sent to live in Colombo.

My life was full of contradictions. I came from a poor peasant background, I attended a Catholic 'public school' and lived with an impoverished uncle in a Sinhalese slum. I was a Tamil and a Hindu having to attend Catholic religious knowledge classes, sometimes attending mass and benediction, and at the same time going to temple on a Friday with my uncles, aunts and cousins like any Hindu should. Inside me then, Western culture and religion were being mixed up with Hinduism; the urban with the rural; the aspiring poor boy who wanted to become middle-class was learning the culture of the slum.

I suppose that is rather an abstract way of describing my conflicts (with the benefit of hindsight). The way I lived through them was often agonising. There was, first and foremost, behind everything, the knowledge that it was my duty as the eldest son of a fairly poor family to go through school and college, hopefully to university, and then get a good job and so be able to help my parents to look after the family. That sense of responsibility – that sense of what Nyerere meant when he said 'We must return our education to the people who gave it to us' – overlaid most of the conflicts I suffered. And yet there were experiences that tore me apart. Going back every holiday to my village, it was a wrench when I realised little by little that my cousins there were being left far behind me in educational terms. Even when it came to playing village cricket, I, as a fourteen-year-old, would play for the first eleven, which showed that the boys who went to public school in Colombo had a prowess beyond the boys in the village. There was a searing gap between me and my contemporaries which was painful because I wanted so much to belong to the village. And then again there was the other side of me – the one that wanted to belong to Colombo and my English school and my pukka friends. I remember most acutely my sense of betrayal when I disowned my favourite aunt when she came to visit me in school, because she was shabby and unshod, and I made out to my school-friends that she was some sort of family servant.

You were being formed educationally in the colonial image, you were being educated for a typical comprador class. But you didn't end up there. Why do you think that was?

I think that it's a mistake to think of colonialism as a one-way street, as something that is done to you, as something that takes you over, something so powerful you can't resist it. There is always a resistance somewhere that comes out of your own culture, your language, your religion. And that resistance first takes the form of an existential rebellion – a rebellion against everything that goes against your grain.

Maybe the fact that, though I was Hindu, I was forced by some of the fathers to go to church, to follow catechism classes, gave me occasion for rebellion. I remember how much I jibbed at that. There were lots of aspects of that education that I resisted but I still did not find an alternative.

I could have gone one of two ways, I suppose. I could have become totally Tamil, totally Hindu, totally Ceylonese. I could have gone into a retrogressive nationalism, tried to put the clock back and denied the fact that the British and the

3

Dutch and the Portuguese had influenced our cultures, educational system, politics, our sense of ourselves even. (And there *was* a feeling in me that if I went back to the temple, learnt more about my culture, I would find refuge from Catholicism, from colonialism, from the British Raj.) On the other hand, I knew that if I wanted to get places, to look after the poorer members of my family, to become a barrister (as I wanted to at one time), to go to England some day, to the Inner Temple or to university, then I had to go along with the system, I had to become a 'comprador', as you say. But I didn't see it like that, it was just a way of going up in the world, economically and socially. The choice, in other words, was between becoming a nationalist and becoming a comprador.

And which did you choose to become?

One does not actually choose to become this or that in my sort of circumstances. It was more that by the time I was entering university, all the other contradictions we have been speaking about – the urban–rural and all that stuff – had boiled down to this gigantic contradiction between nationalism and cosmopolitanism. And I suppose I was one thing one minute and the other the next.

So by the time you went to university you were caught in this one big contradiction yet you weren't a political person. What was the intellectual trajectory that led you to become political? Presumably you didn't become a Marxist overnight?

I don't know whether I am a Marxist. Marxism for me is not a dogma, a faith; it is a way of understanding the world – in order to change it. As for my being a political person, I don't think you can ever talk about politics (with a small p) being absent from a colony. All colonised peoples have, all the time, a subliminal sense of politics, a sense of power or rather of powerlessness.

4

And therefore one is not removed from politics. All the contradictions I've been talking about are societal conflicts which are personalised for one by the nature of colonial society – by the deracination that one undergoes and then by the way one questions that deracination. Politics is part of the atmosphere of powerlessness in which one is brought up, within which one goes to school, within which one relates to one's family, within which one relates to poorer as opposed to richer members of one's family.

But what the university did was to formulate that politics – especially because I did political science and economics – and tell me how to look at society. What opened me up was looking at various political theories and going through the writings of such people as Hobbes and Locke, Rousseau, Owen and Proudhon and Fourier and finally finding Marx. Or, rather, finding dialectical materialism and, in it, finding a way of analysing my own society, a way of resolving my own social contradictions, a way of understanding how conflict itself was the motor of one's personal life as well as the combusting force of the society in which one lived. That tool of analysis that Marxism gave me in dialectical materialism was 'the moment of a miracle' which, in Dylan Thomas's phrase, is 'unending lightning'. And I was later, much later, to discover with the poets and the novelists that the dialectic was not just a tool of analysis but a felt sensibility.

It's ironic, in a way, that this British education, which was teaching you all that was good about your coloniser and the coloniser's language, was also that which was giving you the wherewithal to fight them.

Yes and no. It was the progressive, anti-colonial, subaltern aspects of British culture, not the dominant aspects of British culture, which influenced me. Those tendencies which were Left, and came out at that time principally from the London School of Economics, were what we principally imbibed. Harold Laski, whose *Grammar of Politics* I was weaned on,

Maurice Dobb, Joan Robinson, the Webbs, the Fabians, those sort of thinkers – and I'll never forget the day I stumbled on T.A. Jackson's *Dialectics* in an old bottle-shop. That was a blinder.

It was after the war – our countries were becoming independent and nationalism both in India and in Ceylon was in its progressive phase, anti-imperialist and pro-working class. Many of our lecturers had been educated at the LSE. And they came back with very radical ideas. They had absorbed some of the British Left traditions and became the conduits through which those traditions passed on to us.

Quite a few of them were members of Left parties – either the Communist Party or, more usually, the Trotskyist Lanka Sama Samaja Party (LSSP). And therefore their teaching was not merely theoretical but also practical and we followed them, in a sense, from the school-house into the street. So politics was not just what we learnt as part of our degree syllabus but also those activities we took part in outside university hours when we went to public meetings, or attended various LSSP study groups and societies.

These teachers opened us up to a Left British culture which was anti-subjugation and spoke to the British working-class struggles for liberty and equality. But they taught us in such a way as to make us see parallels in our own society and open us out to the possibilities for struggle for our own working people. We were not taught English literature without a Left analysis being brought into it. In the *Wife of Bath's Tale* we saw parallels with our own wives' tales, poems, folklore. They taught us to nativise the insights of these authors, so to speak – to appropriate them so as to enrich, not to be a substitute for, our own experience – to take out the universal in them and apply it to our own particularities. They localised Chaucer while still leaving him in England. And that opened us out to all sorts of other possibilities. In music, for instance. I was steeped in Sinhalese and Tamil music – particularly Tamil *thēvārums* (hymns) – but when I now heard the Gregorian chant I could see how it resonated with the religious music of our own people. And your minstrels and early poets harked me back to our Sinhalese poets who went from village to village singing out their social poetry from *ōla* scrolls in the marketplace.

I was formed, I suppose, by that move and mix of cultures fighting for an independent Ceylon. And that is perhaps why I still think that culture is something dynamic, moving, forged in the crucible of struggle, and not some preordained, congealed set of artefacts, folklore (which incidentally is what multiculturalism is about).

Did you then, on leaving university, become an active left-wing campaigner? You also had to get a job, you had people to support.

The whole of the first part of my life, in a manner of speaking, was taken up in resolving one set of contradictions and coming up against others. I left the university with a degree but because I didn't come from a rich family and didn't have connections, the amount of influence that my family could wield was very little. Since nepotism didn't help me I had to go and teach. (Those from poor families who got degrees went and taught, those from rich families who got degrees went into law, medical college or became upper-crust civil servants, police superintendents, prison chiefs.)

I first taught in a small mixed school in the tea country where the pupils were mainly the children of poor Sinhalese workers, with a sprinkling of Indian Tamil children from the plantations who were the poorest of the poor and had no access to proper schooling at all. From there I went to teach in the hill country among the Kandyan peasantry. Both were very important experiences. I had known the Tamil country, I had known the cosmopolitan life of the metropolis and now I had, by living among the plantation workers on the estates, got to understand how debased the plantation workers were, and in Kandy I came across the landless Sinhala peasantry whose paddyfields had been taken over for tea plantations. I was getting an understanding of the social formations of my country first-hand. Later, that helped me to see how it was that British and other colonialisms had impacted on our countries at different historical periods, on different parts of the country, in many different ways, and thrown up such diverse social formations within one small country – left us underdeveloped in different ways and shored up the differences between the peoples of our country which then became defined in ethnic or racial terms.

Was it a smooth transition, your development from teacher in the plantation areas of Sri Lanka to left-wing thinker here in Britain?

Oh no. I suppose the colonised go through violent contradictions – comprador one minute, reactionary nationalist the next, progressive lefty the next. Teaching was so poorly paid that it didn't give me enough to meet my family obligations. So finally I got into a bank as a Staff Officer and soon Deputy Manager. Those of us who had degrees were few and far between in Ceylon at the time, and as the banks were being nationalised (that is, Ceylonised), Ceylonese nationals were put in positions of authority. If you had a degree you did not rise from the ranks, you went straight away into an administrative job.

I had joined the bank for family reasons but the status it conferred on me predicated a certain lifestyle which required that I wear silk shirts from Hong Kong, run a motor car, have servants, belong to clubs, drink imported German lager from fluted glasses under the temple trees in the garden of some other comprador or other – the income tax commissioner perhaps, or maybe a barrister or an FRCS. But at the same time I was uneasy about that life, partly because when I went home to my parents or back to my village and saw the poverty there, all that made me ashamed of my own prosperity. And I also found that the bank clerks who worked under me, who probably came out of the same slums that I had known, were

8

the people I could be easy with, go drinking with after work. Going to their homes and seeing how they lived, and how exploited they were, affected me. The first sort of bank clerks' union in the Bank of Ceylon was something that was talked about and given form to in my own house.

Because of this I was constantly at loggerheads with the management, which happened to be British, and I was often in a lot of trouble. I never got promoted.

I was also in trouble with my parents at this time because I fell in love with a Sinhalese Catholic girl and had a runaway marriage – you see how the objective contradictions become subjective? Her parents and my parents were both antagonistic towards such 'mixed marriages', let alone unarranged ones.

But then in 1958 the 'riots' broke out between the Sinhalese and the Tamils. My father's house was attacked and I had to go disguised as a cop with an empty rifle in my hand to get my parents away from a screaming mob. I saw people being killed just by virtue of the fact that they were Tamil; people being burnt alive. Meanwhile the Sinhala Buddhist government, devoted to non-violence, did nothing. Educated people in high places did nothing. The press and the radio did nothing. Sinhalese–Tamil friendship ceased at the midnight hour. The whole decadence and degradation of our people stank in my nostrils. I couldn't take it any more. I just wanted to get away from my country. So I chucked in my job, sold whatever belongings I had and just pushed off to England. And I came and lived in Bayswater and walked straight into the 'riots' in Notting Hill.

That was, I suppose, a double baptism of fire – Sinhalese–Tamil riots there, white–black riots here. And I knew then I was black. I could no longer stand on the sidelines; race was a problem that affected me directly. I had no excuse to go into banking or anything else that I was fitted up to do – yes, fitted up. I had to find a way of making some sort of contribution to the improvement of society, to bring about a society where human beings could be human. And I wanted time to read and reflect and to become active. (There was plenty of discrimination; even with a degree and banking qualifications I couldn't get into a bank in any case: blacks, then, were not trusted in banks.) So I started off as a tea-boy in a public library in Middlesex. And I went on to do my library exams by attending evening classes. From tea-boy I became branch manager of that particular library and then finally I went to be librarian at the Institute of Race Relations in 1964.

Most of your political writing, that people are familiar with anyway, has been done since you worked at the Institute but your thinking and writing were actually tied up with transforming the place where you worked. Presumably you saw that transformation as also part of that idea of 'returning your education', that improving of society, that you were talking about?

I have always felt that living and working and doing are not separate things. One should try to change things not only 'out there in society' but in oneself, in the place where one works, in one's everyday life. The 1960s was the period of Black Power, the decolonisation of Africa, the Vietnam War. Black Power, in particular, spoke to me very directly because it was about race and class both at once. More than that, it was about the politics of existence. And therefore I felt the work of a place such as the Institute of Race Relations – set up as an independent body to do objective research into the relations between white and non-white peoples all over the world – could not keep colonialism out of its remit, could not keep out capitalism; it had to look at various aspects of society which were not necessarily conducive to the academic study of race relations. The IRR hierarchy wanted to look at race relations in an abstract sort of way. But I felt that the study of race relations should help towards the abolition of racism. The Institute could not stand on the sidelines, particularly when successive British governments, Labour and Tory, were passing racist immigration laws.

10

Can you describe a little what the organisation was like in the 1960s and what it became?

The Institute was set up as a branch of the Royal Institute of International Affairs in the 1950s and became independent soon after the 'riots' in 1958. It was supposed to be devoted to the objective study of race relations here and elsewhere (in a slightly policy-oriented way). But after the 1962 Immigration Act it began to take the government's view that controlling immigration was necessary to improve race relations. The fewer the blacks, the easier their integration. No blacks, no problem – it was all a matter of numbers. Hitler said the same sort of thing.

The Institute, which was supposed to be independent in its thinking, was funded by big business – Shell, Nuffield, Rockefeller, Ford – and the governing council had people like Oppenheimer (of the Anglo–American Corporation of South Africa), Prain (of the RST Group), Seebohm (of Barclays Bank) and Caine (of Bookers) running the place. Most of the early studies looked into Africa and other newly-developing countries with a view to seeing how business could invest there. That seemed to be the underlying purpose in the international field for the study of race relations. Improving race relations was a way of improving business opportunities in newly-independent countries which would no longer accept British overlordship. So if you were going to work with the comprador classes in the newly-independent countries, you had to stop saying that they were inferior to you, that their cultures were inferior to yours and declare that we were all brothers under the same capitalist skin.

In 1972 the members of the IRR outvoted the old guard and brought in a new Council composed of those who worked in and for the community. Can you say briefly what the new Institute stood for and, more importantly, how it survived? There are a lot of so-called revolutions that took place in institutions in the 1960s that died.

The Institute was part of the Establishment. It was controlled and in part financed by big business; it spoke to government concerns and also had pretensions to establishing race relations as an academic field of study. But all its concerns bore little relation to what black people were undergoing here in terms of racism and in the Third World in terms of colonialism and imperialism. And it was in trying to air these views and concerns at conferences and in the Institute's journal that the staff fell foul of the management and the battle for the Institute began. The details of the actual struggle within the Institute have been related elsewhere but in sum the issues that the staff, backed by most of the Institute's members, fought over were academic and journalistic freedom. Behind these issues, though, was the feeling that the Institute was interested not so much in studying ways of alleviating racism as in providing a rationale for government policies, providing a sort of research credibility for state racism – or that at least was where its policy-oriented research was pointing. And it was inevitable that as racism got worse (with 'Paki-bashing', police violence, ESN schooling, passport raids and so on) that a crisis of conscience should be thrown up in an Institute such as ours. It had to change.

But the second point of your question is the more interesting – how we lived to tell the tale. There were many crises we went through, not least financial (because the old boy network, we found out first-hand, really did control all the trusts and funding agencies). The answer, I believe, lies in the fact that the staff, the members and the new Council of Management, mostly Institute members who had fought alongside us, began to have a real vested interest in the work – vested interest in the sense of wanting to educate the public in combating racism – by putting the resources and services of the Institute to use in a new way, in a way that would benefit 'the victims' of racism, so to speak. The Institute became a sort of think-tank, a think-in-order-to-do-tank, for black and Third World peoples. The function of knowledge, we held (rather grandly perhaps), was to liberate. But, grand or not, we were at last working with, and responsive to, black and Third World groups as had never before been possible.

We were creating our own priorities, changing the terms of debate, charting all those new areas where the fight against racism had to be taken up – in academe, in the media, in government. We perhaps gave a lead in these matters at that time but there were very many people in all sorts of community groups and organisations who had been just waiting for such perspectives. And, in that sense the Institute became far more than a professional organisation or a research body; it was rather a servicer of movements.

In this collection of writings you are taking on questions of both racism and imperialism. In the 1960s this wouldn't have been a surprising connection in writings from the USA or UK. But today the connection is far less in evidence, yet it's a line to which Race & Class, *the journal you edit, consciously adheres. Can you explain that connection, that philosophy if you like, that comprehends this collection?*

Do you remember what W.E.B. DuBois said in 1903? 'The problem of the twentieth century is the problem of the colour line.' Today the colour line is the poverty line is the power line. We are non-white, we are poor, we are powerless. And that which establishes the connection between them is capitalism; that which perpetuates it is imperialism. Except for a handful of black elites who are doing pretty well, the majority of non-white peoples of the world are poor, and powerless to do anything about their poverty. And they are kept that way by imperialism. That is why you cannot fight racism without also fighting imperialism. You cannot fight for the cause of black people without fighting for the cause of working people. You cannot fight black oppression without fighting black exploitation. You cannot, in the final instance, fight oppression without at the same time fighting exploitation – or you end up exchanging one oppression for another.

13

The Third World has been lost to view in the last 15 or 20 years – lost to view in the deliberations of the Left because in today's global factories, the low-paid workers who do the dirty jobs are literally out there in the Third World and not here in public view or, if here, only as invisible migrant sweatshop and service workers. The Left in the West has failed to understand the changes that are going on in terms of the qualitative leap in the level of the productive forces, they fail to see that our standard of living depends upon the exploitation of an international working class. Instead they say 'farewell to the working class' (as though theirs is the only one), elevate the new social movements of women, blacks, gays, greens, etc., as the agents of change and treat the Third World as an object of Western charity.

Race & Class poses a counter view. It sees the relationship of racism and imperialism as a symbiotic one; the fact that black and Third World peoples are in the 'First' World is directly connected to the presence of the 'First World' in the form of multinationals, of superpower machinations in the Third World. Yet *Race & Class* never subsumes race under class. It looks at race in terms of class, while at the same time bringing to an understanding of the class struggle the racial dimension. I suppose that is what distinguishes us from other Left, Marxist or Third World journals. We do not have a line as such but we have certain criteria which emerged in the wake of the struggle to transform the Institute and, in particular, of the struggle over the function of knowledge itself.

Since imperialism has distorted the histories of Third World countries and sought to set Third World peoples against each other, *Race & Class* tries to bring out the common denominators of oppression and exploitation and point the way to a common struggle. There is a task for those of us 'within the belly of the whale' to analyse and write about Third World struggles but I do not think it is our business to be sectarian, to take sides between liberation movements, to tell them how to conduct their struggles. We try in *Race &*

14

Class to guard against a sort of Left cultural imperialism: the tendency to extrapolate from the Western experience onto Third World societies. That might mean turning the equation round to see what we can learn from a particular tendency or movement in the Third World.

Very often *Race & Class* exposes those aspects of traditional scholarship – in sociology, history, philosophy, science, maths or whatever – that have in-built cultural and class biases. It tries to create new scholarships, if you like, new ways of analysing, tries to retrieve the people's history of an event or period – be it the testimony of Broadwater Farm residents or a re-evaluation of Mau Mau. Above all, it tries to bridge the gap between theory and practice, academia and the grassroots. We are trying, all the time, to ensure that the people we are writing for are the people we are fighting for.

The sub-title of this book, 'writings on black struggles for socialism', is intriguing. That juxtaposition, implying that black struggles are for socialism, hasn't been expressed like that before. But you obviously think it sums up your writing, certainly in this collection?

Any struggles of the oppressed, be it blacks or women, which are only for themselves and then not for the least of them, the most deprived, the most exploited of them, are inevitably self-serving and narrow and unable to enlarge the human condition. It's not just a question of having the experience of oppression and missing its meaning but also of failing to make the meaning flesh. Maybe that's why my writings are mainly about the liberatory aspects of black struggle and on the sites relevant to that struggle. The black middle class, Black Sections, blacks in academia do not interest me. The question for me is: what is it in the black and Third World experience, in the experience of the oppressed and the exploited, that gives one the imagination to see other oppressions and the will to fight for a better society for all, a more equal, just, free society, a socialist society?

15

Any liberation struggle which is not socialist in the first instance ends up in tyranny. The means are the ends, there can be no distinction between them. There is no socialism after liberation, socialism is the process through which liberation is won.

And, for you personally, where is your struggle? Do you feel you are in a kind of exile? Where are you at home?

I am at home in myself; and myself is all these experiences, cultures, value-systems that I have gone through. I don't consider myself an exile because I would have to ask myself then what am I exiled from. I may be in the literal sense exiled from my country, but today, at the end of the twentieth century, when all our boundaries are breaking down, we should be looking not to roots in some place but to resources within ourselves for our understanding of our place in society, our place in a particular country, our place in culture. For me to feel truly 'an exile' would be to be exiled from the struggles of the black and Third World peoples I know so well and from whom I come. And the struggle is where I am, the struggle is here and now. But, of course, I carry a double consciousness with me: that of my place in this society, my place in the struggle of black, working-class people here and now, and that of my place in the struggles of Third World peoples in Third World countries both here and there. And I am not exiled from that. I may not be in the vortex of those struggles but I am involved in them. And therefore I do not understand the question of exile. I do not understand the question of domicile. The heart is where the battle is.

Interview by Quintin Hoare and Malcolm Imrie

Reclaiming the Fight

2

All that Melts into Air Is Solid: The Hokum of New Times*

New Times is a fraud, a counterfeit, a humbug. It palms off Thatcherite values as socialist, shores up the Thatcherite market with the pretended politics of choice, fits out the Thatcherite individual with progressive consumerism, makes consumption itself the stuff of politics. New Times is a mirror image of Thatcherism passing for socialism. New Times is Thatcherism in drag.**

Inevitably – since New Times' gestation in *Marxism Today* was marked by the latter's preoccupation with finding an electoral riposte to Thatcherism, in oppositional politics, taking a cue from Tory successes at the polls to formulate a programme for an anti-Thatcherite coalition of forces.[1] What was it about Thatcherism that appealed to such vast cross-sections of people? How could it be turned to Labour's benefit? How should Labour itself change in terms of principles, policies, pacts, in order to wrest the electorate from Thatcher?

---

* Dedicated to those friends with whom, out of a different loyalty, I must now openly disagree.
** I am interested here in the 'economic, social and political shape' of New Times as presented in the special issue of *Marxism Today* (October 1988) and elsewhere, not in the eclectic manifesto for New Times as presented to the Communist Party of Great Britain (CPGB).

There was an appreciation in these questions of the massive changes that Thatcherism was bringing about in society while Labour was still sulking in a troglodyte past, but, as yet, there was no understanding of the basis on which the Tories were able to carry these changes through. The answers owed not a little, therefore, to the Tory vision of change and tended to appropriate those areas in which the Tories were operating successfully (markets, share-ownership, council housing) to see how they could be recast in a Leftish mode or mould. There was no understanding, that is, that the 'ideological hegemony' that *Marxism Today* was so quick to construct for Thatcherism was based on the Tories' instinctive and profound understanding of the sea-change in capitalist society issuing from the technological revolution in production, and of the consequent need to give people direction, guidance, ballast, 'assure them of certain certainties'. Labour was adrift, rudderless, its moorings in the working class unhinged by the dissipation of the class itself, and hanging on to the driftwood of trade unionism, while Thatcherism charted an assured and defiant course through troublesome seas. 'Authoritarian populism' only explained why Thatcherism had found a hold among the people, but not why people were prepared to put up with it.

There was no attempt on the part of *Marxism Today* to rethink society from the ground up in terms of Marxist analysis – no attempt to rethink Marxism itself on the basis of the new liberatory revolution in the production process. But, then, they had already arrived at a reinterpretation of Marxism down a different route: through a disillusion with Soviet communism and a leaning towards its revised mode in Euro-communism. The first acknowledged the failure of 'actually existing socialism' to enlarge bourgeois democracy and enrich individual freedom, and the second subscribed to the view that the only way the working class was ever going to capture power in advanced capitalist societies was through bourgeois electoral politics and not through violent revolution. The split

20

within the CPGB, with the 'old guard' taking the *Morning Star* (the party newspaper) and the new appropriating *Marxism Today* (the party journal), signalled the change in the journal's direction towards a politics of the possible. But as yet it did not know quite what it stood for or where it was going. What was its philosophy? How did it see the world? Throwing out revolution and class war empirically was all very well, but where was the ideological underpinning for it? What was the journal's constituency? To whom was it speaking if no longer to the working class? Where would it locate itself, find domicile?

In the beginning ...

The philosophy came from the theoretical practitioners whose own disillusion with communism and Marxist orthodoxy sent them back to re-examining the original texts in search of the true Marxism, reinterpreting them for our times and setting up schools of thought, in the process, to interpret the reinterpretations and to announce, through sundry disciplines and theories (philosophy, linguistics, semiotics, psychoanalysis, post-structuralism, deconstruction ...), the consummate and conclusive finding that reality itself was a matter of interpretation, construction, presentation – of words, ideas, images. 'Philosophers', they might have said with a nod to Marx, 'have interpreted the world; our task is to change the interpretation.' And in an information society where 'the word is ... as "material" as the world'[2] and a consumer society where the mode of presentation is all, their claims found a ready home in a 'with-it' *Marxism Today.*

The ideology, along with the constituency, came from another strand of intellectual Marxism* which provided theor-

---

* I am not interested here in distinguishing the various strands of Marxism or in periodising their appearance(s).

etical confirmation that economic determinism and class reductionism were non-Marxist and things of the past. The economic base did not determine, even 'in the last instance', the ideological and political superstructure. They were all more or less 'autonomous instances', 'articulating' with each other, influencing and being influenced, in all sorts of 'conjunctures'. Politics, therefore, was a matter of positioning in and through and *vis-à-vis* these conjunctures – and culture was the mode in which such positioning was expressed. Hence there was a cultural politics (as distinct from a political culture) or, rather, all sorts of cultural politics which, having challenged all sorts of 'social blocs' in civil society, would at some auspicious moment of time come together in a network of alliances heralding the transition from capitalism (to what they are not sure). Accordingly, the agent of change in the contemporary world was not the working class – which, in any case, had ceased to be (if it ever was) a class for itself and was therefore incapable of revolution – but the new social forces such as women, blacks, gays (and, soon, greens) who were themselves informed and impelled by the politics of the person. Later, the 'new Marxists' would try to usher in a dimension of class through the back door of 'the politics of difference' but, for the nonce, it was the new social forces, irrespective of their differing class personae, which were the carriers of the new socialism or, rather, the trackers of the transition.

These, at any rate, were the building blocks of new Marxist arguments, refine them how they would. How they put them together, from time to time, as required by various 'conjunctures', would of course differ from the way that I have played around with them here. But that is the great strength of this sort of autonomy: it allows you to be *ad hoc*, opportune, open-ended, pluralist. The only thing you have got to be sure of is your identity – and there was a politics around that too, autonomous of course, that you needed to construct, but to that anon.

22

As for domicile, location, *Marxism Today* was to find these in the thinking of a Left intelligentsia eviscerated of class and the counsels of a Labour Party thrashing around for a showing at the polls. In France and Italy the Eurocommunists were parties in their own electoral right, but in Britain *Marxism Today*, having broken with the 'Stalinists', had no comparable base – nor, presumably, having broken so violently with the theory and practice of the vanguard party, could it countenance one. Labour, besides, was the established party of socialism. The point was to influence it, infiltrate it or, more accurately, 'hegemonise' it. (Old Marxists infiltrate, new Marxists 'hegemonise'.)*

Thus, New Times was born in the throes of political pragmatism under the sign of cultural theory bereft of economic reasoning. And the last proved disabling of the whole project. For, in throwing out the tool of economic analysis along with the ideological baggage of economism, the new Marxists were unable to bring to New Times the understanding that all the seismic changes in society and culture that they were so adroitly and bravely describing stemmed from (and in turn contributed to) the revolutionary changes at the economic level, at the level of the productive forces, brought about by the new technology. Here was an ongoing revolution, the size, scope, comprehensiveness of which had never been known in the history of humankind and it was passing the Left by – till Thatcherism inadvertently brought it to their notice. And even then, what the Left understood was the scientific and technical magnitude of its achievements, summed up in Sir Ieuan Maddock's phrase that electronics had replaced the brain as once steam had replaced muscle. But its sociological size – that Capital had been freed from Labour – had escaped the Left altogether. The Labour Party was too sunk in its own stupor of trade unionism to see that the working class was decomposing under the impact of the new forces of produc-

* If the Militants were the moles, *Marxism Today* was the cuckoo.

23

tion and that old forms of Labour organisation were becoming frangible.

The old Marxists were, similarly, too wedded to orthodoxy to see that the old relations of production were disintegrating and new ones being born in their place. They had for so long been fighting for the emancipation of Labour from Capital that they could not bear to think that it was Capital that was now being emancipated from Labour.[3] So ensconced had they been in their own beliefs and dogmas and sentiments that they were fearful of venturing out into a changing world and taking it by the scruff of the neck.

And the new Marxists, who had daringly abandoned all such fears and inhibitions and acknowledged and celebrated the cultural and social changes that were going on, were unable, because of their premature apostasy, to connect them concretely with the emancipation of Capital from Labour or root that emancipation in the economic basis of production. Instead, they held up the changes to justify their apostasy.

Determinacies

So that when *Marxism Today* finally came to acknowledge the importance of economic change for an understanding of New Times (in the special issue of October 1988), the economic was still given only a walk-on part on to the 'post-Fordist' stage. 'Coming to terms with New Times', wrote Martin Jacques in the editorial, 'means first understanding what New Times are, what they mean. ... At the heart of New Times is the shift from the old mass-production Fordist economy to a new, more flexible, post-Fordist order based on computers, inform-ation technology and robotics.'[4] But there the concern with the economic ceases – for 'New Times are about much more than economic change. Our world is being remade.' Yes, but how? 'Mass production, the mass consumer, the big city, big-brother state, the sprawling housing estate, and the nation-

24

state are in decline: flexibility, diversity, differentiation, mobility, communication, decentralisation and internationalisation are in the ascendant.' That's fine as a description of what's going on, but where's the analysis? 'In the process our own identities, our sense of self, our own subjectivities are being transformed. We are in transition to a new era.'

Of course 'we are in transition to a new era'. Of course things are changing radically. And of course these changes are not just at the economic level. But the changes in society, culture, politics cannot just be juxtaposed with the economic; the economic cannot just be 'read off' from them any more than they could be read off from the economic. They derive from the economic – still.

Or take Stuart Hall's listings in his 'Brave New World' article[5] – one on the economy and the other on the 'broader social and cultural changes'. The first itemises 'a shift to the new "information technologies"; more flexible decentralised forms of labour process and work organisation; decline of the old manufacturing base and the growth of the "sunrise" computer-based industries; the hiving-off or contracting-out of functions and services; a greater emphasis on choice and product differentiation, on marketing, packaging and design, on the "targeting" of consumers by lifestyle, taste and culture rather than by the Registrar General's categories of social class; a decline in the proportion of the skilled, male, manual working class, the rise of the service and white-collar classes and the "feminisation" of the workforce; an economy dominated by the multinationals, with their new international division of labour and their greater autonomy from nation-state control; the "globalisation" of the new financial markets, linked by the communications revolution; and new forms of the spatial organisation of social processes'. Brilliant, clear, to the point, exhaustive: all the elements of the 'post-Fordist' economy are there.

The 'social and cultural' list, general here, but worked out in the course of the article, lists 'greater fragmentation and

25

pluralism, the weakening of older collective solidarities and block identities and the emergence of new identities associated with greater work flexibility, the maximisation of individual choices through personal consumption'.

There is, of course, no causal connection here between the two, the economic and the social-cultural. They are 'associated', they may even be seen to be walking hand in hand, but the one does not follow from the other, influence the other, make the other possible. What is it that makes for 'greater fragmentation and pluralism' (list 2) unless it is the fragmentation of the working class and hence the obfuscation of class in general? And how has that been brought about if not by 'a shift to the new "information technologies"; more flexible, decentralised forms of labour process and work organisation; decline of the old manufacturing base and the growth of the "sunrise" computer-based industries; the hiving-off or contracting-out of functions and services' and a 'decline in the proportion of the skilled, male, manual working class, the rise of service and white-collar classes and the "feminisation" of the workforce' (list 1) – changes, that is, in the mode and relations of production? (Let's keep the old terminology for now because the new is yet to be born with the new post-Fordist 'system'.)

How have 'the older collective solidarities and block identities weakened' (list 2) except through 'the decline of the old manufacturing base', the rise of 'more flexible, decentralised forms of labour process and work organisation', and 'the hiving-off or contracting-out of functions and services (list 1)? And how have these come about if not through 'the shift to the new technologies' which enables Capital not only to do away with mass production lines and the mass employment of workers on the same factory floor but to move the workplace itself around, from one cheap labour pool to another, as required by profit and the market. (Note how, in his refusal to be 'determinist', Hall leaves out of his reckoning the massed-up workers of the Third World, on whose greater immiser-

26

ation and exploitation the brave new Western world of post-Fordism is being erected, and cannot be persuaded back to them even when the item on 'multinationals with their new international division of labour' resonates with their presence.)

Similarly, 'the emergence of new identities' (list 2) cannot just be 'associated with greater work flexibility' (list 1); it is largely made possible by greater work flexibility which in turn is made possible by the new technology. And 'the maximis-ation of individual choices through personal consumption' (list 2) comes also from retailers' ability to lay 'a greater emphasis on choice and product differentiation, on marketing, on packaging and design, on the targeting of consumers by lifestyle, taste and culture' (list 1) based on computerised information and supply systems which allow them to gear supplies to taste, demand and time.*

And what is this 'spatial organization of social processes' Hall is talking about which exists apart from the spatial orga-nisation of economic processes?

All the significant social and cultural changes that we are passing through today are similarly predicated on economic changes.[6] To try to understand New Times without under-standing that fundamental relationship is like trying to comprehend nineteenth-century society and culture without understanding the industrial revolution that gave rise to it. We are living through similar times where everything is being shaped, influenced, conditioned by the revolution in the productive forces.** Economic determinacy might be said to have flagged with the economic decline and 'class failure' of industrial capitalism in its last decades and to have been

---

* Robin Murray says as much in his article 'Life after Henry (Ford)' in the same issue, but, judging from the attention he gets from his fellow contribu-tors, he must have been inserted in the interests of pluralism.
** 'The entire industrial revolution enhanced productivity by a factor of about 100 ...' but 'the micro-electronic revolution has already enhanced productivity in information-based technology by a factor of more than a million – and the end isn't in sight yet'.[7]

discredited by the success of 'the cultural revolutions of the 60s, 1968 itself' and the 'theoretical revolutions of the 60s and 70s — semiotics, structuralism, post-structuralism' (which Stuart Hall assures us were, along with feminism and psychoanalysis, 'key episodes in the passage to "New Times"').* And all of this may have confirmed the theoretics that the economic was one of several ('autonomous', 'articulating') 'instances'. But today, when Capital has come out of its crisis, refurbished, regenerated and radicalised by the revolution in the productive forces — and Capital is nothing if not an economic project — how can we overlook the crucial role of the economic without offering hostages to Capital? Even as individuals, how can we here, now, caught on the crest of that revolution, impacted by it on all sides, believe that the economic shapes nothing? Even the question of personal transformation, the 'reforging of ourselves as individuals', and our preoccupation with our identities stem from the upheavals occasioned by the economic revolution of our times. Yes, we are being remade, but if we overlook the occasion for that remaking, we overlook those myriad others who are being unmade by the self-same revolution.

The economic determines 'in the last instance' still — but shorn of its class determinacy. For the very revolution that restores the base–superstructure relationship to something like its former importance is also that which does away with the working class in its pristine form, shape, size, homogeneity of experience, unity of will, clout, and emancipates Capital from Labour. And the more Labour tries to hold Capital in thrall by withholding its labour, the more Capital moves towards its emancipation through yet more information technology, yet more labourless productive regimes, yet more recourse to the captive labour force in the periphery. The

---

* Stuart Hall must have found it difficult to include the black struggles of this period in his 'key episodes' (despite their being the precursors and inspirers of the feminist movement) because they combined the struggles of a people and a class: rooted the cultural and the political in the economic.

relations of production, that is, have changed with the changes in the level of the productive forces: information (in the sense of data fed to computers, robots, etc.) increasingly replaces labour as a factor of production; Capital no longer needs living labour as before, not in the same numbers, in the same place, at the same time; Labour can no longer organise on that basis, it has lost its economic clout and, with it, whatever political clout it had, whatever determinacy it could exercise in the political realm. What is crucial here is not that the productive forces have altered the balance of dependency between Capital and Labour, but that they have altered it so radically as to allow Capital to free itself of Labour and yet hold Labour captive.

And that is what moves the terrain of battle from the economic to the political, from the base to the superstructure and appears to throw 'the language of politics more over to the cultural side'[8] and render the subjective important. However, the battle itself is neither about culture nor about the subject, but – still – about the ownership and control of the means of production and the exploitation of workers. Only now, the centre of gravity of that exploitation has shifted from the centre to the periphery and, within the centre, to peripheral workers, home workers, *ad hoc* workers, casual, temporary, part-time workers – all the bits and pieces of the working class that the new productive forces have dispersed and dissipated of their strength. Exploitation has not gone out with class determinacy or inequality and poverty with the working class as we know it. The battle is the same as before – only it needs to be taken on at the political/ideological level and not at the economic/political level.

Thatcher's real lessons

Mrs Thatcher saw the time and seized it. That was her genius. The productive forces were pregnant with a new economic

29

and social order. Labour and labourism blocked its passage. It required Mrs Thatcher to take a knife to the unions before the new order could be born. And with that deft bit of political surgery, she determined what course the new economic order should take, whose interests it should serve. And she sold it to the people in a clear, simplistic ideology that spoke to their self-interest and their self-esteem in a time of deep uncertainty and pother – with the help of a press which was itself dying for change and knew it could get it only from her. The time brought forth the woman. And she cast the time in her image.

The new Marxists, in addressing Thatcherism as an electoral and ideological phenomenon, failed to give sufficient importance to the economic and social order it was constructing. Themselves predisposed towards a politics of position, their aim was rather to align the Labour Party with the new class of skilled and semi-skilled workers who were replacing the old Fordist mass worker, the expanding clerical and office workforce of the service sector which was replacing industry as the locus of employment and the new social forces that were increasingly replacing class constituencies.[9] These were the people who could swing the electorate Labour's way. What were their demands and aspirations? How should Labour refashion itself to meet the claims of the new share-owning working class? How could Labour be made to relate to the new social constituencies, such as women, blacks, greens, etc., which had no 'clear-cut class identity'? 'The whole point of Thatcherism as a form of politics has been to construct a new social bloc.' Could Labour do the same? Could it abandon its traditional class perspective and accept that a social bloc has to be 'constructed out of groups which are very different in terms of their material interests and social positions'? And could these 'diverse identities' be welded together into a 'collective will'? Thatcherism in its second term 'did not make a single move which was not also carefully calculated in terms of this hegemonic strategy. It stepped up the pace of privatisation. But it took care, at every step, to harness new social constituencies to it, to "construct" an image of the new share-owning working class, and to expand the bloc, symbolically, around the image of choice.' Could Labour relate to the fact that 'increasingly, the electorate is thinking politically, not in terms of *policies*, but of *images*' – not that policies don't matter but that they don't 'capture people's imaginations unless constructed into an *image* with which they can identify'. If Labour was going to be the majority party in any deep sense, it had to find a strategy for modernisation and an image of modernity; instead of rallying and mobilising the past, it had to find a 'convincing alternative scenario to Thatcherism for the future'.

There is an outline of a programme here for Labour to win over the constituencies on which 'Thatcherism's electoral hegemony continues to rest', but it is not one that speaks to the needs of that third of the nation that Thatcherism has dispossessed, which after all is socialism's first constituency. And (hence?) there is no reference to the ideological shift that Labour would have to make to accommodate these new constituencies, though ideology, we are told, is 'critical' to the construction of new social blocs. What, in any case, is this (new) ideology that could relate to the interests of the new constituencies and the underclasses – and are the new social forces a classless monolith? Or (alternatively?)* is there a 'hegemonic strategy' that needs to be built around images that would 'expand the bloc symbolically'? For 'elections are won or lost not on so-called real majorities but on (equally real) symbolic majorities'. These images, would they be the same sort of images around 'choice', around a new share-owning working class, etc., that Mrs Thatcher constructs? And how shall these speak to the dispossessed, how capture their political imagination? Or are there alternative images/

* The writings of the new Marxists are so non-commital as to make definition difficult.

policies that Labour can construct which can still keep it socialist at heart?

How, again, should Labour relate to the race-, sex-, gender-based social movements? On what terms? What is so profoundly socialist about these new social forces is that they raise issues about the quality of life (human worth, dignity, genuine equality, the enlargement of the self) by virtue of their experiences as women, blacks, gays, etc., which the working-class movement has not just lost sight of but turned its face against. But if these issues are fought in terms of the specific, particularistic oppressions of women *qua* women, blacks *qua* blacks and so on, without being opened out to and informed by other oppressions, they lose their claim to that universality which was their particular contribution to socialism in the first place. And they, further, fall into the error of a new sectarian-ism – as between blacks versus women, Asians versus Afro-Caribbeans, gays versus blacks, and so on – which pulls rank, this time, on the basis not of belief but of suffering: not who is the true believer but who is the most oppressed. Which then sets out the basis on which demands are made for more equal opportunities for greater and more compound oppressions in terms of quotas and proportions and that type of numbers game. That is not to say that there should be no attempt to redress the balance of racial, sexual and gender discrimin-ation, but that these solutions deal not with the politics of discrimination but its arithmetic – giving more weightage to women here and blacks there and so rearranging the distribu-tion of inequality as not to alter the structures of inequality themselves. In the process, these new social movements tend to replace one sort of sectarianism with another and one sort of sectional interest for another when their native thrust and genius were against sectarianism and for a plurality of interests.

Equally, what is inherently socialist about the issue-based new social forces such as the green and peace movements is the larger questions they raise about the quality of the environs we live in or whether we live at all. But to the extent that the green movement is concerned more, say, with the environmental pollution of the Western world than with the ecological devastation of the Third World caused by Western capitalism, its focus becomes blinkered and narrow and its programmes partial and susceptible to capitalist overtures. Or, to come at it from the opposite direction, it is precisely because the green movement overlooks the centrality of capitalism and imperialism in the despoliation of the planet that it overlooks also the narrowness of its campaigns (the US Greens attack 'addictive consumerism' while ignoring the inability of whole sections of the population to consume at all) and the limitation of its vision (the German Greens boast that their movement is 'neither to the right nor to the left but in front').[10] And for that self-same reason it fails, too, in its claim to connect the global and local, the collective and the individual – and therein fails its own trust and promise.

So, too, does a peace movement which does not, for instance, see that to preserve the world from a holocaustal nuclear war also involves preserving the Third World from a thousand internecine wars sponsored and financed by the arms industry of the West.

There are simple, basic connections to be made here within and between the various movements. They are connections which are organic to socialism, but they can only develop if the new social movements open themselves out to the larger social issues and to each other; move out in a centrifugal fashion without losing sight of the centripetal – move out, that is, from their particularities to the whole and back again to themselves, enriching both, in an unending traffic of ideas, struggles and commitments; weave the specific and the universal into a holistic pattern of socialism which, so far from failing the parts, continues to be informed by them.

But that is not how the new Marxists visualise the new social forces. They do not ask what it is in the philosophy and practice of these movements that needs to be constantly reviewed and rectified if they are to make a continuing contribution to a modern progressive socialism. They do not seem to accept that there can be contradictions within and between the movements or that their practice often plays into the hands of capitalism and is therein negated. Instead, they tend to romanticise the movements – feminism especially, as though in a backlash of socialist guilt, romancing the feminine now where once they romanced the class – regarding them as the catalysts or, in their language, 'the leading edge' of change.* Perhaps they needed to, as a tactic, as a gun trained on the male, heterosexual citadels of socialism. But it is one that has backfired precisely because it has not looked to its own fallibility. It is not enough to ask what it is that the new social forces bring to the socialist movement without also asking what it is within these movements that could be corrupting of socialism.

But then, the axes on which the new social movements revolve are single-issue and identity-based politics which are of themselves self-defining and enclosed particularities tending to burrow into themselves for social truths and answers. Identity politics, in fact, seems to claim that the struggles of the self over its various personae – social, sexual, gendered – are by their very nature (for one does not struggle alone) social and political struggles: they impinge on how society regards women, blacks, gays, etc., and challenge the prevailing mores and ideology, in a sort of metaphysical dialectic between the personal and the political. The laboratory of social change, it would appear, is the self, but the self is also in the world and so the world changes with the changing of the self and the self with it.

> At the still point of the turning world. Neither flesh nor flesh-less; Neither from nor towards ...[11]

Eliot was also a dialectical metaphysician.

---

* In pursuing 'the leading edge of change', the new Marxists ignore the basis of change.

The new politics

Politics is not just out there any more, says Rosalind Brunt –
in study groups and meetings and vanguard parties – but here
in the person, in 'the continuous making and remaking of
ourselves, and ourselves in relation to others'.[12] It is in the way
people experience the world through 'the many, and
increasing, identities it offers: ... a colour, a gender, a class, a
nationality; "belonging" to a family, having a child of your
own; relating to colleagues, friends, comrades, lovers.' It can
no longer be said that there is a politics outside ourselves –
politics is in the person – or that to be political is to talk about
'*the* system, *the* state, *the* working class, *the* Third World' –
everything is political. 'What people do as political acts',
remarks Beatrix Campbell in the same issue of *Marxism Today*
(with a caveat that she is possibly being 'trivial here'), 'is they
read, they buy, they refuse to buy, and they commit all sorts of
acts which are about participation in the culture. It's only nut-
cases in ever declining political organisations who think the
only political act is to go to a meeting.'[13]

Power, for Brunt, is 'not simply a force coming from above
and governed by one set of people, the ruling class'. Power is
everywhere and 'it operates horizontally as much as vertically,
internally as well as externally'. Even sex, goes on Rosalind
Brunt paraphrasing Foucault, 'so far from ... being a natural,
biological given, central to our identity ... is socially and
culturally constructed and has a history brimming with power
points'. But 'where there is power there is also a "multiplicity
of points of resistance"', particularly in the way that historical
identities are constructed – in 'reverse discourse', for example,
where a homosexual subject, say, can 'start to speak on his/
her own behalf, and begin to shift to another, more "empow-
ering" discourse that describes an identity that transcends the
original vocabulary of pathology and illness. Hence the self-
defining movements of "gay" and "lesbian" politics – a defiant
and celebratory "coming out".'[14]

That, according to the New Timers, is what is exhilarating about New Times: the shift to the subject, the personal, the individual. Everything is in our hands now. We are not determined by 'impersonal structures', 'objective contradictions' and 'processes that work "behind men's (*sic*) backs".'[15] We are not conditioned by class, class is no more – the working class certainly, not as we knew it, anyway – and the dominance of production relations has gone with it. Everything has been thrown on to the cultural side. 'All interests, including class ones', says Stuart Hall, 'are [now] culturally and ideologically defined.'[16] That is where the struggle is. That is where we challenge the various power blocs in civil society. And 'far from there being no resistance to the system', Hall assures us, 'there has been a proliferation of new points of antagonism, new social movements of resistance organised around them, and consequently, a generalisation of "politics" to spheres which hitherto the Left assumed to be apolitical: a politics of the family, of health, of food, of sexuality, of the body.' Or, as Beatrix Campbell puts it, 'there's a plethora of collective comings and goings in what you might call "civil society" that are outside the political system.'[17] There is, that is, not just one power game any more but several, and not just one political line but a whole lot of political positions – and hence 'a politics which is always positional'.[18]

And personal. Because the personal is the political. And personal politics is also about the politics of consumption, desire, pleasure – because we have got choice now. New Times affords us choices, all sorts of choices, of how we dress, eat, live, make love, choices of style, design, architecture, the social spaces we occupy. The individual has been opened up to the 'transforming rhythms and forces of modern *material* life'. Commodified consumption? Maybe, but 'have we become so bewitched', asks Stuart Hall, 'by who, in the short run, reaps the profits from these transactions and missed the deep democratisation of culture which is also a part of their hidden agenda? Can a socialism of the twenty-first century revive, or even survive, which is wholly cut off from the land-scapes of popular pleasures, however contradictory a terrain they are? Are we thinking dialectically enough?'[19]

Equally, are we thinking socialist enough? And what, in any case, is this dialectic about materialism which is not itself materialist? Should we become so bewitched by 'the deep democratisation of culture' that we miss out on those who reap the profits from 'these transactions'? How do you gauge democratisation – by its spread or the spread of effective choice – and how deep is it that it deprives a third of the population of such choice? And why 'in the short run'? Because profit is short and culture long? Or because subversion is a commercial proposition only in limited runs and the transactors know when to call the tune, change the demand, 'democratise' some other (reactionary) bits of culture. In an age of 'designer capitalism', as Robin Murray terms it, who 'shapes' our lifestyles? Who still sells us the ideas that sell us the things that we buy? Who lays out for us 'the landscapes of popular pleasures'? Should we not be suspicious of those pleasures which, even in a post-Fordist era, tend to be turned out like hamburgers, mass-produced and mass-oriented? Should we not, instead, find pleasure in being creative in ourselves and in our relationships with others now that we have got the time to be creative in? Can a socialism of the twenty-first century survive which does not develop landscapes of creative leisure for people to be human in?

New Times also sets great store by the feminist concept that the personal is the political. But how that concept has been interpreted (because it lends itself to such interpretation) and used has led to disastrous consequences in Left local authority politics, especially as regards race, and in the fight against racism generally. By personalising power, 'the personal is the political' personalises the enemy: the enemy of the black is the white as the enemy of the woman is the man. And all whites are racist like all men are sexist. Thus racism is the combination of power plus prejudice. Remove the prejudice and you remove the cutting edge of power; change the person and you change the office.

Hence the fight against racism became reduced to a fight against prejudice, the fight against institutions and practices to a fight against individuals and attitudes. And those Left councils which carried out anti-racist policies on this basis found themselves not only ineffectual but open to the accusation that their approach to the collective good often ended up in individual injustice. The McGoldrick affair – where a white headteacher was suspended because her alleged (personal) racism was said to stand in the way of Brent Council's wholly valid policy to recruit more black teachers – was a case in point. Another was the lesson introduced into some Racism Awareness Training (RAT) classes whereby people were so sensitised to the pejorative use of the term 'black' that they baulked at asking for black coffee. Which then gave credence to stories such as the one broadcast by the *Daily Mail* that Haringey Council had banned teachers and children from singing 'Baa Baa Black Sheep' in its schools as it was racist.[20]

All of which went to create the image of the 'Loony Left' which, as Stuart Hall so rightly says, bolstered 'Thatcherism's hidden "moral agenda" around those powerful subliminal themes of race and sex' and helped her win the election.[21] But if, as Hall insists, the Left is to learn from its mistakes, it must also be said that it was precisely the 'policies' arising from the personal is the political 'line' (around 'those powerful subliminal themes of race and sex') that played into the hands of the Right and provided them the modicum of truth necessary to sustain the Loony Left image in the public mind.

The 'personal is the political' has also had the effect of shifting the gravitational pull of black struggle from the community to the individual at a time when black was already breaking up into ethnics. It gave the individual an out not to take part in issues that affected the community: immigration raids, deportations, deaths in custody, racial violence, the rise of fascism, as well as everyday things that concerned housing and schooling and plain existing. There was now another venue for politics: oneself, and another politics: of one's sexuality, ethnicity, gender – a politics of identity as opposed to a politics of identification.

Carried to its logical conclusion, just to be black, for instance, was politics enough: because it was in one's blackness that one was aggressed, just to be black was to make a statement against such aggression. If, in addition, you 'came out' black, by wearing dreadlocks say, then you could be making several statements. 'The one which I think is important', declared a black intellectual in a radio programme recently, 'is the statement it makes to the white people that I have to deal with as a professional, as a scholar, as a historian and other things which I do, and it tells them that there are certain things they can't do to me because I have a power behind me that they can't comprehend.'[22] Equally, you could make a statement, by just being ethnic, against Englishness, for instance; by being gay, against heterosexism; by being a woman, against male domination. Only the white straight male, it would appear, had to go find his own politics of resistance somewhere out there in the world (as a consumer perhaps?). Everyone else could say: I am, therefore I resist.

Of course, the individuals who could leave the black community to its problems and mind their own were those who were not directly affected by them: the emerging black middle class of functionaries and intellectuals. The functionaries found commitment, if not profit, in ethnicity and culture, the intellectuals found struggle in discourse. That way they would not be leaving the struggles of the community behind but taking them to a higher level, interpreting them, deconstructing them, changing the focus of struggle on the sites of another practice, theoreticist this time.

The flight of the intellectual, however, is not confined to the black community – that is a particular type of flight: new, raw, immediately noticeable, because the blacks have achieved some sort of upward social and economic mobility only in the last two decades or so. It is part of a larger, smoother, more sophisticated flight of Left intellectuals from class – a flight that was already intimated in the philosophical excursions of theoretical Marxism and the politics of Eurocommunism but found objective justification in 'post-Fordism' and the disintegration of the working class.

The new class

From then saying 'farewell to the working class' to electing themselves the new agents of change in New Times was but a short and logical step. For the shift from industrial to post-industrial society or, more accurately, from industrial to information society did not just remove the industrial working class from its pivotal position but threw up at the same time a new information 'class'. Since, however, information operated differently at two different levels – at the economic, as a factor of production (information in the sense of data fed to computers, robots, etc.), and at the political, as a factor of ideology, so to speak (information as fed to people) – the combined economic and political clout of the old working class also got differentiated, with the economic going to the technical workers and the political to the 'information workers', the intelligentsia. And in a society 'over-determined' by the political/ideological, the intelligentsia, who had hitherto no class as such, had come into their own. Except that the Right intelligentsia knew that the means of information were in the hands of the bourgeoisie and they were merely the producers of ideas and information and ideology that kept the bourgeoisie *in situ*, while the Left intelligentsia were convinced that the ideas and information and ideology they produced would overwhelm, if not overthrow, the bourgeoisie itself.

Every mode of production, as Marx has said, throws up its own classes. Capitalism is still the 'mode' in his sense, but the method of production has undergone such qualitative change

40

as to shift the balance of influence between the economic, political and ideological instances and, with it, the balance of class forces. In today's post-industrial society that balance has shifted to the middle classes and their most vociferous wing, the intelligentsia, who as purveyors of information, ideas, images, lifestyles find themselves in an unusual position of power to influence the way people think and behave – or, as the new Marxists would put it, the way the 'subject' is 'constructed' and, since ideologies 'work on and through the subject', the way politics is constructed, too. For the New Times intelligentsia this means dragging Marxism with them to their own intellectual terrain, altering the battle-lines to suit their bent and equipment, engaging in wars of position that never lead to a war of overthrow or 'manoeuvre', challenging not the coercive power of the state but altering the ideological hegemonies in civil society, not through the instrument of the party as before but through the construction of alternative social blocs that would coalesce existing Left/centre parties. Central to the project, of course, are the new social forces.

But the mode is still capitalist, the struggle is still against its coercive power as embodied in the state. The working class might have disintegrated, but the bourgeoisie has, for that very reason, got stronger. There is still exploitation and oppression and hunger among the vast majority of the world's population. There is poverty and unemployment right here, in our midst, that arises from the unequal distribution of wealth.* That again is in the hands of the state, held there by the state.

There may well be all sorts of 'resistance to the system', as Stuart Hall suggests, in civil society today, all sorts of new social movements and 'a politics of the family, of health, of food, of sexuality, of the body'.[24] And they may even succeed

---

* In May 1988, 8.2 million people in Britain were dependent upon supplementary benefit. In the year 1988–9 tax cuts for individuals in the richest 1 per cent of tax payers were £22,680 per person, a sum greater than the total income of any single person in the bottom 95 per cent of the population.[23]

in pushing out the boundaries of individual freedom. But the moment they threaten to change the system in any fundamental way or go beyond the personal politics of health, food, sexuality, etc., they come up against the power of the state. That power does not need to be used at every turn, just to intimate that it is there is sufficient to change the politics of the new social forces, personal politics, to a politics of accommodation.

Civil society is no pure terrain of consent where hegemonies can play at will; it is ringed around, if not with coercion, with intimations of coercion – and that is enough to buttress the system's hegemony. It is only in challenging state power that you expose the coercive face of the state to the people, sharpening their political sense and resistance, providing the temper and climate for 'the construction' of more effective 'social blocs'. Conversely, you cannot take on the dominant hegemonies in civil society without at some point – at the point of effectiveness, in fact – falling foul of the system.

It is inconceivable that we should go on talking about resistances in civil society and ignoring the power of the state when Mrs Thatcher has used exactly that to limit the terrain of civil society, keep government from the people, undermine local democracy, abrogate workers' rights, hand over water to businessmen, make education so narrow and blinkered as to make the next generation safe for the Tories.* The Greater London Council (GLC) might have succeeded in constructing all sorts of social blocs and movements (the pride and joy of the new Marxists) to challenge Tory hegemony, but all that Mrs Thatcher had to do was abolish it. The abolition, though, might have been stayed if the social blocs and forces that the GLC had generated and/or supported had a politics that could have opened out to each other and formed a solid phalanx of resistance to the encroachments of the Thatcherite

---

* The interests of the state and of the government, declared the Attorney General, later Lord Chancellor, after the Ponting case, are identical.

state. Instead, their politics of position only helped them to take it lying down.

Nor is civil society an even terrain of consent, a plateau of consent, with no 'cliffs of sheer fall'. It drops sharply for the poor, the black, the unemployed. For them, the distinction between the mailed fist and the velvet glove is a stylistic abstraction, the defining limit between consent and force a middle-class fabrication. Black youth in the inner cities know only the blunt force of the state; those on income support (8 million on today's count)[25] have it translated for them in a thousand not so subtle ways. If we are to extend the freedoms in civil society through a politics of hegemony, those who stand at the intersection of consent and coercion should surely be our first constituency and guide – and a yardstick to measure our politics by. How do you extend a 'politics of food' to the hungry, 'a politics of the body' to the homeless, a 'politics of the family' to those without an income?* How do any of these politics connect up with the Third World?

The touchstone of any issue-based or identity-based politics has to be the lowest common denominators in our society. A women's movement that does not derive its politics from the needs, freedoms, rights of the most disadvantaged among them is by that very token reformist and elitist. Conversely, a politics that is based on women *qua* women is inward-looking and narrow and nationalist and, above all, failing of its own experience. So, too, the blacks or gays or whoever. So, too, are the green and peace movements Eurocentric and elitist that do not derive their politics from the most ecologically devastated and war-ravaged parts of the world. Class cannot just be a

---

* In 1985, 5.42 million people (10 per cent of the population) were living in poverty or on its margins, a rise of 33% since 1979). Families with children experienced a steeper rise in poverty than other people on low income; 6.45 million people in families with children (26 per cent of all families with children) were living in poverty or on its margins, an increase of 55% since 1979. In 1987 there were 107,000 households who were homeless; 64 per cent were households with dependent children; 14 per cent had a member who was pregnant (*Poverty*, Summer 1988 and Winter 1988–9).

matter for identity, it has to be the focus of commitment.

But even if, as the new Marxists have it, class is only one of a subject's many identities, it is still his or her class identity surely that makes a person socialist or otherwise. What makes for that identity may be an individual's direct experience of hardship, or it may stem from one's capacity to see in one's own oppression or oppressions as a woman, a black, a black gay, etc., the oppression of others, or it may derive quite simply from 'the truth of one's imagination'. But unless it informs and underlines the subject's other identities, the politics of identity becomes a narrow, sterile, self-seeking exercise. You don't have to live in poverty and squalor to be a socialist, as Beatrix Campbell so derisorily implies,[26] but the capacity to identify yourself with those who do helps. By the same token, the 'politics of pleasure', which the new Marxists warn us we must not knock, could hardly be one of socialism's priorities – nor the pursuit of personal gain its morality. Class, even as metaphor, is still the measure of a socialist conscience.*

But there's the rub. The new Marxists do not see the self as something forged in and forging the struggle to change the world, but as fragmented identities inhabiting different social worlds, 'with a history, "produced", in process. These vicissitudes of the subject have their own histories which are key episodes in the passage to new times' such as 'the cultural revolutions of the 1960s ... feminism's slogan that "the personal is the political" ... the theoretical revolutions of the 60s and 70s – semiotics, structuralism, post-structuralism – with their concern for language and interpretation'.[27] And it is this 'return of the subjective with a vengeance' that New Times proudly presents.

The 'return' of the subject to the centre of the political stage brings with it, of course, the politics of the subject: individu-

---

* From the point of view of the new Marxists, of course, this may well sound like a class reductionism of the mind.

alism, consumption, choice, the market, sexuality, style, pleasure, 'international humanism'.

The big waffle

Individualism, for New Times contributor Charlie Leadbeater, is what the Left now needs 'at the core of its vision of
how society should be organised' – a 'socialist individualism',
of course, a 'progressive individualism', an 'expansive individualism', a 'democratic individualism' even, in contrast to Mrs
Thatcher's 'constrained, narrow, materialistic individualism'.[28] Labour and the Left had abrogated individual rights
and choices through statism, and Thatcherism had seized
upon them to construct its own vision of society. It was time
now for the Left to reappropriate the individual – an individual with responsibilities, however, not just rights. For 'if the
Left stands for one thing, it should be this: people taking
responsibility for all aspects of their lives'. No more nanny
state, no more asking 'what can the state, the council, the
professionals, do to solve this problem for people'. Should this
sound like Thatcherism, Leadbeater hastens to assure us that,
in addition to individual responsibility, there would also be
collective provision. But how, if not through the state and local
authority – and for whom, if not the needy? And are we then
not returning to the 'theological collectives ... of state and
class'? Through 'intermediate collectives', answers Charlie
Leadbeater, composed perhaps of 'individuals, private initiatives, even companies', operating within a 'space' provided
and regulated by the state.[29] But how is this different from
Heseltine's compact for the inner cities?

The individual must also have choice, in consumption,
lifestyle, sexuality and so on, because 'the dynamic area of
most people's lives is where they can assert their difference
from others'. There's 'new Marxism' for you, and yet the old
man whose name they take in vain said that it was 'only in

community with others' that the individual has 'the means of cultivating his gifts in all directions, only in community ... is personal freedom possible'.

But that apart, the question of choice in Leadbeater's scheme of things does not emerge from the position of the choiceless, those deprived of choice, deprived of purchasing power. It relates, in the first instance, to those who already have and stresses, therefore, the importance of the market in delivering choice. When Leadbeater does turn to the problems of the less well-off, it is to tag on feeble provisos to market solutions, such as regulating competition, or to offer up sundry collective actions which are themselves 'conceived and expressed individually'.

The stress on the individual leads Leadbeater to the market and Thatcherism, the anxiety not to be found out leads him to 'collectivism', and he ends up as a man divided against himself in 'individually-based collectivism' – that is, as a social democrat. At one point he even goes beyond 'collective action' to mention 'redistribution', but it is not the redistribution of wealth. That, though, would have been to shift the centre of gravity of new Marxist argument from consumption to distribution – which, after all, is where socialism begins. The fulfilment of choice in an unequal society is always at the expense of others and is, in that, a negation of choice, of freedom.

It is in Stuart Hall's writing, however, that consumption reaches higher, even more lyrical, levels and requires to be quoted at length if only for its poetry. If 'the preoccupation with consumption and style' appears trivial, he warns us, it is 'more so to men, who tend to have themselves "reproduced" at arm's length from the grubby processes of shopping and buying and getting and therefore take it less seriously than women, for whom it was destiny, life's "work". But the fact is that greater and greater numbers of people (men and women) – with however little money – play the game of using things to signify who they are. Everybody, including people in poor societies whom we in the West frequently speak about as if they inhabit a world *outside* of culture, knows that today's "goods" double up as social signs and produce meanings as well as energy. There is no evidence that, in a socialist economy, our propensity to "code" things according to systems of meaning, which is an essential feature of our sociality, would *necessarily* cease – or, indeed, should.'[30]

I do not understand the last sentence and even the previous one seems meaningless to me – or it is in 'code'. But what 'social signs' do 'today's goods' have for the poor in 'poor societies' except that they have not got them, the goods? And what 'meaning' or 'energy' do they produce except that those who have do not give and those who have not must take? Who are these people who, in our own societies – 'with however little money – play the game of using things to signify who they are' unless it is those who use cardboard boxes under Waterloo Bridge to signify that they are the homeless? They know who they are: they are the poor and they do not have 'things' to play games with. It is they – both men and women – who think, who know that 'the preoccupation with consumption and style' is trivial. And Hall's bringing in male sexism in matters of 'shopping and buying and getting' does not elevate consumption any higher. If, on the other hand, what Hall is trying to say is that poor people find meaning, express themselves, in 'consuming' the goods they cannot afford precisely because they are poor, that again is special pleading to bring consumption closer to the heart of socialism.

Consumption is also where Robin Murray, alas, stubs his socialist toe. He first, like the other New Timers, excoriates the Left for being reluctant to take on the question of consumption. And like Stuart Hall, in another passage to New Times, Murray, too, develops a powerful argument for those movements in civil society which have taken on the market and the state over those issues of consumption where 'the social and the human have been threatened' – such as 'the effects of food additives and low-level radiation, of the air we breathe and the surroundings we live in, the availability of childcare and community centres, or access to privatised city centres and transport geared to particular needs.'[31] But he cannot help singing a paean to the market: 'which local council pays as much attention to its users as does the market research industry on behalf of commodities? Which bus or railway service cuts queues and speeds the traveller with as much care as retailers show to their just-in-time stocks?' One would have thought that the motive of market researchers and retailers alike was profit, not use value.

With 'the return of the subjective' has also gone the notion of imperialism out of new Marxist reckoning – the ravaging of the Third World, the exploitation of its peoples, the theft of its resources, ecological devastation. The Third World is no longer out there as an object of struggle; it is here, in the minds of people, as an anodyne to consumption, in the personal politics of the subject – an object of Western humanism, the occasion for individual aid, a site for pop culture and pop politics. The 'famine movement', the new Marxists call it,[32] 'people aid' to the Third World – making the plight of the Third World come through to people through mass gigs, mass runs, telethons – mass culture at the service of 'mass politics' – the politics of selfish consumption relieved by relief for the Third World – altering, if not the fate of the Third World, the views of government to alter the fate of the Third World – (governments tied up with multinational corporations, governments governed by multinational corporations) – altering people's politics, lifting people's horizons 'beyond even the boundaries of Europe, to Africa' – a mass movement for the moment, initiated not by the Left but outside it – by caring people – by pop stars who put '"caring for others" on the map' of rock culture (because 'every fan knows how much it costs a star to give a free performance') – millionaire pap merchants effecting a peaceful transition for the young from pap culture into pap politics.

'Who would have guessed in 1979, or even perhaps in 1983', ask Stuart Hall and Martin Jacques writing in 1986, 'that the plight of the Third World would generate one of the great popular movements of our time?' And not just that: 'with the rise of the Band Aid/Live Aid/Sport Aid phenomenon, the ideology of selfishness – and thus one of the main ideological underpinnings of Thatcherism – has been dealt a further, severe blow'. In fact, 'the famine movement's capacity to mobilise new forces', especially the youth, has 'helped to shift the political centre of gravity'.[33]

On the contrary, all that it shifted was the focus of responsibility for the impoverishment of the Third World from Western governments to individuals and obscured the workings of multinational corporations and their agents, the IMF and the World Bank. Worse, it made people in the West feel that famine and hunger were endemic to the Third World, to Africa in particular (the dark side of the affluent psyche), and what they gave was as of their bounty, not as some small recompense for what was being taken from the poor of the Third World. And, in the language of the new Marxists (more or less), a discourse on Western imperialism was transmogrified into a discourse on Western humanism.

What New Times represents, in sum, is a shift in focus from economic determinism to cultural determinism, from changing the world to changing the word, from class in and for itself to the individual in and for himself or herself. Use value has ceded to exchange value, need to choice, community to i-dentity, anti-imperialism to international humanism. And the self that New Timers make so much play about is a small, selfish inward-looking self that finds pride in lifestyle, exuberance in consumption and commitment in pleasure – and then elevates them all into a politics of this and that, positioning itself this way and that way (with every position a politics and every politics a position) into a 'miscellany of movements and organisations' stretching from hobbies and pleasure to services.[34]

A sort of bazaar socialism, bizarre socialism, a hedonist socialism: an eat, drink and be merry socialism because tomorrow we can eat drink and be merry again ... a socialism for disillusioned Marxist intellectuals who had waited around too long for the revolution – a socialism that holds up everything that is ephemeral and evanescent and passing as vital and worthwhile, everything that melts into air as solid, and proclaims that every shard of the self is a social movement.

Of course, the self is fragmenting, breaking up. But when in Capital's memory was it never so? Capital fragments the self as it fragments society, divides the self as it divides labour, develops some aspects of the self at the expense of others, encourages specialisation, compartmentalises experience and hands it over to professionals for interpretation, conceptualisation, and keeps the self from becoming whole.

Up to now we had the homogenising influence of class to hold us together, but this, as the new Marxists so rightly point out, was a flattening process, a reductive process, mechanical, and as destructive of the creative self as Capital.* That influence of class is gone from us and all its comforting, stultifying adhesions of procedures and organisation. There is nothing 'objective' to hold us together, our selves are let loose upon the world, and even the freedoms won in that great period of industrial working-class struggle are being threatened.

The emancipation of Capital from Labour has left a moral vacuum at the heart of post-industrial society, which is itself material. The 'universalist' bourgeois values which Bill Warren wrote about – 'equality, justice, generosity, independence of spirit and mind, the spirit of inquiry and adventure, opposition to cruelty' – and which sprang precisely from the creative tension between Capital and Labour are endangered by Capital's emancipation. The Factory Acts which took children out of work and women from the mines and gave

* 'Capitalism ... destroys the human possibilities it creates ... Those traits, impulses and talents that the market can use are rushed (often prematurely) into development and squeezed desperately till there is nothing left: everything else within us, everything nonmarketable, gets draconically repressed, or withers away for lack of use, or never has a chance to come to life at all.'[35]

50

them the light of day, the Education Acts that opened their minds out to other worlds and the world, the Public Health Acts which stopped the spread of disease and plagues – all came out of the tension, the hostility, between Capital and Labour.

Freedom of speech, of assembly, the right to withhold one's labour, universal suffrage, sprang not from bourgeois benefice but from working-class struggle. All the gains of the period of industrial capitalism were the creative outcome of social contradictions – the heart of dialectical materialism. The welfare state was its apotheosis.

Those contradictions are not as eloquent any more. The 'service class' of the post-industrial society which has displaced the working class of industrial society does not contest Capital but is accommodating of it and secretes a culture of accommodation, a petit-bourgeois culture. Where once the tension between the bourgeoisie and the working class produced 'bourgeois' culture and 'bourgeois' freedoms, the lack of tension, of hostility, of 'class hatred' even, produces a petit-bourgeois culture and petit-bourgeois values.

But there are still the values and traditions that have come down to us from the working-class movement: loyalty, comradeship, generosity, a sense of community and a feel for internationalism, an understanding that unity has to be forged and reforged again and again and, above all, a capacity for making other people's fights one's own – all the great and simple things that make us human.

Communities of resistance

Where those traditions have taken hold and come alive today are in the struggles of the people in those spaces that Thatcherism and new Marxism alike have obscured from public view: in the inner cities, among the low paid and the poor, in the new underclass of homeworkers and sweatshop workers, casual and part-time workers, *ad hoc* and temporary workers, thrown up by the putting-out system in retailing, the flexi-system in manufacturing, and the hire and fire system in the expanding service sector, and among refugees, migrants, asylum-seekers: the invisible workers who have no rights, no claims, no roots, no domicile and are used and deported at will.

By their very nature and location, the underclass are the most difficult to organise in the old sense of organisation. They do not submit to the type of trade union regimen which operates for the straight 'official' workforce – but they come together, like villagers, through hearsay and common hurt, over a deportation case here or a death in custody there, to take on the immediate power of the immigration officer or the police and to go beyond it, if that is where it takes them, to oppose the power of the state itself as it presents itself on the street. They come together, too, over everyday cases of hard-ship to help out each other's families, setting up informal community centres to help them consolidate whatever gains they make. These are not great big things they do, but they are the sort of organic communities of resistance that, in a sense, were prefigured in the black struggles of the 1960s and 1970s and the insurrections of 1981 and 1985.

Broadwater Farm was such a community. Relegated to a concrete ghetto and deprived of basic amenities and services, jobless for the most part and left open to crime, the inhabit-ants of the estate came together to create a life for themselves. They set up a nursery, provided meals and a meeting-place for pensioners, established a recreation centre for youth and built up, in the process, a political culture that resisted police intru-sion and proceeded to take on the judiciary and the press over the mistrial (the press trial in fact) of Silcott, Braithwaite and Raghip.

In 1979 the whole of Southall – Asian, Afro-Caribbean, white; the young, the old; women and men; shopkeepers and householders – shut up shop and went off to demonstrate against the incursion of the National Front into their town and were savagely beaten up by the police. Hundreds were injured when mounted police and riot police charged into the crowds – and Blair Peach, a white anti-racist campaigner and teacher, died at the hands of the Special Patrol Group. But that death did not die in the memories and campaigns of white groups and black organisations who took up the question of police accountability and brought it to the attention of a larger and larger public. From these campaigns came the setting up of local police-monitoring groups and council police committees. People were alerted now to the deaths, especially of young blacks, in police or prison custody, and from that has grown a distrust of inquest procedures and the demands for public inquiries in their stead. In April 1989, on the tenth anniversary of Blair Peach's death, activists from all over the UK and Europe gathered in Southall to commemorate his memory and pledge themselves to his legacy of struggle against racism and fascism.

It was also from the failure, wellnigh wilful, of the police to protect working-class Asian families from racial harassment and attack, following Mrs Thatcher's 'this country might be rather swamped by people with a different culture' pronouncement, that the call for the self-defence of the black community arose. And when a few months later Judge Argyle imposed savage sentences on the Virk brothers for defending themselves with spanners and jacks (they were repairing their car at the time) against the unprovoked attack of a racist gang, the Asian community, elders and youth alike, realised that it was as futile to look to the judiciary for justice as it was to the police for protection. From that 'self-defence is no offence' campaign sprang similar campaigns – in Newham, for instance, on behalf of Asian youth who had defended young children against racist attacks on their way from school (the case of the Newham eight). Which in turn raised the question of the pastoral role of teachers in protecting children against racial harassment.

The most celebrated of these campaigns arose from the defence of Manningham against impending fascist attack by twelve young Asians (allegedly) armed with Molotov cocktails. They were charged with conspiracy, a charge so wholly disproportionate that it outraged ordinary people and brought to the defence campaign support from a whole cross-section of groups – women, gays, students – who had hitherto not made the 'racial attack' issue their own.* Meetings across the country, regular newsletters and mass marches were to alert communities everywhere to the issues involved: problems in policing, attacks by fascists and racists in black areas, racism and political bias in the criminal justice system, a wish by the state to smash militant black organisations. It was the success of the community defence campaign as much as the legal representation in court (which was itself 'changed' by the community) which got the twelve acquitted.

These campaigns in turn were to strengthen the resolve of local authorities to outlaw racism, from council housing for instance. And in November 1984 Newham Council took the unprecedented step of evicting a white family, the McDonnells, for persistent harassment of their black neighbours.

Similarly, the issue of deportation and of the rights of children to join their parents, taken up by trade unions and legal and civil rights bodies, were initially raised by women's organisations – black and white. And from these issues the realisation arose that the question of deportation and children's rights had got to be seen and fought in the larger context of the quality of family life generally – and gave rise to the campaigns over child benefit, unsavoury surveillance by the state of marriages (to make sure they were not bogus), the racist and sexist nature of nationality laws and the 'internal',

---

* Among those who sat in on the trial each day was a young white home-help. Her anger and commitment was later to be channelled into a series of biting cartoons in the Institute of Race Relations publication *How Racism Came to Britain* (which the Secretary of State for Education then tried to ban from schools).

unseen, unknown, unaccountable control of black families –
via the police, education, welfare and social services.

It is a community of women again, predominantly middle-
aged women, which has helped keep alive in Britain the issue
of Israeli terror in the Occupied Territories, protested against
the treatment of women Palestinian prisoners, collected funds
for the children detained during the *intifada*, confirmed their
fellow women in Israel in their struggle against the occupation. Week in and week out for two years a Women in Black
picket has stood each Saturday in silent protest outside the
Israeli airline office in London – informing people, collecting
signatures, arguing the issues with passersby. The irony is that
these women are for the most part Jewish women and that the
catalyst for their movement came from a realisation in Jewish
feminist circles that their politics of identity was too narrow,
historicist and self-indulgent – and betraying of a sisterhood
that should embrace Palestinian women as well.

Recently, the campaign to prevent the deportation of Tamil
asylum-seekers from the UK involved a fight between the judiciary and the Home Office over their legitimacy. But the
whole issue of the would-be-refugees, tortured by the Sri
Lankan government, brought up Britain's role in the training
of the armed forces and intelligence networks of repressive
regimes and the implications of tourism in such countries.
And when two Tamil asylum-seekers working (for want of
work permits) as night security guards in a Soho amusement
arcade were burnt to death, the issue became one of the super-
exploitation of a new rightless, peripatetic section of the
working class and led to an exposé of the profits made by the
leisure industry.

It was, again, the migrant workers and the Refugee Forum
which fought for the rights of Kurds who had to flee Turkey in
1989. The feeding, housing, clothing of the Kurds, help with
translation, appeals for the right to remain, were all under-
taken by community groups themselves. Outrage over arbitrary detentions and deportations by the Home Office (which

led to the self-immolation of two Kurdish asylum-seekers) brought out various migrant and black communities onto the streets in demonstrations and meetings.* Just as in the case of the Tamils, the Kurds, too, threw up crucial issues which the 'movement' had to embrace: the conditions of work in East London's sweatshops (where the Kurds found employment), the use of chemical weapons (by Iraq) on the Kurds, Britain's collusion through NATO with Turkey's armed forces and, therefore, its harassment and torture of the Kurdish minority.

The joint struggles of refugee, migrant and black groups in Britain not only help to sustain the links between racism and imperialism and between racial oppression and class exploitation, but have also been at the forefront of the attempts to build a network of European groups against a new European racism[36] in the run-up to 1992. And only last month (November 1989) activists from black settler groups, migrants, refugees and asylum-seekers based in Holland, Germany, France, Denmark and the UK came together in a conference in Hackney to launch a Communities of Resistance Campaign across Europe.

All these activities may constitute a 'miscellany of movements', 'a plethora of collective comings and goings' outside mainstream party politics, as the new Marxists describe them. But there the resemblance to anything they have in mind ceases. In the first place, these are collectivities, movements, that issue from the grassroots (if the term may still be used) of economic, social and political life, from the bare bone of existence, from people who have nothing to lose but their chains, nothing to choose but survival, and are therefore dynamic, open, organic. They are not inward-looking, navel-gazing exercises like identity politics or narrow self-defining particularities like single-issue politics. They do not, in other words,

---

* These are not the party-hacks' meetings that Beatrix Campbell inveighs against but practical meetings to work out rotas for volunteers at community centres, panels of lawyers to take up cases, etc.

issue from the self but from the community, not from choice but from need, and are organic in the sense of sharing a common life.

Secondly, these movements do not stop at the bounds of civil society or confine their activities to its boundaries. They know from experience that beyond civil society lies the state, behind civil society lurks the state, on every street corner the state, at the Job Centre and the town hall, in the schools and at the hospital, whether demanding your rights or asking for guidance or just trying to lead an ordinary family life – local state or central, it matters little, as Thatcherism goes on eroding local authority, except that that, too, is now their fight. The struggles stretch from civil society to state and back in a continuum, effecting material changes in the life and rights of ordinary people and extending, in the process, the bounds of civil society itself.

Thirdly, what these movements throw up, by their very nature, are not diverse cultural politics but a multi-faceted political culture which finds authority in practice, tests theory in outcome, and works towards a wider political movement commensurate with our times, but unrelenting still of its struggle against Capital. The point is to overthrow capitalism, not to join it in order to lead it astray into socialism.

Hence and fourthly, these movements have little sympathy with the notion of the personal is the political because this has tended in practice to personalise and fragment and close down struggles. The personal is the political is concerned with what is owed to one by society, whereas the political is personal is concerned with what is owed to society by one. The personal is the political is concerned with altering the goal posts, the political is personal is concerned with the field of play. The personal is the political may produce radical indi-vidualism, the political is personal produces a radical society. The personal is the political entraps you in the self-achieving, self-aggrandising lifestyle of the rich, the political is personal finds value in the communal lifestyle of the poor.

Finally, there is an unspoken morality about these movements which stem from a simple faith in human beings and a deep knowledge that, by himself or herself, the individual is nothing, that we need to confirm and be confirmed by each other, that only in the collective good our selves can put forth and grow.*

This means that to come to consciousness of one's own individual oppression (which the new Marxists so eloquently point to as a sign of New Times) is to open one's sensibilities out to the oppression of others, the exploitation of others, the injustices and inequalities and unfreedoms meted out to others – and to act upon them, making an individual/local case into an issue, turning issues into causes and causes into movements and building in the process a new political culture, new communities of resistance that will take on power and Capital and class.

Moralistic? Morality is material when it is forged on the smithy of practice into a weapon of ideology. 'If you want to know the taste of a pear', a Chinese saying goes, 'you must change its reality by eating it.'

References

1. Stuart Hall, 'Thatcher's lessons', *Marxism Today* (March 1988).
2. Stuart Hall, 'Brave New World', *Marxism Today* (Special issue, October 1988).
3. See A. Sivanandan, 'New circuits of imperialism' p. 169, this volume; and Zygmunt Bauman, 'Fighting the wrong shadow', *New Statesman* (25 September 1987).
4. Martin Jacques, *Marxism Today* (October 1988).
5. S. Hall, 'Brave New World'.
6. See A. Sivanandan, 'New Circuits'.

* Whether this is a 'moral agenda' in the electoral way the new Marxists speak of it I do not know, but it is certainly the basis of another morality than Thatcher's and one that she would want to abolish along with socialism.

7. Carver Mead quoted in Walter B. Wriston, 'Technology and sovereignty', *Foreign Affairs* (Winter 1988–9).

8. S. Hall, 'Brave New World'.

9. S. Hall, 'Thatcher's lessons'.

10. Bharat Patankar, 'Monochromatic green gathering', *Race & Class* (October–December 1989). See also *Race & Class* special issue *Un-greening the Third World* (January–March 1989).

11. T.S. Eliot, 'Burnt Norton' in *Four Quartets* (London, 1970).

12. Rosalind Brunt, 'Bones in the corset', *Marxism Today* (October 1988).

13. Beatrix Campbell in 'Clearing the decks: a roundtable discussion', *Marxism Today* (October 1988).

14. R. Brunt, 'Bones in the corset'.

15. S. Hall, 'Brave New World'.

16. Ibid.

17. B. Campbell in 'Clearing the decks'.

18. S. Hall, 'Brave New World'.

19. Ibid.

20. Anthony Doran, 'Baa, baa, green sheep!' *Daily Mail* (9 October 1986).

21. S. Hall, 'Thatcher's lessons'.

22. *After dread and anger* (BBC Radio 4, 21 March 1989).

23. Frank Field, *Losing out: the emergence of Britain's underclass* (London, 1989).

24. S. Hall, 'Brave New World'.

25. Frank Field, *Losing out*.

26. Beatrix Campbell in 'Clearing the decks'.

27. S. Hall, 'Brave New World'.

28. Charlie Leadbeater, 'Power to the person', *Marxism Today* (October 1988).

29. Charlie Leadbeater in 'Clearing the decks'.

30. S. Hall, 'Brave New World'.

31. Robin Murray, 'Life after Henry (Ford)', *Marxism Today* (October 1988).

32. Stuart Hall and Martin Jacques, 'People Aid – a new politics sweeps the land', *Marxism Today* (July 1986).

33. Ibid.

34. Beatrix Campbell in 'Clearing the decks'.

35. Marshall Berman, *All that is solid melts into air: the experience of modernity* (London, 1983).

36. A. Sivanandan 'Racism 1992', p. 153 this volume.

Reclaiming the Fight against Racism

For two decades black people had had to fight their battles unaided by – and, in fact, impeded by the racism of – the labour movement and the Left generally. But after the inner-city rebellions of the 1980s the established Left, led by the Greater London Council's example, took up the 'black cause'. And the fight against racism moved from the streets and the shop-floor to the town halls and the committee rooms where bureaucrats sought neatly packaged solutions to throw at 'the problem' and its vocal spokespeople. In the process the definition of the problem, the object of struggle and its outcome all became changed. The fight against racism became a fight for culture and ethnicity; and personal racism rather than institutional racism became the site of struggle – thus providing a venue for a class of professionals and a platform for middle-class aspirants to Parliament. Black struggle and black issues became taken up not so much for the betterment of the community as for individual career prospects.

Each of the pieces here – a speech, an article and an interview – were crucial interventions in the fight against the ethnicists, the professionals and 'the aspirants' and helped dampen the divisive ethnic policies of local authorities, kill off racism awareness training (RAT) and its practitioners and inform the thinking of the new Black Manifesto.

3

Challenging Racism:
Strategies for the 1980s*

I am delighted that I have been asked to speak here today because what I want to say has to be said here, under the auspices of the GLC's Ethnic Minorities Unit – here in this very temple of ethnicity – because I come as a heretic, as a disbeliever in the efficacy of ethnic policies and programmes to alter, by one iota, the monumental and endemic racism of this society.

On the contrary. What ethnicity has done is to mask the problem of racism and weaken the struggle against it. But then, that is precisely what it was meant to do. It was the riposte of the system – in the 1960s and 1970s – to the struggles of black people, both Afro-Caribbean and Asian, both in the workplace and in the community, as a people for a class, extra-parliamentary and extra-trade union. It was the riposte of a system that was afraid that the black working-class struggles would begin to politicise the working class as a whole. It was, in particular, the riposte of the class-collabor-ationist Labour governments of Wilson and Callaghan which

* This is a revised version of a talk given on 12 March 1983 at the Greater London Council Ethnic Minorities Unit Consultation on Challenging Racism.

sought in ethnic pluralism to undermine the underlying class aspect of black struggle and black politics. But the massive onslaught of Thatcherite Toryism on blacks and the working class has shown Labour – or, at least, the Labour councils in the inner cities – the error of their ways and the inadequacies of multiculturalism to combat the new racialism. There is room for manoeuvre here, for a war of position if you like – and it is up to the black communities to return ethnic struggle to black struggle and socialism to Labour.

To work out the more immediate and short-term strategies, therefore, we need to go back into our history, black history, in Britain and look at the changing nature of racism, the corresponding changes in the sites and locales of struggle – and in the process take a closer look at how the language of struggle was changed from anti-racism to multiculturalism.

Racism does not stay still; it changes shape, size, contours, purpose, function – with changes in the economy, the social structure, the system and, above all, the challenges, the resistances to that system. And to understand the dynamics of this racism and its relationship to the class forces in society, I want to take you back to the 1950s and 1960s.

We came here when a war-torn Britain needed all the labour it could lay its hands on. It had stockpiled, through exploitation and another racism, whole reserves of cheap black labour in the colonies and it was inevitable that the countries in which they were stockpiled should supply Britain with the labour it needed for its factories and services. So that what we came to in the 1950s was a kind of *laissez-faire* discrimination and a racism, a racial prejudice, which carried over from the colonial period. It was not structured, institutionalised – though colour was written into discrimination: the system discriminates in order to exploit, and in the process of exploiting, it discriminates. Because Britain needed all the labour it could get, the discrimination that obtained was in terms not of getting jobs but rather in our social life, in housing, schooling and so on. We faced a racial discrimination which depended on market forces. Colour only gets written into legislation via the Immigration Act of 1962; and from then on it began to get institutionalised. And that is a crucial difference: the difference between the *racialism* of the 1950s and the *racism* we began to confront from 1962 onwards. It is a difference abjured in the higher reaches of sociology and by avant-garde 'theoretical practitioners' of the Left. But it is a distinction we need to make if we are going to understand how to sort out the struggles against people's attitudes and the power to act out those attitudes in social and political terms. It is an essential distinction to make for the purposes of practical struggles and, as you will see, a distinction that came out of struggle. People's attitudes don't mean a damn to me, but it matters to me if I can't send my child to the school I want to send my child to, if I can't get the job for which I am qualified and so on. It is the acting out of racial prejudice and not racial prejudice itself that matters. The acting out of prejudice is discrimination, and when it becomes institutionalised in the power structure of this society, then we are dealing not with attitudes but with power. Racism is about power not about prejudice. That is what we learnt in the years of struggle in the 1960s – when we met it in the trade unions, on the shop-floor, in the community, at the ports of entry. We learnt it as we walked the streets, in the social and welfare services, in the health service – we learnt it everywhere. And inevitably our struggles involved all our peoples and all these areas.

In the workplace and the community, Afro-Caribbean and Asian, we were a community and a class, we closed ranks and took up each other's struggles. We had such a rich infrastructure of organisations, parties and self-help projects. Self-help was what we did, exactly, because we were outside mainstream society. We built a whole series of projects which grew out of organisations in the community. And all the parties, like the United Coloured People's Alliance, the Black Unity and Freedom Party, the Black Liberation Front, the Black Panthers, had their projects, newspapers, newssheets, schools.

Organisations went to the factories and the strikes were taken from place to place – strike committees up and down the country learning from one another, and learning in the process to weave from the differing but common traditions of our anti-colonial struggle a common struggle against racism. We related to both the struggles back home and the struggles here, the struggles then and the struggles now, the struggle of Gandhi and Nehru, of Nkrumah and Nyerere, of James and Williams, of Du Bois and Garvey, and the ongoing struggles in Vietnam and 'Portuguese Africa' – Guinea-Bissau and Cape Verde – and the struggles for Black Power in the United States of America. They were all a part of our history – a beautiful massive texture that in turn strengthened the struggles here and fed back to the struggles there – and, of course, we were involved in the struggles of the oldest colony, Ireland. And *black* was a political colour.

But as the 1970s began to dawn and the recession began to bite, labour was being laid off. It was a period on the international scene when capital was moving to labour in Third World countries, instead of importing it to the metropolis. It was a period when Britain, like the rest of Europe, no longer needed cheap black labour. The Immigration Act of 1971 stopped all immigration dead, breaking up families and damaging the whole fabric of family life; the 'Sus' laws criminalised the young – and our priorities became separated. The Asian community, by and large, was concerned to get their dependants in before the doors shut on them; and struggles had to be waged, too, against arbitrary arrests and deportations. And because these were legal issues, issues connected with the law, the Asian community tended to take them on in a very legal way, a defensive way, through law centres and defence committees – one-off committees which no longer collated and co-ordinated struggles. The concern of the Afro-Caribbean community, on the other hand, focused predominantly around issues like 'Sus' and the criminalisation of their young, police brutality and judicial bias. That is not to say that there were no struggles in the workplaces (take Imperial Typewriters, STC or Perivale Güterman, for example) or that Afro-Caribbean and Asians did not continue to make common cause. But we did not have the newspapers which would have co-ordinated those struggles, we did not have the political organisations which had produced the papers.

The infrastructure we had built up was being eroded. It was only the black women's movement that continued from the 1970s and into the 1980s to hold together the black infrastructure. It was the women – both Afro-Caribbean and Asian – who were to continue to collate the struggles, to connect the Third World issues, to publicise and organise and, above all, to uphold the unity between Asian and Afro-Caribbean communities.

At the same time, on the ideological level a new battle was being mounted by the state against *black* struggles whereby they could be broken down into their ethnic and, through that, their class components. Ethnicity was a tool to blunt the edge of black struggle, to return 'black' to its constituent parts of Afro-Caribbean, Asian, African, Irish – and also, at the same time, to allow the nascent black bourgeoisie, petit-bourgeoisie really, to move up in the system. Ethnicity delinked black struggle – separating the West Indian from the Asian, the working-class black from the middle-class black. (And a certain politics on the black Left itself was beginning to romanticise the youth, separating their struggle from those of their elders – destroying the continuum of the past, the present and the future.) Black, as a political colour, was finally broken down when government moneys were used to fund community projects, destroying thereby the self-reliance and community cohesion that we had built up in the 1960s.

Ethnicity began life as a pluralist philosophy of integration – 'equal opportunity accompanied by cultural diversity in an atmosphere of mutual tolerance' – floated by the then Home Secretary, Roy Jenkins, in 1967 and taken up by the other Roy, Hattersley, and by all the other roys and girls of the labour movement, and transformed into ethnic policies and programmes by the pundits of the Community Relations Commission, the Race Relations Board and the Runnymede Trust, aided by bourgeois sociologists and educationalists, and funded by the Home Office's Urban Aid Programme. Government moneys for pluralist ploys – the development of a parallel power structure for black people, separate development, bantustans – a strategy to keep race issues from contaminating class issues.

Where that pluralist philosophy was first put into effect – where it was formulated and defined – was in education, in the schools, precisely because it was there, among the young blacks, the 'second generation', that the next phase of revolt was fermenting. And the name of the game was multicultural education.

Now, there is nothing wrong with multiracial or multicultural education as such: it is good to learn about other races, about other people's cultures. It may even help to modify individual attitudes, correct personal biases. But that, as we stated in our evidence to the Rampton Committee on Education, is merely to tinker with educational methods and techniques and leave unaltered the whole racist structure of the educational system. And education itself comes to be seen as an adjustment process within a racist society and not as a force for changing the values that make that society racist. 'Ethnic minorities' do not suffer 'disabilities' because of 'ethnic differences' – as the brief of the Rampton Committee suggests – but because such differences are given a differential weightage in a racist hierarchy. Our concern, we pointed out, was not with multicultural, multiethnic education but with anti-racist education, which by its very nature would include the study of other cultures. Just to learn about other people's cultures is not to learn about the racism of one's own. To learn about the racism of one's own culture, on the other hand, is to approach other cultures objectively.

But multiculturalism has become the vogue; it gives the

'ethnic' teachers a leg up and it exculpates the whites: they now know about my culture, so they don't have to question their own. Worse – and this was demonstrated clearly in a confrontation we recently had with a group of head teachers who stumbled on the Institute in the course of their multicultural expedition – they know more about my culture than I do, or think they do! And this gives them a new arrogance, based no longer on feelings of superiority about their culture but on their superior knowledge of mine. One sahib even tried to talk Hindi to me – and I don't even know the language.

Education, however, was not the only area in which culturalism abounded. It began to spread to other areas too – like the media and policing – but let's look at these at a later period, after Thatcher's ascendancy, when they become more clearly defined.

The pluralist philosophies and ethnic programmes which had begun to set up parallel (ethnic) structures within society were, of course, part of Labour policies. What happened when Thatcher came into power was that she couldn't give a damn about blacks or pluralism or the working class. The Tories, in fact, had stolen the clothes of the National Front and moved British society so far to the right as to be near-fascist. (That is why the NF does not do well in the elections; they do better on the streets – look how racial attacks have become part of the popular culture, with the state as a party to it.)

Thatcher herself began life, her racist life – and she is a sincere racist – with a clarion call to the nation to beware that 'this country might be rather swamped by people with a different culture', a call which unleashed the fascist maggots of the inner cities on our children. Her policy-makers spoke of internal controls and passport checks. Enoch Powell, the Permanent Minister of Black Affairs, spoke of 'induced repatriation' and local Tory authorities like Slough literally paid black people to go home.

The nature and function of racism was beginning to change. The recession and the movement of capital to the labour reserves of the Third World, as I pointed out before, had stopped the importation of labour. The point now was to get rid of it. Hence the rationale of racism was no longer exploitation but repatriation, not oppression but repression – forged on the ideological level through the media (directly) and the schools (indirectly and long-term) and effected on the political level through the forces of law and order: the police and the courts principally.

The sites of struggle, in other words, had moved from the (predominantly) economic to the ideological and political, and the protagonists were no longer the state and the 'first generation' but the state and the 'second generation', no longer employers and workers but the state and the workless.

And so the locale of struggle moved from the factory floor to the streets, from the one-time employed, now unemployed, to the never employed. And that is a very important distinction to make when we talk about black youth – for they have not only, like their white counterparts, never been socialised into labour and therein found some stake in the system, but have, unlike them (their white fellows, that is), been kept out of work and indeed out of society by the dictates of institutionalised racism. And so they take nothing as given, everything is up for question, everything is up for change: capitalist values, capitalist mores, capitalist society. And their struggles find a resonance in the struggle of the unemployed white youth and the cities burst aflame.

And it is then – after the burning of Brixton and Toxteth and Southall – that Thatcher sends for Scarman to rescue ethnicity for the Tory Party and create another tranche of the ethnic petit-bourgeoisie, this time in the media and the police consultancy business: chiefs for the bantustans.

Just look at the ethnic media today – especially the ethnic television (newspapers and radio programmes were there before, though in a smaller way). Look at *Black on Black* and *Eastern Eye* in particular. On the one hand, we have the idea of letting blacks get places, so that they can teach their young that they don't have to take on the system when they can become part of it. On the other hand, we have the idea of *positive* black culture, with Eastern cookery classes and Indian films, reggae and 'black humour'. These programmes merely replicate the white media; black plays and comedies do the same. *No Problem* is a problem: we are laughing at ourselves. The system wants that type of replication and 'balance', presenting both sides of a question, as the BBC says it does. What *we* want on *Black on Black* and *Eastern Eye* is an unbalanced view. We don't want a balanced view. The whole society is unbalanced against us, and we take a programme and balance it again?

Look at what *Eastern Eye* did with the John Fernandes case. Fernandes, if you remember, is the teacher who exposed the extent of racism in police cadets and in the teaching at Hendon Police College when its head, Commander Wells, refused to accept Fernandes's findings. *Eastern Eye* gave both Fernandes and Wells a hearing and then, for good measure, allowed Wells the benefit of two black cadets (an Asian and an Afro-Caribbean, a man and a woman) who denied there was any racism at Hendon Police College. That's ethnicity for you. And the worst of it is that these media wallahs think they got up there on their own merit or because they huddled together and called themselves a trade union. Whereas the fact of the matter is that they got there on the backs of the kids who burnt down Toxteth, Brixton and Southall.

So, too, have the rebellions of 1981 helped to get more Afro-Caribbeans and Asians into the police force. Some police chiefs have even brought down standards of recruitment in the cause of 'positive discrimination' – all part of the Scarman scheme. And there are the community consultative committees, with blacks on them to help the police to police the community – a Scarman production, of course.

Such consultative committees should, in fact, be seen in the larger context of the other 'consultations' that are going on – between the police and the social and welfare agencies of the state – what is fondly termed community policing. But once Metropolitan Commissioner Newman's neighbourhood watch schemes get off the ground, spying, too, will be open to Thatcherite private enterprise.

These developments alone tell us why it is important to take on Thatcherism on the ideological and political terrain. But there are other more fundamental reasons connected with the massive changes in the capitalist system itself, which make these two areas paramount. I do not agree with Ken Livingstone that there is ever going to be full employment again. Full employment is a thing of the past, an artefact of the industrial revolution. What today's microelectronic revolution predicates is unemployment. With the silicon chip, microprocessors, robotics, lasers, biogenetics and so on, we are moving into an entirely different ball game, a different capitalist order if you like, where the division of labour is between the skilled and the unskilled and the classes are increasingly polarised into (simply) the haves and the have-nots. Of course, the technological revolution can also make for a society in which there is greater productivity with less labour (fairly distributed), improved consumption for all and more time to be human in. But Thatcher and monetarism do not allow for such a scenario. Instead, what you will have is microelectronic surveillance, computerised data and centralisation of information – and Big Sister watching you. In such a society – and we come to the same conclusion as when we viewed it from the other direction, through the prism of racism – ideology and politics become paramount. The sites of our struggle, therefore, are in education and the media, on the one hand, and against Tory law and order, on the other – meaning not just the police, but unjust laws as well, laws which repress trade unions, women, gays, children and call for extra-parliamentary struggle.

And in that connection, we must not overlook the one positive thing that Thatcher has done – which is to throw up the contradictions within the Labour Party and move certain sections of it closer to us. Remember that the pluralist politics

72

of division which emerged in the 1960s and 1970s came out of the social democratic wing of the Labour Party. The left wing (as it began to emerge) has been left with the ethnic baby; it does not know in which direction to turn, and I think that it is up to us to point them in the right direction. Don't let's be purists and stand outside, for we can't fight the system bare-handed. We don't have the tools, brothers and sisters; we've got to get the tools from the system itself and hope that in the process five out of ten of us don't become corrupt. If we've got the tools and Ken Livingstone's GLC is prepared to give them, we should not hesitate to use them.

Now I'd like to go, quickly, into the programmes and strategies of struggle. In the field of education, as we have seen, it is important to turn ethnicity and culturalism into anti-racism. But this involves not just the examination of existing literature for racist bias (and its elimination) but the provision of anti-racist texts – like the two booklets, *Roots of racism* and *Patterns of racism*, that we at the IRR have published – and not just an examination of curricula and syllabuses but of the whole fabric of education: organisation and adminis-tration, methods and materials, attitudes and practices of heads and teachers, the whole works.

Similarly, in the media we need not only to combat racist bias, but also to stop replicating the white media and propagate instead radical black working-class values. To do that, ethnic programmes (the English language ones anyway) will have to stop tackling only ethnic themes and look at every aspect of British society from the vantage point of the black experience. Conversely, we should demand the introduction of black views and analyses into the mainline programmes (like *Panorama* or *Weekend World*) without being shoved off into ethnic slots.

Others have already spoken on the police and on the Police and Criminal Evidence Bill which will extend to the rest of the population – certainly in the inner cities – the harassment and brutalities hitherto inflicted on the black communities. Here I want only to point out that even while local Labour authorities are making every effort to make the police accountable to elected police committees, the police themselves have deftly side-stepped the issue – first, as we have seen, by their version of 'community policing', and second, through media legitimation of their actions. And, if you remember, it was ex-police chief Sir Robert Mark who made the studied cultivation of the media a central aspect of police policy. The GLC's police monitoring groups are, of course, looking into the whole question of police accountability, and we ourselves are doing research into the media and the police; but, if the Fernandes case is anything to go by, we need to look, too, at the training for that accountability – for how can we expect cadets trained in racism to be accountable to local black communities?

The Fernandes case also suggests another strategy that we must look to: the turning of cases into issues. Cases are one-off, local, disconnected; issues are national and anti-state. The trial of the Bradford twelve, for instance, brought to national prominence the issues of self-defence and conspiracy law; the murder of Blair Peach at the Southall demonstration brought into question the role of the Special Patrol Group and the validity of internal police investigations; the New Cross massacre and the case of Colin Roach showed, among other things, the bias and inadequacies of the coroner's court.

We need to concentrate on cases which raise a number of issues and so bring together the various aspects of our struggle and the different groups involved in them. The Fernandes case, for instance, raises a number of issues – education, policing, the media, trade union racism* – thereby providing us with a more holistic view of our struggle and a basis for mutual support and joint action.

And we need to mobilise blacks everywhere around our

---

* Fernandes' union, the National Association of Teachers in Further and Higher Education, refused to take up the issue of racism in the teaching of police cadets and ultimately sided with the police against both its local branch union and Fernandes.

common experiences of racial attacks. Colin Roach should not just affect Stoke Newington – we should look at the whole aspect of struggle around Colin Roach, the Newham eight, the attacks in Sheffield and in Leicester. We must collate our struggles, cross-fertilising the Afro-Caribbean and Asian experiences, and find unity in action.

We must look, too, to the various levels of struggle – on the streets, in the media, in the council chamber. We must begin to see how we can take our issues into the media and make the media responsible to the communities, instead of legitimating the actions of the system. Similarly, we must make our black councillors responsible to us – they must be seen on the ground participating in our struggle (not just exposing themselves to it), using whatever power they have for the benefit of the community. We must make the black petit-bourgeoisie, which is a petit-bourgeoisie on (white) sufferance, return its expertise, power and education to the working-class blacks whom ethnicity has left defenceless.

And, finally, we must look at the whole area of alliances. Against Thatcherism, there is no question that the objective conditions are there for all sorts of alliances – and alliances do not mean the subservience of one group to another. But, at the same time, we must beware the opposing tendency – and it is a contradiction that has been growing for some time – of too much autonomy. In the 1970s black people said they would not subsume their struggle to the class struggle, that their struggle had got to be autonomous. But we made alliances with the white working class. For instance, during the trial and imprisonment of the Pentonville Five, when the trade unions were planning a march on Pentonville Prison, they appealed to black groups to join in the march. The Black Unity and Freedom Party agreed that the unions' struggle was also black people's struggle, but because of trade union racism they would not join the official march. Instead, they led a different march down a different road to the same spot on behalf of the Pentonville Five. That is what I mean by autonomy and alliances.

Too much autonomy leads us back into ourselves; we begin to home in on our cultures as though nothing else existed outside them. The revolutionary edge of culture that Cabral spoke of is taken away, leaving us with a cultural nationalism that is ineffective in terms of social change. The whole purpose of knowing who we are is not to interpret the world, but to change it. We don't need a cultural identity for its own sake, but to make use of the positive aspects of our culture to forge correct alliances and fight the correct battles. Too much autonomy leads us to inward struggles, awareness problems, consciousness-raising and back again to the whole question of attitudes and prejudices.

Alliances between the anti-racist and the working-class struggle are crucial, because the struggle against racism without the struggle against class remains cultural-nationalist. But class struggle without race struggle, without the struggles of women, of gays, of the Irish, remains economistic.

Let me end by saying this: it's still possible to make use of the good offices of left-wing Labour councils and the ethnic minorities units which left-wing councils have got landed with and turn them towards anti-racist struggle. We must return ethnicity to anti-racism and socialism to Labour. And, in order to do that, we must begin, now, to collate and co-ordinate our struggles – so as to build, in 1984, here, in London, a mass movement. Why not?

RAT and the Degradation of Black Struggle

There is a class war going on within Marxism as to who – in the period of the deconstruction of industrial capitalism and the recomposition of the working class – are the real agents of revolutionary change: the orthodox working class, which is orthodox no more, or the 'ideological classes' who pass for the new social force or forces. It is a war that was engendered, on the one hand, by the growing disillusionment with Soviet communism and, on the other, by the receding prospect of capturing state power in late capitalist societies where such power was becoming increasingly diffuse and opaque. The solution to both, on the ground, pointed to a variant of social democracy under the rubric of Eurocommunism. The solution, for theory, pointed to a rereading of Marx, a rehashing of Gramsci and a return to intellectual rigour accompanied by activist mortis. The working class, as a consequence, was stripped of its richest political seams – black, feminist, gay, green etc. – and left, in the name of anti-economism, a prey to economism. Conversely, the new social forces, freed from the ballast of economic determinism (and class reductionism), have been floated as the political and ideological 'classes' of the new radicalism. But that flight from class has served only to turn ideological priorities into idealistic preoccupations,

and political autonomy into personalised politics and pallia-
tives – which, for all that, have passed into common Left
currency and found a habitation and a name in Labour local
authorities. The clearest expression of these tendencies and
the mortality they bring to the new social movements is to be
seen in the philosophy and practice of Racism Awareness
Training (RAT), the blight of the black struggle – itself a
result of the flight of race from class.

Culture, community and class

What, however, had led to the flight from class within the
black movement in Britain was the demise of the black
community. That community – of Black, Afro-Caribbean-
Asian – had been created in the post-war years by a culture of
resistance to racism in the factories and the neighbourhoods of
the inner cities to which Afro-Caribbeans and Asians had been
condemned to work and live. As workers, they were initially
separated by a colonial division of labour which, by and large,
assigned Afro-Caribbeans to the service industries and Asians
to the foundries and factories. But, as denizens of the same
ghetto, they found common cause against a racism that
denied them their basic needs in housing, schooling and social
and welfare services and brought them up against racist land-
lords, racist teachers, racist social workers and racist
policemen. Common problems and common interests led to a
common culture of resistance – and to community.

That sense of community was reinforced by a common
(albeit different) tradition of struggle against colonialism in
Africa, Asia and the Caribbean. Nkrumah, Nehru, Garvey,
Padmore, James and Williams were all stars of a common
constellation, and the struggles of one continent flowed and
ebbed into the struggles of the other. So that when the trade
unions refused to take up the cause of the Afro-Caribbean or
Asian workers over industrial disputes or racial discrimination

78

and/or exploitation, black communities closed ranks behind them and gave them the sustenance and the support to mount a protest or conduct a strike. And that then wove the interests of the class into the concerns of the community and made for a formidable political force far in excess of its numbers.

The direction for that political force and its ideological tenets came from a variety of black Marxist organisations (the Indian Workers' Association (IWA) and the Universal Coloured Peoples' Association (UCPA) foremost among them) which, in reaction to the Eurocentrism of the white metropolitan Left and its attempts to subsume race to class, held this much in common: that the unity and autonomy of black struggle could only enrich and politicise the struggles of the class as a whole. That did not mean that they were culturally exclusive. On the contrary, their struggles, though informed by a resistance to the oppression of black people, were directed towards the liberation of the class. And in this they were guided by the understanding that any struggle against racism which deepened and extended the class struggle was the right struggle. Conversely, any struggle that led to the cul-de-sac of reactionary nationalism was the wrong one. Hence their stand: for the blacks and therefore for the class.

This politics was, in turn, fed back to the community, in the temples and the churches and Sunday schools, and through meetings and marches and newssheets and pamphlets that linked the struggles here to the struggles back home and made common cause with the movements in Africa, Asia and the Caribbean. And it was this common and burgeoning culture of active resistance to racism and imperialism that cohered black community, linked race to class and engendered the struggles of the second generation.[1]

It was no accident, therefore, that the state should, as of nature, go for the cultural jugular of the black movement, with strategies to disaggregate that culture into its constituent parts – and then put them up for integration. And integration, as defined by Home Secretary Roy Jenkins in May 1966, was to be seen 'not as a flattening process of assimilation but as equal opportunity accompanied by cultural diversity, in an atmosphere of mutual tolerance'. But 'equal opportunity' never got off the ground, nor was meant to, and the plea for 'mutual tolerance' proved to be conclusively cynical with the passage of yet another racist Immigration Act two years later. The emphasis was on 'cultural diversity' – and the integration of those cultures into a 'cultural' pluralist set-up. Racism was not a matter of racial oppression and exploitation, of race and class, but of cultural differences and their acceptability. The 1965 White Paper had got it wrong in trying to get the National Committee for Commonwealth Immigrants (NCCI) to teach British culture to 'coloured immigrants'. But the Race Relations Act of 1968* was going to teach immigrant cultures to the white power structure instead – through a national Community Relations Commission (CRC) and its myriad provincial progeny – and so minimise the social and political cost of racial exploitation. And to facilitate that process in the most fraught areas of urban deprivation, the government would provide special financial aid – some of which might even trickle down to 'the Coloured quarter'.

But that type of multiculturalism did not quite work out either. Explaining West Indian and Asian peoples to white groups and individuals in positions of power – as the CRC did – or picking (ineffectually) at racial discrimination – as the Race Relations Board (RRB) was wont to do – seemed to have little effect in managing racism or breaking down black resistance. Nor had urban aid reached the parts (of society) that would have lubricated such a strategy; and, though a class of black collaborators was springing up in the shadows of the CRC and the RRB, they were still too few in number to take

---

* This was meant to balance out the Commonwealth Immigrants Act of a few months earlier (which denied British citizenship to British Asians in Kenya). For, as Hattersley had said, 'without integration limitation is inexcusable, without limitation integration is impossible'.

the heart out of black protest. And to make matters worse, the (Tory) government brought in yet another Immigration Act (1971)* stopping dead all primary immigration and putting all dependants on a hit list (those, that is, who were waiting in their countries of origin to join their families in Britain).[2]

A different struggle ...

The Act may have diverted the struggles of the black community, and the Asians in particular, from the (political) fight against racism to the more legalistic fight for entry permits for their dependants. But, by creating an official category of illegal immigrants (and overstayers) and setting up a special police unit (IIIU) to pursue them, the Act served also to stoke the fires of black resistance. Already, Afro-Caribbean youth were being brutalised by the police and criminalised by the 'Sus' law; now, the Asians were suspected of being illegals and so open to arrest in their workplaces or their homes. And on the streets, the sport of Paki-bashing had grown, with police indifference (if not connivance), into more generalised and organised racial violence. In education, the relegation of Afro-Caribbean children to ESN schools and the dispersal of Asian children to schools outside their neighbourhoods combined to agitate black parents. On the shop-floor, the power of the employers (heightened by the Industrial Relations Act of 1971) was compounded by the racism of the unions.

And as racism intensified, the resistance to it intensified, too – but in different ways from the 1950s and 1960s. Whereas the

---

* The Tory government is mentioned not because there is any difference between Tory and Labour Immigration Acts – Callaghan, the Home Secretary in the previous Labour government, had in fact foreshadowed the 1971 Act by preventing the entry of fiancés – except that with every one of its Acts to restrict numbers, Labour had a balancing Act to restrict social dislocation.

struggles of that period had been taken up with the 'first-generation' fight against a brutal racism that denied basic needs and services to Afro-Caribbeans and Asians, those of the late 1960s and early 1970s had to address themselves to creating a social and educational infrastructure for the second generation – in self-help groups and social centres, supplementary schools and neighbourhood schools, workshops and bookshops, hostels for the unemployed and the homeless, youth clubs and associations. And because of the differential racism now visited on the different communities, these activities themselves became differentiated as between Afro-Caribbean and Asian. But they still found their expression in and through political groups and organisations – which, if they tended to be less 'universal' than the UCPA (1967–71), less generalised than the IWA (now split three ways), still came together to gather the community and mount a protest, organise a march, set up a picket. And through their newspapers and bulletins and demonstrations, they continued to connect the struggles of black people in Britain to the struggles of the Third World, the struggle against racism with the struggle against imperialism. The parameters of struggle were still the same as in the decade before – except that now, with the second generation, the priorities of resistance were beginning to change. And, though there was still a culture of resistance that held black communities together and made for race/class struggle, this owed more to the selfconscious ideology of black political parties and organisations than to spontaneous local community initiatives.

Besides, the deployment of black workers itself had changed from the earlier period: they were scattered now in various industries and not necessarily concentrated (race-wise) in a few. Hence the strikes of 1972, 1973 and 1974 in the East Midlands (Nottingham, Loughborough, Leicester), Birmingham and Greater London were distinguished not only by the support they received from black political organisations but also by their attempts to break down the racism of the trade unions and involve them more directly in black workers' struggle.* 'Unions, after all, were the organisations of their class and, however vital their struggles as blacks, to remain a people apart would be to set back the class struggle itself: the struggle against racism was still a struggle for the class.'[3]

The politics of the black youth, however, were of a different order. They were not prepared to do the 'shit work' that their (immigrant) parents had been forced to do – they wanted what they were entitled to as of right – and their politics was therefore insurrectionary. Nor were they prepared to put up with mounting police harassment and brutality – which, in 1972, had received the blessing of the press and, in 1973, the government's imprimatur.** A series of running battles with the police marked the early years of the 1970s – at Brockwell Park Fair (1973), for instance, and at the Carib Club (1974) and in Chapeltown, Leeds, on bonfire night (1975) – and exploded into direct confrontation with bricks and bottles and the burning of police cars at the Notting Hill Carnival of 1976.

... and a different state strategy

Already, by 1974, the anxieties of the state had begun to shift from the resistances of the first generation to those of the second. The 1968 version of multiculturalism cum urban aid had clearly failed because it was aimed primarily at the white power structure. All it had done was to spawn a nursery of comprador blacks – in the race relations industry. The new labour strategy of multiculturalism with urban aid, therefore, would be aimed at the black communities – financing in particular the *respective* self-help projects of Asians and Afro-Carib-

* From this emerged the first National Committee for Trade Unions Against Racialism (1973).
** The White Paper on Police-Immigrant Relations (1973) warned of 'a small minority of young coloured people ... anxious to imitate behaviour amongst the black community in the United States'.

beans, which were starved of funds. Accordingly, in January 1975, the Home Office announced the granting of aid to 'urban areas facing special social problems' to the tune of £7 million, funding a host of black community groups in the process.[4] And in September of that same year, the (Labour) government indicated in a White Paper on Racial Discrimination its intention this time to include effective equal opportunities programmes into its multicultural strategy. For 'the character of the coloured population resident in this country has changed dramatically over the decade ... and the time is not far off when the majority of the coloured population will be British born' – and it was 'vital to tap the reservoirs of resilience, initiatives and vigour in the racial minority groups and not to allow them to lie unused or to be deflected into negative protests on account of arbitrary and unfair discriminatory practices'.[5]

The strategy and purpose of the White Paper, and the Race Relations Act that followed from it (1976), have been anticipated and analysed in 'Race, class and the state' (1976).* For my argument here, what is important to note is that the combined strategy of promoting individual cultures, funding self-help groups and setting down anti-discriminatory and equal opportunity guidelines, not least through the collapsing of the RRB and CRC into a single Commission for Racial Equality (CRE), began finally to break down the earlier cohesion of culture, community and class. Multiculturalism deflected the political concerns of the black community into the cultural concerns of different communities, the struggle against racism into the struggle for culture. Government funding of self-help groups undermined the self-reliance, the

* 'Within ten years Britain will have solved its "black problem" – but "solved" in the sense of having diverted revolutionary aspiration into nationalist achievement, reduced militancy to rhetoric, put protest to profit and, above all, kept a black underclass from bringing to the struggles of the white workers political dimensions peculiar to its own historic battle against capital.'[6]

self-created social and economic base, of those groups: they were no longer responsive to or responsible for the people they served – and service itself became a profitable concern.

Anti-discriminatory action was either ineffectual or touched only the cultural fringes of discrimination – so that you could wear a turban and still get a job – and behind equal opportunity, based as it was on the concept of racial disadvantage (as opposed to institutional racism), hovered the notion of differential opportunities for Asians and West Indians, respectively.[7] If opportunity there was, it was opportunity for the 'black' compradors, preened and pruned by the CRE to blossom into the new 'black' leadership, and later the 'state-class', that would manage racism and keep the lid on protest – or at least deflect it from political struggle. And as a further bonus, Labour had, under the previous Tory administration, been gifted a cross-section of Asian business men from Uganda (passing for refugees), presumably to add to 'the leaven of energy and resourcefulness that immigrant communities brought with them'.[8]

Underlying the whole of the state's project was a divisive culturalism that turned the living, dynamic, progressive aspects of black people's culture into artefact and habit and custom – and began to break up community.

In fact, the collapse of the long-standing strike at Grunwick at the end of 1977 owes not a little to this process. The strikers (predominantly Asian women in a predominantly Asian work-force), it has been argued by some black activists, would have done better to rely on the black community and black organisations for their support than to look to the trade unions – who finally betrayed them.[9] But except for the support of women and of the odd black organisation, that community, which as recently as 1973–7 had rallied to a series of black strikes in the East Midlands, was no longer there. And even in the strikes that followed Grunwick's in the next couple of years – as at Futters, and Chix – it was the women in the black community who turned out to help the class.

Black women had 'held up half the sky', without getting half the recognition, during the Black Power era. But now, when the rest of the community was falling away, it was they who stood out against the skyline. And, informed not only by their struggles against racism and sexism but by those of their sisters against sexism and imperialism in the Third World, it was they who found common cause with the class.*

It was the women, besides, who had to bear the brunt of the cuts in health, education and welfare which marked the last years of Callaghan's Labour government. These affected Asian and Afro-Caribbean families in particular, and it was the women from the communities who took up the issues of childcare (Afro-Caribbean and Asian), black prisoners' rights (Afro-Caribbean), the virginity-testing and X-raying of immigrants (Asian), the enforced use of depo-provera (Afro-Caribbean and Asian), the neglect of 'ethnic diseases' such as sickle cell anaemia (Afro-Caribbean) and rickets (Asian), the easy relegation of (Afro-Caribbean) children to adjustment units (sin-bins), and the fight against the deportation of 'illegal' (Asian) mothers or for the entry of 'illegal' (Asian) children to join them. But, of their very nature, these issues had a differential impact on the two communities and tended to make for separate struggles on the ground. And although ideologically the black women's movement still tried to cohere the common interests of race, gender and class, the black culture of resistance of an earlier period was now being put under review by a feminist culture of resistance which was still not confident enough to create new black parameters.

* By 1978, black women's groups had sprung up all over Britain and came together to form one powerful national body, the Organisation of Women of Asian and African Descent (OWAAD), with a national newspaper, FOWAAD.[10]

From black struggle to anti-racist struggle

The struggles of the youth, already divided by the propagation of multiculture, had also taken off in different directions. The trouncing the police had received at the hands of the Afro-Caribbean youth at the Notting Hill Carnival (1976) had only led to a more sophisticated, mailed-fist velvet-glove, approach to policing. The tactic of using the media to legitimate the criminalisation of black youth, first begun under Police Commissioner Robert Mark, was continued by his successor, David McNee – only he, taking to heart his nickname, 'The Hammer', now brought riot shields to the 'defence' of his force. And increasing police authoritarianism itself found legitimacy in the policies of a Labour government which, with an eye to the forthcoming elections, had begun to backpedal on its anti-discriminatory programme (however ineffective) and rely instead on the forces of law and order to smother black discontent.

Labour had earlier – as part of its balancing act between restricting immigration and improving integration – started yet another Dutch auction on immigration control through, this time, a Green Paper on Nationality Law. The Tories, under Thatcher, upped the ante and promised pass laws to control 'internal immigration' and 'arrangements' to facilitate voluntary repatriation. And the National Front, thus released into respectability, became more brazen in its attacks on the Asian community – and so occupied the attention of Asian youth. But since the Front's bravery was invariably under 'police protection', the Asian youth were up against the police as well. The killing of Gurdip Singh Chaggar in 1976 by young fascist thugs in the heart of Southall had led to clashes with the police (who held that the murder was not necessarily racial). In 1977, the Front, under police escort, had staged virulently racist and provocative marches through black city areas and were stopped by the youth of both communities. In 1978, Judge McKinnon ruled that the National Party leader

Kingsley Read's pronouncement on Chaggar's murder – 'one down, one million to go' – did not constitute incitement to racial hatred.* In 1979, the Front, abetted by the policies of the local Tory council and the police, flaunted its fascist election programmes in Southall Town Hall and was repelled by the citizenry, but at the cost of the life of a teacher, who was battered to death by the Special Patrol Group.

The rise of the Right had, three years earlier, brought together radical whites and blacks in the inner-city areas in an Anti-Racist Anti-Fascist Co-ordinating Committee (ARAFCC) with its own newspaper, *CARF*. Their battle was joined a year later by white organisations under the broad banner of the Anti-Nazi League (ANL). But, in the process, the direction of the battle got deflected from a fight against racism and, therefore, fascism to a fight against fascism and, incidentally, racism. The whites from the local committees of ARAFCC defected to the ANL, which, with its spectacular events such as rock concerts and fêtes and carnivals, its youth organisations such as School Kids Against the Nazis and its paper *SKAN*, and its mass leafleting drives, was able to attract more (white) support and mobilise more (white) people. The fascists, as a result, were stopped dead in their electoral tracks; but they were also driven from the (white) high streets into the (black) alleyways of the inner city, there to continue their depredations and their recruitment. And when, after the general election of 1979, the ANL (its mission accomplished) disbanded, the issues of racism and fascism had become separated, and the joint struggles of Asians and Afro-Caribbeans likewise. The black struggle (for community and class) was becoming more narrowly a struggle against racism, and the anti-racist struggle itself was tending to divide into struggles that concerned Asians (mainly) and the struggles that

---

* 'In this England of ours', the good judge observed, 'we are allowed to have our own view still, thank goodness, and long may it last.'

concerned Afro-Caribbeans (mainly).* The protest over Akhtar Ali Baig's murder (July 1980) in Newham, for example, was mostly an Asian affair, and the massive march following the burning to death of thirteen young Afro-Caribbeans in a fire in New Cross (January 1981) chiefly an Afro-Caribbean one.

And then, in the summer of 1981, the youth of the benighted inner cities, black and white, Afro-Caribbean and Asian, came together again, not so much in joint struggle as in a blinding moment of spontaneous insurrection against the impossibility of their common condition. For, in the course of two brief years, Thatcherite monetarism had blighted the future of all working-class youth, not just black, and left them a bleak landscape of 'rocks, moss, stonecrop, iron, merds' over-shadowed by policemen.

The rebellions shook the government. The danger now was not the black community as such. There was no *black* community. The promotion of cultural separatism (euphemistically known as cultural diversity or multiculturalism) was keeping Asians and Afro-Caribbeans apart; the development of a youth culture and a women's culture was further decomposing the forces within the community, without, as yet, realigning them in a new black configuration; and the emergence of an Afro-Caribbean managerial class in the race relations industry (and sub-managers in the nationalised self-help groups), together with the flowering of Ugandan Asian entrepreneurship, was breaking up community into classes. The danger to the state stemmed from the never-employed youth of the inner cities, both black and white, hounded and harried by the police. But the blacks, by virtue of their racial oppression, were the insurrectionary tinder.**

* But not before the Indian Workers' Association, the Black Socialist Alliance, Blacks Against State Harassment and various black women's groups had organised one final national demonstration against state harassment and fascist thuggery in June 1979.
** 'To allege that unemployment or social deprivation is the cause of the "riots" is to pretend that racism is not also the cause of unemployment and social deprivation – among blacks.'[11]

Hence, while a Task Force of town planners and bankers and business men under the Minister for the Environment was sent to study mixed areas like Toxteth in Liverpool, to see how such areas could be regenerated, black (mainly Afro-Caribbean) areas like Brixton got the attention also of a quasi-judicial inquiry under Lord Scarman to investigate the 'disorders' and their causes (in racism and police–black relations). Little of substance came out of the first of these initiatives for Toxteth (or Smethwick) as such, but the Urban Aid programme, which, under the Tories, had fallen into disfavour, now received a 'dramatic re-awakening of interest ... as a vehicle for social measures in multi-racial areas', and the CRE, which the Tories had threatened to close down, was open for business again – the business of channelling funds to black 'self-help' groups.* Consequently, 'funding for the total urban programme ... was dramatically increased, against the trend, to a 1982/3 level of £270m.'**

The rise and rise of ethnicity

It was Lord Scarman's report, however, that pointed to a new ethnic strategy, which was received with enthusiasm (and relief) by Tory and Labour alike.*** The foundation for that

* Though Section 11 of the Local Government Act of 1966 is the 'major vehicle of ... government support for local authority programmes designed to combat racial disadvantage', 'the Urban Programme is the major source of funding for voluntary sector schemes designed to combat racial discrimin-ation'.[12]
** 'Nationally, over 200 new "ethnic projects" have been approved for 1982/3; in the Partnership authorities these are valued at £2m (£0.77m in 1981/2) while Traditional Urban Programme expenditure on "ethnic projects" has increased still more sharply to £7m (£2.7m in 1981/2). It is estimated that £15m is currently being spent on ethnic projects under the urban programme.'[13]
*** But then, it was in essence an elaboration of the multicultural strategy initiated by Labour in 1976 – and in hard times, the Tories were not averse to taking lessons from their masters in social control.

strategy, however, had already been intimated in the report of the Home Affairs Committee on Racial Disadvantage (1981) – which was itself informed by a whole school of ethnicity that had emerged (at Bristol University's Social Science Research Council Unit on Ethnic Relations) to take on the 'problem' of British-born blacks.

Whereas multiculturalism, addressing itself to the revolt of the first-generation 'immigrant', diagnosed the problem as one of cultural misunderstanding, the ethnicists, in trying to relate to the ongoing revolt of British-born blacks, connected it with the cultural limbo to which racism had ostensibly condemned them. Neither Asian/Afro-Caribbean nor British but afflicted by both, the second generation was adrift of its moorings and rudderless, caught in a cross-current of emotion in its search for identity – not least, to fight racism with. And in that search, it kept returning to its ethnicity and, redefining it, found refuge therein. Ethnicity refers, therefore, to the creation of a new reactive culture on the part of British-born Asians and West Indians alike. But where Asians tended to go into their cultures to make the new ethnicity, West Indian ethnicity came out of a mixture, a 'creolisation', of Afro-Caribbean culture with the 'host' culture. 'Those who were born in Britain', states Watson, 'are caught between the cultural expectations of their parents (the first-generation migrants) and the social demands of the wider society. Young Sikhs and Jamaicans, for instance, often feel that they do not "fit" in either culture ... Largely in response to racism, these two minorities have begun a process of ethnic redefinition – or "creolisation"'.[14] Or, in Weinreich's language: 'West Indian boys have conflicted identifications with the general representatives of their own ethnicity and the native white population.' Hence, the 'changes' in the second generation should be seen as 'redefinition of their ethnic distinctiveness'.[15] It is racism, however, according to the Ballards, that has 'precipitated a reactive pride in their separate ethnic identity'.[16] Ethnicity itself, for Wallman, is a 'perception' of difference, a 'sense' of it, something that was 'felt', a clue to identity.[17]

By acknowledging the resistance to racism on the part of the second generation only to banish it to 'conflicted identification' and 'ethnic redefinition', the ethnicists deny the connection between race and class and between racism and imperialism – and reincarcerate the second generation in the castle of their skin. Identity is all. The Home Affairs Committee then takes on the ethnic theme and, making ethnicity official, signs up institutional racism as racial disadvantage – leaving it to Scarman to tie it up with ethnic need.

Like the Race Relations Act of 1976, the main planks of the Scarman report were racial discrimination (direct and indirect) and racial disadvantage. Racial discrimination Scarman, too, was prepared to leave to the 'existing law', and presumably the CRE.* But racial disadvantage, which the 1976 Act – steering its way gingerly between the Scylla of institutional racism and the Charybdis of inherent inferiority – had left (undefined) to the vagaries of equal opportunity, was in Scarman to be (specifically) treated in terms of special ethnic needs and problems.** And it is here at the point of cure, in the act of applying the ethnic poultice to the ethnic wound, that racial disadvantage begins to smell of inherent disability.

The West Indian family, implies Scarman, is comparatively unstable, 'doubtless because of the impact of British social conditions on the matriarchal extended family structure of the West Indian immigrants'.[18] For instance, 'the percentage of children in care and of single-parent families in the black community is noticeably higher than one would expect in relation to the proportion of black people in the community as a whole. Fifty per cent of single-parent families in ... Lambeth in 1978 were non-white'. Besides, 'the two wards where the April disorders were centred – Tulse Hill and Herne Hill –

* The CRE was under inquiry by the Home Affairs Committee at the time and Scarman would not commit himself.
** 'The special problems and needs of the ethnic minorities', is how Scarman put it.

contain some 22 per cent of all the single-parent households in Lambeth and 2.1 per cent of the 0–18 group in those wards are in care. Of the 185 children in care of those two wards on 10 September 1980, 112 (61 per cent) were black'. In addition, it was estimated that '200–300 young blacks are homeless, sleeping rough or squatting in Brixton'.

Young West Indians, for Scarman, are 'a people of the street ... They live their lives on the street, having often nothing better to do: they make their protest there: and some of them live off street crime.' Inevitably, they must come into conflict with the police, 'whom they see as pursuing and harassing them on the streets'.* And this hostility of black youth to the police has 'infected older members of the community'. The street-corners are 'social centres' for old people too, and 'young and old, good and bad have time on their hands and a continuing opportunity ... to engage in endless discussion of their grievances', so that 'in Brixton even one isolated instance of misconduct can foster a whole legion of rumours which rapidly become beliefs firmly held within the community'.

If this is not as elaborate as Moynihan's 'tangled pathology' of the American 'Negro family',** it is because Scarman's brief was to investigate the 'Brixton disorders' not the West Indian community. But, given his determination to acquit the state of institutional racism, it was inevitable that he should find the West Indian community guilty of inherent disability – and so give racial disadvantage a meaning which even the Home Affairs Committee report on the subject (July 1981) had been careful to avoid. But the committee, since its brief was racial disadvantage as such, also referred to the disadvantage

---

* By contrast, the 'chief complaint of Asian leaders appears to be that the police do not do sufficient to protect their community from alleged attacks by racist members of the white community.'[19]

** 'Once or twice removed, it [the weakness of the family structure] will be found to be the principal source of most of the aberrant, inadequate or anti-social behaviour that did not establish, but now serves to perpetuate the cycle of poverty and deprivation.'[20]

suffered by the Asian community and located it in language, religion, custom and (peasant) illiteracy. (Only the 'East African Asians' were an exception.) Between them, the two reports set out the terms of West Indian and Asian ethnic need and provided the criteria on which the government based its (ethnic) programmes and allocated its (ethnic) funds.

The ensuing scramble for government favours and government grants (channelled through local authorities) on the basis of specific ethnic needs and problems served, on the one hand, to deepen ethnic differences and foster ethnic rivalry and, on the other, to widen the definition of ethnicity to include a variety of national and religious groups – Chinese, Cypriots, Greeks, Turks, Irish, Italians, Jews, Moslems, Sikhs – till the term itself became meaningless (except as a means of getting funds). This 'vertical mosaic' of ethnic groups, so distanced from the horizontal of class politics, then became even more removed by the policies of 'Left' Labour councils who, lacking the race/class perspective which would have allowed them to dismantle the institutional racism of their own structures, institutionalised ethnicity instead. And it was left to a handful of genuinely anti-racist programmes and/or campaigns, such as those against deportation, police harassment and racial violence (sustained largely by GLC funding), to carry on the dwindling battle for community and class.

The other cure for racial disadvantage propounded by Scarman was 'positive action', which meant no more than a determined effort at promoting equal opportunity or, more precisely, reducing unequal opportunity for ethnic minorities, but backed up this time by a system of monitoring. And this, too, was taken up avidly by inner-city administrations who, having set up their own race relations units (to administer ethnic programmes and ethnic funds), required now an ethnic staff – not least, to keep an eye on jobs for ethnics.*

---

* The local CRCs were pushed on to the sidelines in the process and the central CRE was left the statutory task of taking up cases of discrimination.

Underlying the whole of Scarman's report is a sociopsychological view of racism, resonant of the ideas of the ethnic school, which, when coupled with his views on racial disadvantage, verges on the sociobiological. Institutional racism, for Scarman, is not a reality of black life but a matter of subjective feelings, perceptions, attitudes and beliefs. Ethnic minorities have a 'sense' of 'concealed discrimination'. Young blacks have a 'sense of rejection' and 'a sense of insecurity'. They do not 'feel' secure socially, economically or politically. They 'see' policemen 'as pursuing and harassing them on the streets' – and the older generation have come to share this 'belief'. (The 'belief' in the Asian community is that the police do not protect them against 'alleged' racist attacks.) Community 'attitudes and beliefs' (caused by a lack of confidence in the police) underlie the disturbances. 'Popular attitudes and beliefs' themselves 'derive their strength' from the 'limbo of the half-remembered and the half-imagined'. The 'image' of a hostile police force is 'myth' and 'legend'.[21]

Equally, if the police force was guilty of anything, it was not institutional racism but racial prejudice – which 'does manifest itself occasionally in the behaviour of a few police officers on the street'. And the breakdown of police–community relations was, on the part of the police, due to the fact that their 'attitudes and methods' had not quite caught up with 'the problem of policing a multicultural society'. Part of the policeman's training, therefore, should be directed to 'an understanding of the cultural backgrounds and attitudes of ethnic minorities'.

Racism, for Scarman, was in the mind – in attitudes, prejudices, irrational beliefs – and these were to be found on both sides of the divide, black and white. Institutional racism was a matter of black perception, white racism was a matter of prejudice. Or that, on the face of it, was what Scarman seemed to be saying – and at best, it was even-handed, liberal even. But what he had effectively done was to reduce institutional racism to black perception and replace it with personal prejudice –

and so shift the object of anti-racist struggle from the state to the individual, from changing society to changing people, from improving the lot of whole black communities, mired in racism and poverty, to improving the lot of 'black' individuals.

It was a plan that the nascent 'black' petit-bourgeoisie, nourished on government (and local government) aid for ethnic need and positive action for ethnic equality, leapt to embrace. By and large, the ethnics were content to fight each other in their quest for office. And it was only when there was a white blockage in the system, preventing them from going up further, that the ethnics turned 'black' and pulled out all their oppressed 'black' history to beat the whites with. Hence the demand for Black Sections in the Labour Party; the rise and fall of the Black Media Workers' Association (BMWA) (the fall coming after the white media made room for them in ethnic slots – since when they have gone back to being Afro-Caribbeans and Asians, respectively); and the emergence of a black trade union aristocracy, the Black Trade Union Solidarity Movement (BTUSM).* None of these gives a fart for ordinary black people, but uses them and their struggles as cynically as any other bourgeois class or sub-class.

Ironically enough, most of the support for these groups has come from the 'left wing' of the labour movement which, having failed to incorporate black working-class struggles and black working-class leadership into its own history and organisation, now feels compelled to accommodate black sects in its vaunted broad church. Taking black out of the context of the struggles in which it was beaten into a political colour, the white Left now believes that any self-seeking middle-class group that calls itself black has an automatic right to appropriate that history and is automatically political or progressive. What is even more ironical is that this should be happening at a time when, in the rush for office, even such reconstituted

---

* The personnel of one group were frequently the personnel of another, as in an interlocking directorate.

96

blackness is breaking up into Afro-Caribbean and Asian, with the Afro-Caribbeans claiming a prior right to black history on the basis, simply, of a darker colour – thereby emptying 'black' of politics altogether.* Black Sections are no more representative of black working people than the Labour Party is of white. In fact, black politics has to cease to be political for blacks to get into politics. The BTUSM is no more interested in the lot of the rank and file than their lordships Chapple and Murray were as erstwhile leaders of their unions. The BMWA, in the short period of its fight-to-get-into-Channel-4 existence, never did anything for the lower ranks of black workers or, for that matter, demanded to make political black plays or programmes that would have improved the lot of ordinary Afro-Caribbeans or Asians – unless exposing the foibles and manners of one's own people to white voyeurs, but from the inside this time, can be considered funny or political. But then, an ethnic media can only reproduce the cult of ethnicity. And a culture of ethnicity, unlike a culture of resistance, has no community and has no class.

And to undergird it all, undergird the efforts of the new ethnics to move up and away – up through the white blockages in the system and away from the black communities and their troubles – there is a whole school of thought and enterprise which promises to change white minds and white attitudes so that a thousand black flowers can bloom in the interstices of the white structure. Felicitously, it calls itself RAT (Racism Awareness Training)** – and it is to this final degradation of black struggle that I now turn my attention.

---

* This degradation of 'black' has now passed into vulgar usage and separated Afro-Caribbeans from Asians – as in 'black and Asian', which is itself a nonsense, as one refers to colour (not politics) and the other to geography.
** Some RAT practitioners have recently changed the name to TIRA (Training in Racism Awareness); but a RAT by any other name still smells.

The birth of RAT

RAT began life in HAT (Human Awareness Training) on a military base in Florida at the end of the 1960s, when the reverberations of black rebellion in American cities began to resonate in the military installations in the USA and Japan and drove the Defense Department to a Human Goals Proclamation upholding individual dignity, worth and equal opportunity in its ranks. The training of human relations instructors at the Defense Race Relations Institute (DRRI), therefore, was meant to inculcate a knowledge of minority cultures and history, together with an understanding of personal racism.

HAT, of course, had formed part of human relations training for some time, but the race relations element came to prominence only after the Kerner Commission (1968) declared that racism in America was a white problem and that it inhered in the very structures of society. 'What white Americans have never fully understood – but what the Negro can never forget – is that white society is deeply implicated in the ghetto. White institutions created it, white institutions maintain it and white society condones it.'[22] On the face of it, the Kerner report looked like a radical statement (as radical as Scarman appeared liberal), and though it connected racism with white institutions, nowhere did it connect the institutions themselves with an exploitative white power structure. So that oppression was severed from exploitation, racism from class and institutional racism from state racism.

The US Commission on Civil Rights (1970) echoed the Kerner Commission and went on to define racism (which Kerner had left undefined) as 'any attitude, action or institutional structure which subordinates a person or group because of his or their color', adding that an 'institutional structure was any well-established, habitual or widely accepted pattern of action' (that is, behavioural) or 'organizational arrangements whether formal or informal' (that is, administrational). The

Commission also made a distinction between 'overt racism' and 'indirect institutional subordination' (which was to become direct and indirect discrimination in the British context). And combating racism, stated the Commission, involved 'changing the behaviour of whites' and 'increasing the capabilities of non-white groups' (which in Britain was to become known as tackling racial disadvantage). But the principal responsibility was 'with the white community rather than within the non-white communities'.[23]

Following the two reports, a whole host of literature sprang up in education, psychology and the churches, rescuing racism from structural taint and interiorising it within the white psyche and white behaviour – and formulating programmes for combating racism on that basis. The New York-based Council for Interracial Books, Integrated Education (Chicago), the Foundation for Change and the Detroit-centred New Perspectives on Race were particularly active in the educational field. Writing in *Integrated Education*, Paul Goldin formulated a 'Model for racial awareness training of teachers in integrated schools' which 'pushes one (through inter-racial confrontation) into an identification with the minority position'.[24] In *Developing new perspectives on race*, however, Michigan's school superintendent, Patricia Bidol, advocated a more cognitive approach, emphasising that 'only whites can be racists because it is whites that have control over the institutions that create and enforce American cultural norms and values' – and it is whites who benefit from it. She distinguished, therefore, between overt (Archie Bunker type) racism and covert (unintentional) racism – and defined racism itself as 'prejudice plus institutional power'. And it was Bidol and Detroit's New Perspectives on Race who pioneered in the development of racism awareness training for educators.*[25]

---

* Bidol's influence is also prominent in Britain, as for instance in the use of her slide show, 'From racism to pluralism', at RAT sessions run by the Racism Awareness Programme Unit (RAPU).

But the work of the Detroit Industrial Mission – following the burning of the city (1967) and the rise of black militancy in DRUM (Dodge Revolutionary Union Movement) and FRUM (Ford Revolutionary Union Movement) – pointed to the need to create a 'new white consciousness' through both attitudinal and behavioural change. The emphasis hitherto, wrote its Associate Director, Robert W. Terry, in *For whites only*, had been on changing attitudes to change behaviour or changing behaviour (through law, for instance) in order to change attitudes. But though both attitudes and behaviour were critical and both needed to be changed, 'attitudes will be misplaced and behaviour misdirected if consciousness remains untouched'. For even the most well-intentioned person, argues Terry, taking on from where the Civil Rights Commission had left off,* without being 'personally involved in overt acts of racial injustice', can perpetuate racism in institutions merely by the way the American 'cultural or belief system ... sets his orientation in the decision-making process'. Hence, it was important to be conscious of cultural (historical, linguistic, etc.), institutional (direct and indirect) and individual racism all at once.[27] Cultural racism had to be examined wherever it occurred (language, textbooks, media), 'confrontation' was a good way of challenging personal racism and, for institutional racism, Terry provided a model check list designed by the Chicago Campaign for One Society: 'Inventory of racism: how to look for institutional racism'.**

The elements of the RAT credo were already set by the time Judy Katz came to write her D. Ed thesis: 'Systematic handbook of exercises for the re-education of white people with

* 'Even many whites who sincerely abhor racism in principle and openly combat overt racism, sometimes feel themselves resisting clearly anti-racist actions for "intuitive" reasons they do not fully understand. This usually means such anti-racist actions threaten to reduce certain almost subconsciously perceived psychological benefits these whites have been gaining from living in a society where they are considered members of a "superior" group.'[26]
** This same checklist is reproduced in Katz's handbook.

respect to attitudes and behaviourisms' (1976) – except that by now she could also draw on the women's movement for an even more personal interpretation of oppression and the need for consciousness-raising. That perspective would, in addition, also allow her (and her followers) to distort the language, style and analysis of the black movement and further remove racism from its exploitative context and render it classless.

Racism, states Katz, is indeed a white problem, and white people had better take conscience of it – for the sake of their own mental health. As far back as 1965, she points out, the Commission on Mental Health described racism as the number one mental health problem in the United States. 'Its destructive effects severely cripple the growth and development of millions of our citizens, young and old alike.'[28] Even before that, the Myrdal 'report' on 'The American Dilemma' (1944) had drawn attention to the hiatus, the schism, the rupture in the (white) American psyche: between 'American ideals of equality, freedom, God-given dignity of the individual, inalienable rights' and 'the practices of discrimination, humiliation, insult, denial of opportunity to Negroes and others in a racist society'.[29] New research had sprung up to show that racism was a 'psychological problem ... deeply imbedded in white people from a very early age both on a conscious and an unconscious level'. And even black commentators, according to Katz, confirmed the diagnosis, pointed to a cure – like Whitney Young, for instance, head of the National Urban League: 'most people are not conscious of what racism really is. Racism is not a desire to wake up every morning and lynch a black man from a tall tree. It is not engaging in vulgar epithets ... It is the day to day indignities, the subtle humiliations that are so devastating ... The Kerner Commission has said that if you have been an observer; if you have stood by idly, you are racist.' Katz even rallies radical blacks like Du Bois to her cause: 'Am I, in my blackness, the sole sufferer? I suffer. And yet, somehow, above the suffering, above the shackled anger that beats the bars, above the hurt that crazes, there surges in me a vast pity – pity for a people imprisoned and enthralled, hampered and made miserable for such a cause.' And more recent black militants, like Stokely Carmichael, taken out of the context of struggle: 'if the white man wants to help, he can go home and free his own people',[30] or Malcolm X: 'whites who are sincere should organize themselves and figure out some strategies to break down race prejudice that exists in white communities'.*[31]

Racism, for Katz, is an 'essence' that history has deposited in the white psyche, like sexism is an 'essence' deposited in the male: oppressors oppress themselves.** It is a part of the psychosocial history of white America, part of its collective unconscious. It is in American customs, institutions, language, mores – it is both conscious and unconscious at the same time, both overt and covert. There is no escaping it. And because the system is loaded in their favour, all that whites can be, even when they fight racism, is anti-racist racists; if they don't, they are just plain, common or garden racists.

Hence, any training programme that intends to bring individual whites to a consciousness of themselves should also take conscience of American culture and institutions. And it should be done at two levels at once – the cognitive or informative and the affective or emotional – at the level of thinking and at the level of feeling. The techniques that had hitherto been used in human relations training erred on one side or the other; or, like multicultural or ethnic studies, they were too other-oriented, not self-aware enough; or they were, like inter-racial encounters, too exploitative, once again, of Third World peoples. Only white on white techniques promised any success, and it was on that basis that Ms Katz had devised a systematic training programme which was influenced as much by the shift in psychotherapy towards a teaching role as by the

* RAT practitioners in Britain even quote Stokely on institutional racism.
** 'Our sexual and racial essences have an enormous influence on our perspectives and experiences.'

shift in education towards a counselling role.* The point, after all, was not to change attitudes, but to change behaviour – to change the world.

Since then (1976), the Katz technique of racism awareness training – an intensive six-stage programme of forty-eight exercises crammed into two weekends but adaptable 'to many different settings' – has become widely used in the United States, 'in school systems, with teachers, counsellors and administrators, as part of Affirmative Action Programmes with managers; at university communities with students, faculties, and administrators'.[32]

Part of its appeal lay, of course, with the American penchant for therapy, but part of it was also due to the political climate in which it grew: the collapse of the Black Power movement into culturalism and theological liberation, the personalisation of power in the women's movement and the diaspora of guilt broadcast by Israel in the wake of its imperial adventures.

Taking a leaf out of the Black Power book, Ms Katz defines racism as a 'white problem'. But whereas the white problem in Black Power ideology referred to the white capitalist power structure, in Ms Katz it is reduced to a personal one, a problem of individuals who, because they are white, have power over non-whites. Having so established white guilt as irreversible, almost in-born, Ms Katz takes infinite pains to warn whites that they should not feel guilty, for guilt is 'a self-indulgent way to use up energy'.** On the other hand, whites suffer from racism – as much as men suffer from sexism. And 'we have learnt from the Feminist Movement that men as well as women are adversely affected by oppressive sex roles'. Her

---

* Which is why her trainers carry the exotically hybrid name of 'facilitators'.
** In one of the exercises in the *Handbook*, Ms Katz advises the 'facilitator' that 'one way to manage feelings of guilt is to emphasise that racism is deeply ingrained in our system and that we are clearly products of our system' – and then proceeds illogically to demand that one changes oneself rather than the system.

programme of anti-racist sensitivity training, therefore, promises through a 'process of self-examination, change and action that we will someday liberate ourselves and our society'.

It is the sort of psychospiritual mumbo-jumbo which, because it has the resonances of the political movements of its time – capitalists have changed the world, our business is to interpret it – and, by reducing social problems to individual solutions, passes off personal satisfaction for political liberation, and then wraps it all up in a Madison Avenue sales package promising instant cure for hereditary disease, claimed the attention not just of Middle America but of a grateful state. For what better way could the state find to smooth out its social discordances while it carried on, untrammelled, with its capitalist works?

The spread of RAT

It was not, on the face of it, a package that would have appealed to the British 'character', but it seemed the logical extension to the work of a group of teachers and community workers (mostly black) whose campaign against racial symbols in children's books had derived its message and method directly from the Council for Interracial Books in the USA – who were themselves proponents of RAT. Accordingly, in 1978, the group founded the Racism Awareness Programme Unit (RAPU) on the rock of Katzian teaching – and was joined soon after by renegades (mostly black) from the multicultural faith, disaffected by its inability to speak to white racism. In the following year, some of the RAPU people, along with others, set up the National Committee on Racism in Children's Books and began to produce a quarterly magazine, *Dragons Teeth*. The journal's aim of investigating (and challenging) racial bias in children's books, however, was centred around black images and stereotypes. And this, over the next two years, led to a preoccupation with black identity and reclaiming the past – and found its obverse in white identity and RAT.

RAT, by now, had begun to make inroads into the public sector. Some interest in human relations training (including race relations) had been evinced in official circles with the rise of black youth militancy in the mid-1970s. But these, where they did obtain – principally in education, police and probation services – took the form of the occasional conference or seminar or lecture. Industry paid a little more attention to race relations, but strictly for O and M purposes, and was therefore limited, as in the work of the Industrial Language Training Centres (ILTCs), to things like difficulties in communication between employers and employees because of language and culture.

By 1980, Nadine Peppard, who as Race Relations Adviser at the Home Office was responsible for developing race relations training, and advising the police, prison and probation services, was arguing for the type of affective techniques that had been developed in the USA – at the DRRI in Florida, among others, and by the Council for Interracial Books. Although a more conscious effort, she felt, had recently been made in the 'practitioner services' to include 'the general question of attitudes and the psychology of prejudice', group work techniques, such as role-playing and training games, were still restricted to the industrial field (in the work of the ILTCs, for instance). 'A practical analysis of what is required', urged Ms Peppard, 'clearly shows that those attitudes or beliefs which underlie actual behaviour must be seen as the heart of the matter and that to construct a training scheme which tries to ignore them is to beg the question.'[33] An essential aspect of group work, she suggested, was the type of 'sensitivity training', 'consciousness-raising' or 'awareness training' that was 'a standard aspect of training' in the USA. As a reference point and guide, she cited the 'experimental training programme' mounted at the University of Oklahoma by Professor Judy Katz.

In education, too, the end of the 1970s saw a general shift of emphasis, often within multicultural teaching itself, from imparting information to challenging attitudes. Before students could understand other people's customs, they would, it appeared, have to be opened up to such understanding, made receptive to it, emotionally and mentally. Hence, a psychological or affective approach was necessary – for the 'affective component "leads" the cognitive in attitude change'.[34] Information, in other words, did not change people's attitudes and behaviour. On the other hand, if you changed people's attitudes and behaviour, they would be more receptive to the information. The sociological approach of multiculturalism was yielding to the psychological approach of racism awareness training.

But not till after the riots of 1981 and Scarman did either the official race relations courses or RAPU take off seriously into RAT. For one thing, Scarman had changed the terms of debate from the material effects of racism on poor blacks to the cultural effects on and the job prospects of middle-class ethnics. For another, he had, in his recommendations on local authority spending and police training, provided a breeding-ground for RAT and the reproduction of 'imagined communities'[35] and their ethnopsychological struggles for identity against ethnocentrism.*

A flurry of reports, working groups and conferences on local authority strategies to combat racial disadvantage ensued.[36] The Minister of State for Home Affairs, declaring that 'it cannot be unfair to give help to those with a special handicap',[37] pledged central government support for local authority endeavours. Race relations subcommittees, ethnic advisers, RAT courses – and even (elected) black councillors – began to spring up in every inner-city borough in London and the conurbations. The GLC, Brent, Haringey, Hackney, Camden,

---

* Identity is the personalisation of nationalism, ethnicity its group expression – all points in the same continuum.

Islington, Lambeth, Newham, Northamptonshire, Coventry, Bradford, Nottingham, Leicester, Sheffield, Birmingham, Greater Manchester, Liverpool – they all had their ethnic units and ethnic officers and ethnic projects, their ethnic monitoring units and, above all, as an investment in an ethnic future, their RAT courses, some of them even compulsory for local authority staff, some of them with their own RAT inspectorate. (They were also, not fortuitously, the areas that had 'rioted' or were ripe for 'riot' in 1981.)

And yet, in terms of the material conditions of the workless, homeless, schoolless, welfareless blacks of slum city, all this paroxysm of activity has not made the blindest bit of difference. The GLC Housing Committee Chairman admitted in 1984 that racial harassment on some East London estates was 'on a scale not seen in this country for 40 to 50 years'.[38] In the same year, the Policy Studies Institute survey concluded: 'the quality of the housing of black people is much worse than the quality of housing in general in this country.'[39] And unemployment for blacks, already twice the average for whites at the end of 1982, has worsened considerably.

All that has happened is that the centre of gravity of the race relations industry has moved from the central government and the CRE to the local state – and with it, the black struggle, not for community and class any more, but for handouts and position.* And racism awareness, not Black Power, was the new ideology.

The same tendencies to ethnicising and RATifying racism were observable in education. In 1981, the Rampton Committee of Inquiry into the Education of Children from Ethnic Minority Groups, though acknowledging racism in the teaching profession, identified racism with 'a set of attitudes

---

* By the very same token, however, a certain black radicalism has moved into the town halls and helped local organisations in the battle against the local state, as witness the Camden 'occupation' of the Town Hall in 1984 over the treatment of homeless families (many of whom are black), following the burning to death of a family in a sub-standard bed-and-breakfast joint.

and behaviour towards people of another race which is based on the belief that races are distinct' and went on to repeat the shibboleths of the American school.* Racism could be 'both intentional and unintentional' and 'a well intentioned and apparently sympathetic person, may, as a result of his education, experiences or environment, have negative, patronising or stereotyped views about ethnic minority groups which may subconsciously affect his attitude and behaviour towards members of those groups.'[40] And Rampton, like Scarman, emphasised 'the particular educational needs' of particular ethnic groups – which doubtless helped the National Association of Schoolmasters and the Union of Women Teachers to pass off their 'negative, patronising or stereotyped' view of West Indian children for 'educational need': 'many West Indian children suffer from the fact they belong to a subculture of British culture with no readily identifiable distinctiveness' – in contrast, that is, to Asian children who are 'largely the products of a stable cultural background'.[41]

But Rampton also gave a fillip to RAT in schools. The Birmingham Education Department even got its 'multicultural outreach worker', David Ruddell, to devise its own teaching kit – on Katzian lines, of course, but adapted to British needs (as Katz had said one could do). So that although the basic 'philosophy' remained the same ('white racism is a white problem', 'racism = prejudice plus power' and all that stuff), the reality in British inner-city schools also demanded that some attention was paid to the racist violence of the National Front (NF), at whose instigation ('intentional or unintentional') innumerable black kids had been attacked and quite a few killed. But Ruddell gets over the difficulty with his opening salvo. 'One of the barriers to the recognition and

---

* The report of the Swann Committee, the successor to Rampton, emphasises attitudes and behaviour as Rampton does – but, unlike Rampton, does not see teacher racism as crucial to black underachievement.

tackling of racism today', he writes in his introduction to 'Recognising racism: a filmstrip, slide and cassette presentation for racism awareness training',[42] 'is the equating of racism with strong personal prejudice, with violence and the National Front. This is a vision of racism no less widespread among the teaching and caring professions than among the rest of the public. And it is a convenient and restrictive vision, for it allows the vast majority of racist thought and action to go unchecked.' Not all black people come face to face with 'this most extreme expression of racism', but 'all black people suffer the effects of the subtle but endemic institutional racism that permeates our society and our culture'. And then, as though catching himself in the act of too brazenly writing off the experience of a whole class, Ruddell attempts to bring it back through culture – 'cultural racism comes as the luggage of our history, our language and probably our class structure' – but is baulked by the opposing culture of Scarmanite ethnicity and the cult of RAT. From there on, his pamphlet takes off into the higher reaches of psychologism to reach a screeching crescendo in Brenda Thompson's 'I am a white racist – but willing to learn'.

Another school of thought, emanating from the Inner London Education Authority, however, feels that there is an anti-racist element in multicultural education which they, as radicals, can exploit. Accordingly, they call themselves the Anti-Racist Strategies Team. But their 'Pilot Course' for teachers, for all its political posturing and anti-RAT rhetoric, has the same RAT outlook and even some of its training methods – such as 'Concentric Circles: an exercise to help participants to get to know each other', 'Simulation Game', 'Brainstorming and commitments to changing institutions and practices – a sharing of ideas' (and this under 'Strategies for Action'!) and 'a heavy video' of Salman Rushdie's 'Viewpoint on Racism' for Channel 4 (which, because it errs on the side of rhetoric, as opposed to analysis, has become meat for RAT courses).[43]

The Language Training Centres for industry, on the other hand, have gone over to psychological and affective techniques without necessarily espousing the Katz philosophy. They have, for instance, moved away 'from a narrow definition of language to one which encompasses all aspects of effective communication training and probes behind the actual words used to the attitudes beneath'.[44]

The churches fell for RAT much more easily and as of second nature: its credo, after all, was no different from theirs: you must change yourself before you can change the world. Racism, in RAT eyes besides, had the look of original sin. And there was a certain set ritual and ceremony about RAT exercises, even a RAT confessional and a RAT priesthood to facilitate your entry into a raceless heaven, and an aura of piety surrounding it all. But, of course, the different church groups stress different aspects of RAT, as churches are wont to do. The Methodist Leadership Race Awareness Workshop (MELRAW), for instance, speaks of the need for 'becoming aware of the sin of racism and seeking forgiveness so that we can begin truly to work for reconciliation'.[45] On the other hand, the Ecumenical Unit for Racism Awareness Programmes (EURAP) sees 'Racism Awareness Workshops' as 'designed to help people to get free of the clutter of upbringing, of misinformation and prejudice in order to be equipped to tackle the abuse of power'. EURAP also stresses the need for periodical assessment 'to see whether effective practices have emerged'. If tackling the abuse of power is the goal, the churches have the example of the World Council of Churches' material support (albeit short-lived) of revolutionary movements in Africa. By comparison, they have had 1,985 years to assess whether or not changing minds changes society. But then, that is why RAT belongs in the church, but not, necessarily, the church in RAT.

Where RAT afforded immediate sanctuary to racism, however, was in the police force. The 1981 rebellions against the police and their state had discredited the police force on all

counts and at every level. The Brixton 'disorders', in particular, had shown up the endemic and unrelenting racism of
the force in its entirety. Scarman, in rescuing them and the
state from such public and universal opprobrium, had let
them off with a reprimand for 'racially prejudiced attitudes'
(in the lower ranks) and a severe course of multiculturalism
and attitude-training. Gratefully, the police accepted the sentence.

They had, immediately after the inner-city 'riots', made a
stab at multicultural studies at the Hendon Police Training
College – and even appointed a black lecturer, John
Fernandes, to carry it off. But, after Scarman, the police were
threshing around for a training programme that would change
attitudes and behaviour rather than educate and inform. A
Police Working Party was set up the following year, but even
before it could report (February 1983), the Metropolitan
Police Force, influenced by the work of the DRRI in Florida,
went off into HAT, with all its attendant simulation games,
'experiential exercises' and role-playing. At the same time it
entered into a joint study and experiment in RAT with the
ILTC.

Multiculturalism, meanwhile, had died at Hendon:
Fernandes's attempt to find an anti-racist strain in multiculture had brought him up against the hard rock of police
racism, both at the recruit level and the senior officers' – and
put paid both to Fernandes and multiculturalism. But RAT
was waiting in the wings and, no sooner had Fernandes been
suspended, found its way into the Police Training College –
through RAPU, whose leading black light was also a member
of the Police Working Party and Ethnic Adviser to Haringey
all at once. The Fernandes case had, by then, blown up into
an important political issue for blacks – leading to a campaign
highlighting the racism not only of the police force but
of the unions.[47] But RAPU and its black facilitators gave
no thought or mind to dividing black struggle or placating
the police with RAT placebos – reputedly for £600 a

throw.*[49] But then, that is the type of commerce that RAT lends itself to.

RAT also abounds in the voluntary sector – among youth workers, community theatres, housing groups, advice centres, community workers, nursery managers, who, because of the sense of vocation and commitment that have brought them to their jobs, are particularly susceptible to RAT potions.**[50] And lest their commitment should let the voluntary sector stray from their particular briefs, the Home Office has made it a point (through Voluntary Service Unit funding) to corral them into umbrella organisations in Leicestershire, West London and Manchester.

Then there is black RAT for black people – as in RAPU and LRATU (Lewisham Racism Awareness Training Unit), for instance – concerned with recovering black identity and raising black consciousness and, in the stated case of the Lewisham Unit, with enhancing and strengthening 'practices that lead to power acquisition particularly within the confines of white dominated organisations and society in general'.[51] Interracial RAT (not advocated in Katz) has tended to dwindle of late, but still holds sway in bodies like URJIT (Unit of Racial Justice in Tooting), whose confused thinking and flagellatory rhetoric, as expressed in Tuku Mukherjee's *I'm not blaming you: an anti-racist analysis,* would border on the

* The police have gone into all sorts of RAT experiments since this, but a recent Home Office assessment on 'RAT for the police' has doubts whether RAT fits into the 'traditional culture of police training'. 'What the trainers were offering ... were courses bearing upon the relationship between black people and white people. What the participants were expecting were courses dealing not just with this, but with the relationship between black people and the police.' Clearly, the police did not want to be treated as whites suffering from racism but as police suffering from blacks. And RAT did not seem to be able to help them there, but a revised RAT, it was expected, has possibilities.[48] The Home Office has, in any case, removed police RAT from private enterprise by setting up the Police Training Centre in Community and Race Relations at Brunel University (1983).
** I am grateful to the workers of the voluntary sector – discussion with whom at the GLC/IRR Seminars on Racism helped inform my views.

risible but for the seriousness with which they take themselves.

Finally, there are the professional RAT operators who appear to have come out of management training and business rather than from an involvement with black issues – and make a business of RAT. Foremost among them is Linda King and Associates: Anti-Racist Consultants in Public Relations, Management and Staff Development. Founded by a black American woman, the firm has a leaning towards American concepts and American terminology such as 'internalised oppression', 'peoples of colour', 'parenting', etc. It even has courses for 'parenting in an anti-racist way' – for mixed couples, that is. It also has cut-price courses, and gets written up in up-market (and sexist) journals like *Cosmopolitan*, where you might be surprised to come across words like 'slavery' and 'colonialism', but not after they have been treated to RAT. 'People can't help being racist', Linda King is quoted as saying. 'It is a form of conditioning which comes from our history of slavery and colonialism and present inequalities in the economic structure. But we can unlearn it.' And, of course, you must then 'choose to put into practice what you have learned'.[52]

The business propensities of RAT have also begun to be recognised in RAPU, the first and true church. Riven by schisms and sects and internal quarrels, its missionary zeal blunted by heresies and tainted by consorting with the police, and disappointed at seeing the moneychangers arrive in their temple (when they themselves were being funded by the GLC), RAPU has fallen from grace.* But its (black) high priestess, taking note of the times, has set herself up as 'Affirmata', a 'Race and Sex Equality Training and Consultancy' in the manner of King. White racism, it appears, is no longer a white problem,** but a business proposition.

---

* RAPU's anxieties were particularly noticeable at a seminar at the CRE to assess RAT (31 October 1984).
** But if white racism is a white problem, why do black people not leave it to them to get on with it?

RAT fallacies and falsehoods

The confusion and fallacies of RAT thinking, as well as its metaphysics, have come through in the presentation. Thus racism is not, as RAT believes, a white problem, but a problem of an exploitative white power structure; power is not something white people are born into, but that which they derive from their position in a complex race/sex/class hierarchy; oppression does not equal exploitation; ideas do not equal ideology; the personal is not the political, but the political is personal;* and personal liberation is not political liberation.

Some of the confusion arises from the wrong use of terms. Racism, strictly speaking, should be used to refer to structures and institutions with power to discriminate. What individuals display is racialism, prejudiced attitudes, which give them no intrinsic power over non-whites. That power is derived from racist laws, constitutional conventions, judicial precedents, institutional practices – all of which have the imprimatur of the state. In a capitalist state, that power is associated with the power of the capitalist class – and racial oppression cannot be disassociated from class exploitation. And it is that symbiosis between race and class that marks the difference between the racial oppressions of the capitalist and pre-capitalist periods.

The fight against racism is, therefore, a fight against the state which sanctions and authorises it – even if by default – in the institutions and structures of society and in the behaviour of its public officials. My business is not to train the police officer out of his 'racism', but to have him punished for it – if, that is, he is meant to be accountable to the community he serves. Nor does changing the attitude of an immigration officer stop him from carrying out virginity tests – but changing immigration law (or merely the instructions from

* Changing society and changing oneself is a continuum of the same commitment – else neither gets changed.

114

the Home Office) would. Nor can (middle-class) housing officers who have undergone RAT change housing conditions for
the black working class, as long as the housing stock is limited.
Nor, finally, does disabusing the minds of the owners and
editors of the yellow press of their 'racism' prevent them from
propagating their poisonous ideology of racism (when it sells
papers); only a concerted continuing, public and political
campaign can do that.

RAT, however, professes to change attitudes and behaviour, and thereby power relations – not in reality, but by
sleight of definition: by defining personal relations as power
relations.*

That is not to say that RAT does not act as a catharsis – for
guilt-stricken whites – or as a catalyst, opening them out to
their own possibilities and those of others, leading even to a
change in their individual treatment of blacks. (The unit of
oppression for RAT is the abstract individual.) It might even,
for a rare few, open up a path to political activism, but such
people will already have had such a potential, anyway – and
all that RAT could have done was to catalyse it. But its preten-
tiousness to do more is at once a delusion of grandeur and a
betrayal of political black struggle against racism and, therefore, the state.

More importantly, in terms of strategy, the distinction
between racialism and racism – the distinction between power
relationships between individuals (however derived) and the
power relationships between classes (however mediated)** –
helps distinguish between the lesser fight (because attitudes
must be fought too) and the greater, and allows of different
tactics for different fights, while clarifying at the same time the
different strands of the same fight – so that the state does not
play one against the other.

* Multiculturalism, on the other hand, denies power relations by denying
the hierarchical structure of society.
** In Stuart Hall's brilliant and comprehensive phrase, 'race is the modality
in which class is lived'.[53]

But then, the use of the term 'racism' to mean both (personal) racialism and (structural) racism – influenced partly by the use of the term 'sexism', which itself arose from the tendency in the women's movement to personalise politics by personalising power (there is no 'sexualism' in the women's movement)* – has passed into common usage, itself a sign of the decline of black struggle. And it would be pedantic not to accept it as such – till, that is, struggle again changes the terminology.

In the meantime, RAT has to be hoist with its own petard – it invites that sort of metaphor to explain itself, mixed and confused. Racism, for RAT, is a combination of mental illness, original sin and biological determinism (which, perhaps, explains its middle-class appeal). It is 'the number one health problem in America', according to Katz – and if her disciples in Britain have not proclaimed it as clearly for this country (they have had no Mental Health Commission to back up such a view), they have, in their therapy, certainly treated racism on that basis.

Racism, according to RAT, has its roots in white culture, and white culture, unaffected by material conditions or history, goes back to the beginning of time. Hence, racism is part of the collective unconscious, the pre-natal scream, original sin. That is why, in the final analysis, whites can never be anything more than 'anti-racist racists'. They are racist racists to begin with, born as they are to white privilege and power; but if they do nothing about it, 'collude' (consciously or unconsciously) in the institutional and cultural practices that perpetuate racism, then they are beyond redemption and remain racist racists. If, on the other hand, they 'take up arms' – or, in this case, RAT, against such privileges – 'and

---

* The women's movement (in the West) personalised power – legitimately – to mean the immediate, direct and personal physical power of men over women, but then extrapolated it – illegitimately – to black and Third World struggle, which are connected more immediately and directly to economic exploitation and political power.[54]

opposing, end them', in their own lives, at least, they could become 'anti-racist racists'. Racists, however, they remain in perpetuity. It is a circular argument bordering on the genetic, on biological determinism: racism, in sum, is culture and culture is white and white is racist. And the only way that RAT can break out of that circle is to acknowledge the material conditions that breed racism. But then, it would not be RAT.

For that same reason, RAT eschews the most violent, virulent form of racism, the seed-bed of fascism, that of the white working class – which, contrary to RAT belief, is racist precisely because it is powerless, economically and politically, and violent because the only power it has is personal power. Quite clearly, it would be hopeless to try and change the attitudes and behaviour of the poorest and most deprived section of the white population without first changing the material conditions of their existence. But, at that point of recognition, RAT averts its face and, pretending that such racism is extreme and exceptional, teaches teachers to avert their faces, too. And that, in inner-city schools, where racism affords the white child the only sport and release from its hopeless reality, is to educate it for fascism.* David Ruddell, Antoinette Satow and even blacks like Basil Manning and Ashok Ohri specifically deny the importance of the battles against the NF on the basis that such an extreme form of racism is not necessarily the common experience of most blacks and, in any case, lets off the whites with fighting overt racism out there and not covert racism in themselves, in their daily lives and in their institutions (meaning, really, places of work, leisure, and so on).[55] But that is because they, like the activists of the Anti-Nazi League, but for different reasons, do not see the organic connection between racism and fascism. Martin Webster, the National Activities Organiser of the NF, saw it, though, when he declared that 'the social base of the NF is made up of the

* Ideas for RAT, as for the 'ideological classes', matter more than matter.

desperate and the dispossessed among the white working class'.[56]

Nor does RAT, because it ignores all but the middle class, make a distinction between the different racisms of the different classes – the naked racism of the working class, the genteel racism of the middle class and the exploitative racism of the ruling class – if only to forge different strategies and alliances to combat the different racisms.

But then, to ask RAT to do anything so political is, as a Tamil saying has it, like trying to pluck hairs from an egg. RAT plays at politics, it is a fake, a phoney – a con trick that makes people think that by moving pebbles they would start an avalanche, when all it does is to move pebbles, if that, so that the avalanche never comes.

And because, in Britain, black people have been involved in this con trick – in introducing it, practising it, reproducing it – RAT has been able to misappropriate black politics and black history, and degrade black struggle. For if black struggle in Britain has meant anything, it has meant the return of politics to a working-class struggle that had lost its way into economism, the return of community to class,* the forging of black as a common colour of colonial and racist exploitation, and the opening out of anti-racist struggles to anti-fascism and anti-imperialism both at once.

Equally, if black and Third World feminism has meant anything, it has meant, on the one hand, a corrective to the personalisation of politics and the individualisation of power in the white women's movement and, on the other, an attempt to forge a unity of struggle between race, gender and class. RAT (which in Britain boasts black women in its ranks, some of them one-time activists) not only works in the opposite direction on both counts, but, in dividing the women on race

---

* It was that understanding of community and the resolve not to let it die that brought to the miners the unstinting support of Afro-Caribbean and Asian workers.

lines, reflects and reinforces the opposing feminist tendency to divide the 'race' on sex lines, and further disaggregates the struggle. Such fragmentation of struggle, while helping perhaps to overcome the personal paranoia that capital visits on different groups differentially, sends them off in search of their sectional identities, leaving capital itself unscathed.

Which is why even if there is no longer a classic working class to carry on a classic class struggle, the struggles of the new social forces must, for that very reason, focus on the destruction of the ruling class – for that there is, under whatever guise or name it appears before the respective movements: patriarchy, white racism, nuclearism, or is conjured up by the 'new Marxists': power blocs, hegemonies, dominant factions. And particularly now, when the technological revolution has given capital a new lease of life and allowed the ruling class to disperse and dissimulate its presence – in so many avatars – while centralising and concentrating its power over the rest of us.

References

1. A. Sivanandan, 'From resistance to rebellion' in *A different hunger: writings on black resistance* (London, 1982).

2. A. Sivanandan, 'Race, class and the state' in *A different hunger*.

3. A. Sivanandan, 'From resistance to rebellion'.

4. See A. Sivanandan, 'Race, class and the state'.

5. Secretary of State for the Home Office, *Racial discrimination*, Cmnd 6234 (London, 1975).

6. A. Sivanandan, 'Race, class and the state'.

7. See, for example, Select Committee on Race Relations and Immigration, Session I 1974–75, *Report on the Organisation of Race Relations Administration*, HC 448–I (London, 1975), and David Smith, *The facts of racial disadvantage* (London, 1976).

8. Home Office, *Racial discrimination*.

9. See 'UK commentary: Grunwick (2)', *Race & Class*, vol. XIX, no. 3 (Winter 1978), pp. 289–94.

10. A. Sivanandan 'From resistance to rebellion'. See also Beverley Bryan, Stella Dadzie and Susanna Scafe, *The heart of the race: black women's lives in Britain* (London, 1985).

11. 'Editorial', *Race & Class*, vol. XXIII, nos 2/3 (Autumn 1981/ Winter 1982).

12. House of Commons Home Affairs Committee, Session 1980–81, *Racial disadvantage*, HC 424–I (London, 1981). paras 52 and 67.

13. K. Young, 'Ethnic pluralism and the policy agenda in Britain' in N. Glazer and K. Young (eds), *Ethnic pluralism and public policy* (London, 1983).

14. J.L. Watson, 'Introduction: immigration, ethnicity and class in Britain' in J.L. Watson (ed.), *Between two cultures: migrants and minorities in Britain* (Oxford, 1977).

15. P. Weinreich, 'Ethnicity and adolescent identity conflicts: a comparative study' in Verity Saifullah Khan (ed.), *Minority families in Britain: support and stress* (London, 1979).

16. Roger Ballard and Catherine Ballard, 'The Sikhs: the development of South Asian settlements in Britain' in Watson, *Between two cultures*.

17. Sandra Wallman, 'The scope for ethnicity' in Sandra Wallman (ed.), *Ethnicity at work* (London, 1979).

18. *The Brixton disorders, 10–12 April 1981: report of an inquiry by ... Lord Scarman* (London, 1981).

19. Ibid.

20. US Department of Labor, *The Negro family: the case for national action*, compiled by D.P. Moynihan (Washington, DC, 1965).

21. See also Martin Barker and Anne Beezer, 'The language of racism – an examination of Lord Scarman's report on the Brixton riots', *International Socialism* (Winter 1982–3), pp. 108–25.

22. *Report of the National Advisory Commission on Civil Disorders*, chairman Otto Kerner (New York, 1968).

23.. US Commission on Civil Rights, 'Racism in America and how to combat it' (Washington, DC, 1970).

24. P.C. Goldin, 'A model for racial awareness training of teachers in integrated schools', *Integrated Education*, no. 43 (January–February 1970), pp. 62–4.

25. P. Bidol and R.C. Weber, *Developing new perspectives on race: an innovative multimedia social studies curriculum in race relations for secondary level* (Detroit, 1970); and P. Bidol, 'A rap on race – a mini lecture on racism awareness', *Interracial Books for Children*, vol. 3, no. 6 (1974), pp. 9–10.

26. R.W. Terry, *For whites only* (Detroit, 1970).

27. Ibid.

28. See Judy H. Katz, *White awareness handbook for anti-racism training* (Norman, OK, 1978).

29. Quoted in ibid.

30. Quoted in ibid.

31. Quoted in ibid.

32. Ibid.

33. Nadine Peppard, 'Towards effective race relations training', *New Community*, vol. 8, nos 1/2 (Spring–Summer 1980), pp. 99–106.

34. Phil Baker and Elizabeth Hoadley-Maidment, 'The social psychology of prejudice: an introduction' (Southall, National Centre for Industrial Language Training, 1980).

35. See Benedict Anderson, *Imagined communities: reflections on the origin and spread of nationalism* (London, 1983).

36. See the CRE report, *Local government and racial equality* (London, 1982); Joint Government/Local Authority Association Working Group, *Local authorities and racial disadvantage* (Department of the Environment, London, 1983); and the Conference which followed, 'Local authorities and racial disadvantage', London, 21 March 1984 (Bichard Report); 'Race equality – strategies for London boroughs', report of the LBA/CRE/LACRC conference for councillors, Sussex, 1–3 July 1983.

37. Home Office Press Release, 21 March 1984.

38. *Evening Standard* (16 October 1984).

39. Colin Brown, *Black and white in Britain: the third PSI survey* (London, 1984).

40. Committee of Inquiry into the Education of Children from Ethnic Minority Groups, 'West Indian children in our schools', chairman Anthony Rampton (London, June 1981).

41. NAS/UWT 'Multi-ethnic education' (Birmingham, 1984).

42. D. Ruddell and M. Simpson, 'Recognising racism: a filmstrip, slide and cassette presentation for racism awareness training' (Birmingham, Education Department, 1982).

43. 'Towards anti-racist strategies: a course for teachers' (ILEA Centre for Anti-Racist Education, London, 1984).

44. Nadine Peppard, 'Race relations training: the state of the art', *New Community*, vol. II, nos 1/2 (Autumn/Winter 1983), pp. 150–9.

45. Quoted in T. Holden, *People, churches and multi-racial projects* (Methodist Church, London, 1984).

46. Ecumenical Unit for Racism Awareness Programmes, Annual Report, 1983–4.

47. National Convention of Black Teachers, 'Police racism and union collusion – the John Fernandes case' (London, 1983).

48. P. Southgate, 'Racism awareness training for the police: report of a pilot study by the Home Office' (London, 1984).

49. See 'Scabbing against Fernandes', *Asian Times* (28 October 1983) and 'Racism Awareness Programme Unit', *Asian Times* (25 November 1983).

50. For a description of a RAT course, and a critique, see the CARF articles in *Searchlight*, nos 115 and 116 (January and February 1985).

51. Lewisham Racism Awareness Training Unit, Black awareness programme, 9–10 August 1984.

52. Denise Winn, 'Would you pass the colour test?' *Cosmopolitan* (January 1985).

53. Stuart Hall, Chas. Critcher, Tony Jefferson, John Clarke and Brian Roberts, *Policing the crisis* (London 1978).

54. See Jenny Bourne, 'Towards an anti-racist feminism' (London, Insti-

tute of Race Relations, 1984), *Race & Class* pamphlet no. 9.

55. See D. Ruddell and M. Simpson, 'Recognising fascism'; Ashok Ohri, Basil Manning and Paul Curnow (eds), *Community work and racism* (London, 1982).

56. Martin Webster, in *Spearhead* (May–June 1979).

5

Blacks and the Black Sections

The continuing failure of the Labour Party to nominate black candidates for Parliament has led to the demand by some of its black members for special 'Black Sections' to represent black interests. The suggestion has been denounced as 'repellent' by the Labour leadership, and as 'divisive of the class' by a section of the Left. On the eve of the 1985 Labour Party Conference, the Campaign Against Racism and Fascism asked Sivanandan for a race/class perspective on the subject.

The issue of Black Sections is likely to come up again at the next Labour Party Conference. A lot of anti-racists and Left socialists are confused about what position to take vis-à-vis Black Sections, whether the demand is progressive, anti-racist and so on.

Yes, there is confusion and I believe that it stems from the fact that there are actually two perspectives we have to understand: that of the Labour Party and that of the black movement. Black Sections belong in the Labour Party, not to the black movement. They belong in the Labour Party precisely because the labour movement had failed first to support the struggles of working-class blacks and then to incorporate the history of that struggle within their own history and traditions. Black Sections were thrown up by and a response to that failure. If the Labour Party wants now to be seen to be taking an anti-racist stance (and, make no mistake, the Labour Party has proved itself to be a thoroughly racist party) 'Black Sections' is the easy option and Kinnock is a fool not to see it.

Secondly, if the Labour Party prides itself on being a broad church, a federation of interests, why is there no room for Black Sections? They are no more outlandish than Women's Sections – and I bet they will be just as ineffective in getting anything done for the working class. 'Black Sections', you must understand, is not a radical demand. It is Kinnock's refusal to entertain the notion that gives it an aura of radicalism.

But why do you say Black Sections don't belong in the black movement?

Because they have not been thrown up by black people in the course of black struggle, they are not organic to black working-class struggle. They are, instead, the demand of a handful of aspiring middle-class blacks who, finding their way to the top of the Labour hierarchy blocked by racist structures, first set up their own parallel organisations and cabals within the trade union set-up – such as the Black Trade Union Solidarity Movement and Black Media Workers' Association – before graduating as Black Sections into the Labour Party set-up. They do not come out of the struggles of ordinary black people in the inner cities – and they do not relate to them – but they have attached themselves to black struggles, like limpets, the more readily to gain office. And, because they have – by virtue of their education and class background – a knowledge of how the system works and are familiar with Labour Party structures and bureaucracy, they are able to come up with a technical, constitutional 'black' position. They know the machinery – and they know how to make it work for them. That makes them machine politicians, not grass-roots politicians.

124

Do you know the kind of demands the Black Sections are making – representation on the NEC, demands that constituency parties only select black candidates and so on? You know what it reminds me of – the reserved seats in the Executive and Legislative Council system in the British colonies. They are not people prepared for the hard graft at the community level – the proving of themselves on the ground by serving the people. They are after some short-cuts to power – and they are appropriating black history to justify those short-cuts. But of course they are no different from their counterparts in the upper echelons of the (white) Labour Party and trade unions.

But couldn't it be argued that if the Black Sections were in the Labour Party, they could help transform it, make it less racist for example?

Transform it? No. Less racist? Perhaps – but only in terms of the discrimination faced by middle-class blacks – in the matter of jobs, promotions, economic mobility, social acceptance. And don't tell me that to aid them would be to aid blacks lower down the scale. That would be to subscribe to the IMF/World Bank 'trickle-down' theory that aid given to Third World bourgeoisies gradually finds its way down to the people. Black Sections will neither 'blacken' the Labour Party nor benefit the black working class. And the changes they can make from within will be cosmetic. Worse, it will change not the Labour Party but black politics, by drawing away black expertise from where it is needed most – in the ghettos.

Are you actually saying that there are now different forms of racism facing different sections of the black community?

Yes, of course. Not to say that would be to equate 'Black Sections' with black struggle – that would be to ignore the class stratification that has taken place in the black community. There is no such thing as a black-*qua*-black movement any more. There are middle-class blacks fighting for a

125

place in the (white) middle-class sun and there are workless and working-class blacks fighting for survival and basic freedoms.

Black Sections, in fact, are a distraction from the main issues facing ordinary black people – most importantly, the tremendous increase in racial attacks, arson and murder, the impunity with which these are carried out and the failure of the police even to acknowledge them as racial attacks, let alone their failure to bring the culprits to book. And then when the people set up their own organisations to defend themselves, they are penalised and outlawed by the courts – and left defenceless. My point is not just that Black Sections don't relate to this, but, worse, that they have changed the terms of debate about racism. Black Sections are what the media want to concentrate on when it ought to be discussing the resurgence of fascist groups, which is much worse than it was in the 1970s – only now it is hidden from view, it affects mostly the black communities; it does not affect the electoral chances of the Labour or Tory parties as it did in the local and general elections in the 1970s. And that also explains why there is no Anti-Nazi League today. The nazis are not trying to win seats any more, they are altering whole areas of working-class culture – and where is the Left in all this, where are the Black Sections? In a society polarised into classes by Thatcherite monetarism, the Left and anti-racists have to choose which type of racism they want to deal with – the Black Sections' middle-class concerns or the fundamental issues of life and liberty that confront the black working class.

Your view on Black Sections, as on Racism Awareness Training, is quite controversial, though always with a race/class perspective. Could you clarify for us the relationship you see between black struggle and working-class struggle?

First, working-class blacks bring a tradition of community politics which can enrich the labour movement and the

Labour Party. It was that same tradition that brought massive black support to the miners' struggles and it was not an accident that the miners were fighting for their communities, too. It was ordinary black people you saw taking food, clothing, money to the miners' pickets, not the Black Sections. Second, it is the rumpus about Black Sections that has thrown up black candidates in a number of constituencies – not the needs of the black community, not their 'nominees' if you like, not candidates who will necessarily represent their interests. That will come, in the course of struggle, and then we can expect it to radicalise Labour politics. But 'Black Sections' is a hybrid, looking for its legitimacy to the struggles of black people and for its habitation and name to the Labour Party. It has no life of its own, it's a pastiche, it's disorganic.

For Socialism

As Thatcherism began to bite more deeply into the fabric of the inner city and the lives of black people, the anti-racist response from the Left became more sustained and yet more off target. And in taking issue with the Left over its interpretations of racism, black struggle entered more centrally into the shaping of a new Left politics while rediscovering at the same time the socialism inherent in the black condition.

The first three pieces gathered here are essays in interpretation, analysis and rectification on different topical issues, but they all point to one end: that the fight against racism is also the fight for socialism. The last piece is an essay in prognostication, outlining the shape of the Pan-European racism to come.

6

Britain's Gulags

September and October 1985 saw violent confrontations between young people and the police on the streets of Handsworth (Birmingham), Brixton and Tottenham (London). In Handsworth, two days of street fighting followed the arrest of a black man for an alleged motoring offence and the beating by police of a black woman who intervened. In Brixton, police shot and seriously wounded a black woman in her house, while searching for her son. In Tottenham, a black woman collapsed and died when police entered and searched her home. What ensued was described by the Metropolitan Police chief as 'the worst rioting ever seen in mainland Britain'.

Racism is as English as Shakespeare and as old as slavery – and the British police force is not only riddled with it but accepts it, tacitly, as a structured line of its macho culture. In a monetarist social order, such attributes are prime assets in enforcing the lines of demarcation between the haves and the have-nots and the never-will-haves. To have allowed a handful of blacks to enter into middle-class Britain through Scarmanite policies of 'positive discrimination' and urban aid says nothing to the youth trapped in the benighted inner cities – and forgotten. To then make periodic law and order incursions into whatever life they have made for themselves comes

131

across not as an attempt to ensure law and order for their own communities (the police are never there when blacks come under fascist attack) but as a muscle-flexing exercise on the part of the police on behalf of the society outside – recalling thereby their own condition and provoking a spontaneous uprising against it. A degenerate press then whips up racial (and now inter-'ethnic') bigotry, a repressive government sets afoot yet more authoritarian law enforcement, and the Labour Party draws even further back from the regenerative politics of socialism into Scarmanite policies of patch up and make do. Handsworth is a classic example of the syndrome, Brixton and Tottenham its variants.

If the blacks who were deposited in the port towns of Liverpool and Bristol and Cardiff were the result of slave and long-distance trade, those who were brought to shore up the heavy industries of the Midlands and the North and the service and light industries of the South in the post-war years signified an industrial era, albeit in decline. And as industry began to recede before the advance of technology, or simply died of the silicon age, it left once vital inner-city areas mired in poverty and decay, and peopled largely by a black underclass that had stemmed their decline for a while. But Thatcherism has accelerated that decline by knocking out even the meagre underpinnings of the inner city with the policies of a thousand cuts and the politics of the stick.

Handsworth lost its foundry and engineering industries by the late 1960s, and by the end of the decade banks and businesses had moved out. The urban programme, instituted by Labour in 1968 and directed to largely white working-class communities (like Saltley), did not reach the black ghetto till after the White Paper of 1975 spelt out the anxieties of the state *vis-à-vis* disaffected black youth. And even then, such aid was directed not at building houses or schools or hospitals but at subsidising and buying up black self-help groups which had sustained emergency housing, supplementary schooling and legal assistance, and had in the process built up a militant black politics. Since then, the devastating cuts of the Tory government in housing (by 65 per cent since 1979 in terms of capital allocation to local authorities), in health and, through other cuts in grant aid, in local authority spending on schools and social and welfare services – compounded by the creation of unemployment (40 per cent of Handsworth is unemployed, and half its youth never-employed) – have eroded the infrastructure of the area. And to prop it up, Handsworth was granted £20 million in urban aid which failed to 'trickle down' into the black community. To patch it up, Handsworth, like other inner-city areas, was provided with a rag-bag of voluntary organisations and Youth Training Schemes which, in reproducing racial discrimination within their own structures, have become self-defeating. And to keep it in place, Handsworth got a community policing scheme (1979) in which the police played fairy godmother and godfather, both at once – providing young blacks with a well-equipped and expensive youth centre and then coming down heavily on those who did not want to use it. The Lozells Project, as the youth suspected, turned out to be an information-gathering and keeping-tabs exercise.

A similar pattern of neglect and decay obtains in Brixton and Tottenham, though the decline in these areas – given over as they were to distributive trades and services rather than to heavy industry – was more gradual and prolonged, stretching back to the 1930s. But Tory cuts – and now rate-capping – have had an equally devastating effect on them. Brixton has the second largest number of substandard dwellings in the city, and '200–300 young blacks' were discovered by Scarman in 1981 to be 'homeless, sleeping rough or squatting'. Half the single-parent families in Lambeth were 'non-white' and 'the two wards where the April disorders were centred ... contain some 22 per cent of all the single-parent households in Lambeth'. If Scarman were to extend his enquiries to Tottenham today, he would find that almost half of the Broadwater Farm estate consists of single-parent families and some 70 per cent of its residents are on one sort of benefit or another.

But to Scarman, convinced of the tangled pathology of the West Indian family, these are not indicators of poverty or of how racism structures such poverty as to make for black over-representation. And although he made some glancing remark that unemployment and social deprivation may be the cause of the 'riots', he failed to see that racism was also the cause of unemployment and social deprivation. He could not understand, that is, that racism is so institutionalised in British society as to defy solutions based on changing prejudiced attitudes and interpersonal behaviour. Hence, his recommendations did nothing more than put new gloss over old policies. A police–community liaison committee, for instance, had existed in Brixton long before Scarman, but had collapsed under the impact of heavy up-front policing which preceded Operation Swamp '81. All that Scarman's consultative committee served to do was to mask the change in police tactics from reactive policing to surveillance, intelligence-gathering and targeting – all of which accounts for the breaking and entering into the Groce and Jarrett homes. The consultative committee, like the liaison committee before it (and those elsewhere), has proved to be a one-way street – from the community or, rather, its state-sponsored 'elders' to the police – pretending to go some way towards police accountability, but leading to a dead-end of police arrogance and inflexibility. Or, where was the consultative committee between 7 a.m. when Mrs Groce was shot and 5 p.m. when the first attack on Brixton police station was mounted?

It is that same arrogance that failed to acknowledged that, despite all the dereliction visited on them, the blacks on Broadwater Farm estate had made a bearable life for themselves and the other residents – with a play group, a youth centre, and an old people's club (for blacks and whites) – which could not be lightly invaded. But as in the case of the Lozells Project, the police feel threatened if any black scheme in the ghetto is not controlled or approved by them. Broadwater Farm, like Handsworth or Brixton, has a history of such

134

incursions, most notoriously in November 1982, when a riot squad occupied the estate for two whole days.

The distrust, if not hatred, of the police is common to both Afro-Caribbean and Asian youth of the inner city, except that the one is harassed and criminalised directly, while the other is left vulnerable to the harassment of the National Front before being criminalised for defending itself. The story of black struggles in the 1970s has almost always been the story of confrontations with the police: Notting Hill, Chapeltown, Cricklewood, Southall, Burngreave, the Oval, Liverpool 8, and the names of police stations – Thornhill Road, Brixton, Moss Side, Hornsey, Stoke Newington – have passed into black legend as the castles keep of racist police. To allege in the light of this history that outside agitators caused the 'riots' is not to understand the deep animosity that the police have generated in the black community and the way that its members automatically defend each other when set upon by the police. The incident that set Handsworth afire, according to the youth of the area, was the brutal police treatment of an Afro-Caribbean woman who had gone to the aid of an Asian man, who was himself being harshly treated for a motoring offence.

The popular press, however, chose first to play down and then to ignore this sequence of events when the 'riots' proceeded to unfold a possible scenario of interethnic conflict more to their liking. And so the looting and burning of shops *qua* shops became the looting and burning of *Asian* shops – and not by youth in general (Afro-Caribbean, Asian and white), but by Afro-Caribbean youth exclusively, who deliberately caused the death of the two Asians in the Lozells' post office. But little was made of the fact that a white youth was later charged with their murder. Nor in all the clamour about the death of a policeman, on duty, was there more than a whisper of protest from white press or politician to mourn the death of a black woman, in her home. And when a black politician did speak her name and give voice to the grief and rage of his constituents, not even the ranks of Labour could scarce forbear to damn him. Nor, again (over Handsworth), was any attention paid to the statements put out by the African-Caribbean Community of Handsworth and the local Asian Youth Movement asserting that 'the rebellion was not racially motivated' but 'directed against property and the police'. The *Asian Youth News* also pointed out that 'African youths ran from shop to shop getting the shop-keepers and their families out of the buildings and to safety; one Asian shop was defended by the African youths because there were children in bed upstairs'. The paper also referred to a statement that the 'small shopkeepers of Lozells Road' had made to the effect that there was 'no enmity whatsoever between African and Asian'.

But even without these statements, it should have been clear to an unprejudiced or, at least, an enquiring press that these small Asian shops are to Handsworth what Barclays and Burtons are to Brixton. Ironically enough, it was they, when the banks and the businesses and the insurance companies fled the place, who stayed on to prop up Thatcher's ghetto economy. But at the point of 'riot' they, too, or rather, their meagre shops proclaim them as a class – not a race – apart.

Once again, the black communities' view of the press as liars and bigots who fit up stories to their preconceptions and then, pooling them, present a phalanx of opinion which passes for truth, has been reinforced. (Very little, incidentally, was made of the fact that the police in Tottenham had let themselves into Mrs Jarrett's home with a key taken from her son's possessions when he was arrested for stealing his own car.) The press is also, for young blacks, the legitimating arm of the police, serving to stigmatise them as thieves and muggers and orchestrating public opinion on behalf of indefensible police actions – which, in turn, helps to further distance them (the police) from their accountability to the public, to the point indeed of putting the public itself 'on notice'!* The more genteel press is then seen to turn out the same views in more literate and crafted garb, but attacking this time not 'the people of the street' (Scarman) but the 'subversives' who speak up for them. The top people's paper finally finds a name for such subversion in 'Marxism' and a habitation in 'the enemy within'.

What has occurred in Handsworth and Brixton and Tottenham are no more riots than the uprisings of the unemployed in London a century ago – only now it is the never-employed black underclass, interned in the workless gulags of Britain, who have taken up that tradition of protest. And what they, like the miners, point to is the combination of ideological, political and economic forces that Thatcherism *in extremis* has begun to mount against the people.

---

* Immediately after Tottenham, Metropolitan Police Commissioner Kenneth Newman put all the people of London on notice that he would not hesitate to use CS gas and plastic bullets if circumstances warranted it.

7

Race, Class and Brent

Increasingly, over the past year, the Tory government (supported by its satraps in the gutter press) has given up even the pretence of attacking the crucial issues of racial discrimination, police racism and inner-city decay and has gone over to attacking instead the 'anti-racism' of local Labour parties and their radical black councillors. Unfortunately, this shift from tackling racism to tackling the discourse on racism (via anti-anti-racism) was a red herring that the Labour Party was bound to follow, given its inability, refusal even, to recognise and develop the inherent compatibility of socialism and black struggle. And it was precisely in the London Borough of Brent that the possibility of such a rapprochement was being held out. But the national Labour Party, in disowning the struggles there, and in implicitly accepting the dominant propaganda that the Left in Brent was indeed 'loony', was able neither to ameliorate the stylistic excesses of 'anti-racism' nor to validate its vaunted socialist thrust and principles.

Two incidents in Brent focused national attention. First, there was the disciplining of the white head teacher, Maureen McGoldrick, for allegedly telling a council employee not to send her any more black teachers to fill vacant posts. Second, there was the decision to appoint black teachers to 180 specialist posts as race advisers, which were funded under the government scheme aimed at areas of special deprivation and high 'ethnic' concentration. But, in the hands of the media, Brent has come to symbolise left-wing totalitarianism – a place where 'thought police' and 'race spies' are used to hound and persecute decent, English teachers who just cannot get on with the job they are paid to do because of unwarranted political interference.

It is a view which has met with little, and largely ineffective, opposition. Even those Left analysts who tried to disentangle the threads of the Brent debate have, by and large, confined themselves to 'anti-racism' and missed, therefore, many of the wider ramifications of the struggles in Brent over education. For, though the issue came to the fore in Brent over increasing the appointment of black teachers, the issue itself was not black teachers *per se*, but entrenched class disparities in the provision of education. In other words, *an issue of class was being fought out on the terrain of race.*

Every 'fact', therefore, needs to be analysed twice, once on the touchstone of race and once on the touchstone of class. To do that, however, it is first necessary to look at the social geography of Brent. The most startling thing about Brent is that it displays within one borough a microcosm of Thatcher's 'two nations'. Though, statistically, Brent as a whole has some of the worst housing, highest overcrowding, and highest unemployment in all London, the deprivation is not equally distributed. On the contrary, the north and west of the borough (north of London's North Circular Road), formerly the Borough of Wembley, is predominantly middle-class with a high degree of owner occupation. It is an area which tends to return Tory or Alliance councillors and still campaigns, even now, to return to its former 1960s boundaries, so as to maintain the area's suburban essence, free from the contamination of the adjacent inner-city wards. All this is not to say that there are no black residents in this part of the borough. There are northern wards which have as many black residents as do the more deprived wards of the south and east. But in the north and west, the majority of the blacks are Asian professionals or business people – many of whom came relatively recently from East Africa.

The south and east of Brent (formerly the London Borough of Willesden) is, socially, completely different. It has some of the worst indices of deprivation in the whole of Britain. Here, the housing stock is very old and often overcrowded; its residents are skilled or unskilled workers – many of whom are now unemployed. In the southern and eastern wards are concentrated the poorer blacks, most of whom are working-class and the majority Afro-Caribbean.

The councillors who now hold power in Brent have had the experience of living in the more deprived areas of the borough. In May 1986, Labour won forty-three seats; eighteen black councillors were elected, eight of whom were women. These are not machine politicians, borrowing a line from time-worn institutionalised politics. They are, in the main, committed local people who have themselves been at the butt-end of local government ineptitude, indifference and racism. Their political impetus comes from the simple wish to change things for their own children.

Hence the local education authority's genuine concern about the underachievement of black children in its schools. The dissatisfaction among parents (especially Afro-Caribbeans) about education is no secret. The independent investigation into Brent's secondary schools[1] (commissioned by a Tory-controlled council) bears this out, as does the recent report by HM Inspectors.[2] Though over half the schools' children are black, until very recently only 10 per cent of teachers were. One way of helping black children gain confidence in themselves and in their schooling is by employing more black teachers. And so Brent embarked on an ambitious recruitment drive for black teachers who were to be deployed throughout the whole borough.

In Sudbury, the ward in which Ms McGoldrick is head

teacher (and which is solidly Tory), it was the belief amongst the middle-class parents – *black and white* – that white teachers would, *ipso facto*, mean higher standards and better education for their children. The 'Wembley mentality' and the 'colonial mentality' were in agreement. Having a black skin – as a governor, as a parent or as a teacher – did not necessarily mean siding with the borough's most oppressed, or caring about the underachievement of the majority. That many black parents, teachers and governors went over to Ms McGoldrick's 'cause' reflected, instead, their preoccupation with maintaining 'standards'. Or, to put it differently, blacks and white were united in their attempt to uphold a common class interest.

Even if the idea of a borough-wide campaign to raise standards and find teachers with whom children could relate did not appeal to certain 'better-off' schools, it should have appealed to the union which represented Brent teachers. Schools were chronically short of staff. But it was in fact the union, represented locally by the Brent Teachers' Association, which intensified all the contradictions between the teachers and the education authority. Not only did it refuse to co-operate with the independent investigation, it also withdrew its earlier support for the provision of the specialist advisory posts, once the commitment was made to appoint black teachers (on the grounds that it had not been consulted). A black teacher who questioned the union's commitment to anti-racism has allegedly been threatened with disciplinary proceedings. Effectively, the union rubbished the council's policies and, in the course of a series of legal actions, tended to portray its members as victims of black, racist, Loony Left councillors. The union's only concern, it appeared, was to maintain the power and conditions of its professional members – and they, of course, happened to be mainly white, middle-class and conservative in outlook. The union, in protecting the professional interests of its members was, in fact, perpetuating educational privilege.

Brent has been variously accused by its critical supporters of bad public relations, of trying to do things too fast, or of choosing the wrong cases over which to fight. But such notions do not help us learn – perhaps for another time and another fight – the real and serious mistakes Brent's Labour Council made, not in combating racism, but in the way it chose to do it. For, though it intended to fight racism and thereby enlarge socialism by using perspectives derived from the racial deprivation and discrimination experienced by the new working class – perspectives consistently ignored by the Labour Party – the way the policy was carried out was confused.

The fundamental error was to take up an 'anti-racism' package for want of properly thought-out policies tailored to local needs. Such a package had originally been cobbled together by Labour authorities (and especially the Greater London Council) as an institutional response to the 'riots' of 1981 and to Lord Scarman's discovery of 'racial disadvantage' and 'ethnic need'. Such 'anti-racism' made no distinction between individual racism and institutional racism, between personal power and institutional power, and opened the door to all kinds of 'skin politics' and white 'guilt-tripping'. It was the adoption of such a slick package and the implementation of its ideas by officers that allowed the Council's fight over policies to appear as a personalised vendetta against a few teachers. It was also why its fight ended up as a fight about the right to employ black teachers rather than as a fight for improving the education of all children, in which black teachers were to be the means to an end.

And it was inevitable that a minister in a Tory government so devoted to extending privatisation, to maintaining elitism and to destroying local government power would intervene in Brent to preserve 'individual freedom'. But the fact that the Labour Party leadership was also prepared, in the run-up to a general election, to nail its colours to the same mast (and demand that its Brent members play down the fight for their educational policies) needs to be examined.

Brent's education authority was, despite some error in tactics, fighting for very basic socialist principles. The fight between central and local government was not about racism versus anti-racism but about elitism versus democracy. Brent was trying to extend equality of opportunity to *all* its children and wished most of all to meet the needs of the borough's most deprived. The idea was to raise up the lowest parts of the borough to meet the standards of the highest. The already advantaged areas and schools, which sensed that their privilege was somehow at stake, declared war on such policies. The same battle had been fought twenty years ago by the 'privileged' grammar school sector against Labour's comprehensive school plans. But the Labour Party of today could not see Brent's struggle as part of that same policy to democratise education.

Or, to put it another way, the struggle for a socialist education system in Brent was mediated through the struggle against racism – and therefore stood for greater justice. It was a struggle which should have opened out the Labour Party and the rest of the Left to the fact that this was a *socialist* battle. It should have shown in everyday practice how black struggle – for human dignity and true freedom – far from being divisive of, or in competition with, socialism, actually lies within and advances its best traditions. But the Labour Party, having drifted so far from its own tenets and having failed, because of its own racism, to be informed by the socialist perspectives that the black working class had brought to it, was prepared to look no further than the Tory version of what was happening in Brent. Unable to fight as a party to clarify the politics of Brent and drive home to the nation the common denominators in the fight against racism and the fight for socialism, Labour sold out on itself.

References

1. Jocelyn Barrow (chair), *The two kingdoms: standards and concerns: parents and schools: independent investigation into secondary schools in Brent, 1981–84* (London, 1986).

2. Department of Education and Science report by HM Inspectors, *Education provision in the outer London Borough of Brent* (London, 1987).

8

Left, Right and Burnage

On 17 September 1986, thirteen-year-old Ahmed Ullah was stabbed to death at Burnage High School, Manchester, by a white schoolmate. The local education authority commissioned an inquiry, under Ian Macdonald QC, but refused to publish its findings on grounds of defamation. In April 1988, some of its conclusions were leaked to a local paper. These included, among other things, a strong criticism of the way the school had applied its anti-racist policies. And it was this aspect of the report alone that was seized upon by the right-wing press to mount an attack on anti-racism.

Racism killed Ahmed Ullah on the playing fields of Burnage –
not anti-racism, if by 'anti' we simply mean 'opposed to',
'against'. But anti-racism as practised in Burnage was, on the
showing of the Macdonald Report,[1] an accessory before and
after the fact – merely by virtue of failing its own purpose.
That it did so, however, owes not a little to the confusion and
bewilderment of the Left as to the nature of racism and how to
combat it, on the one hand, and to the sustained attack on
anti-racism by the New Right, on the other.

The fight against racism is, in the first instance, a fight
against injustice, inequality, against freedom for some and
unfreedom for others. But because racism is inextricably

woven into hierarchies of power, of exploitation, and in some instances (as in South Africa) determines those hierarchies, the fight against racism is, in the final analysis, a fight against such exploitative power.

Both power and racism, however, have personal connotations, are easily reducible (and in everyday living are so reduced) to individuals, the positions they hold, the roles they fulfil. And so the fight against racism sometimes takes on the dimension of a personalised fight against an individual – as though to change the person (or his or her personality) is to change the office, the institution. When such confusion is carried over into policy, it tends not so much to alter the course of racial injustice as to damage the larger fabric of natural justice. Ms McGoldrick, for instance, was suspended from her headship by Brent Council on suspicion of being a racist (on the basis of a remark she is said to have made in a telephone conversation) and therefore in contravention of the anti-racist policies that the Council wished to carry out in education. At no point prior to suspension was she afforded a full hearing or accorded the benefit of her past record. And however much the issues might have been muddied by the yellow press or muddled by a reactionary teachers' union, the fact remains that the Council, in its anxiety to do right by black children, did wrong by Ms McGoldrick. Whereas, the fight for racial justice, if rightly fought, must of its very nature improve and enlarge justice for all.

It is also a fact – and a sad one – that black councillors and officers who know how the 'sus law' has been used against their young should themselves administer 'sus' by some other name. They had, in Eliot's grand phrase, had the experience but missed the meaning.

As a result, Ms McGoldrick was handed over as a *casus belli* to the genuine racists in our midst and to the racist media in particular, who were only too willing to espouse her cause in order to discredit the cause of anti-racism – as they now do over Burnage.

It was left to the 'thinkers' of the New Right, however, to mount a 'considered' attack on anti-racism by weaving together – with slovenly scholarship and consummate humbug – its foibles and its failings and presenting these as the fabric of its philosophy. A whole book, *Anti-Racism: an Assault on Education and Value*, was directed to this exercise, and a biased TV programme in the *Diverse Reports* series 'examined' the subject so 'critically' as to still the voices of those, like myself, who tried to say that there was no body of thought called anti-racism, no orthodoxy or dogma, no manual of strategy and tactics, no demonology. What there was in our society was racism, in every walk of life, and it had to be combated – in every conceivable way. And because racism was hydra-headed, and reared its different heads in different ways in different times (prosperity and depression) and in differing areas (employment, housing, schools) and different places (inner city, suburbia), the ways of combating racism were also different and legion. Nor were there any short-cuts to its demise. Racism had been a long time in the making and would take a long time to die. 'Anti-racism', therefore, was a portmanteau word meant to carry all these differing ideas and ways of combating racism. The important thing, however, was to keep racism from corrupting society to decay.

If anti-racism for the irredentists of the New Right was an assault on *their* education and values, it was for the New (Social Forces) Left an essay in cultural politics, personal politics – which, in practice, descended into culturalism, ethnic politicking, interpersonal relations, identity-seeking. The fight against racism became a fight for culture, and culture itself was evacuated of its economic and political significance to mean lifestyle, language, custom, artefact. And black, from being a 'political colour', was broken down into its cultural parts of West Indian, Asian, African – and these in turn reduced to their ethnic constituents. And since local authority funding was largely geared to 'ethnic need', there was a sudden flowering of a thousand ethnic groups. Everybody was ethnic now – Irish, Italians, rastas, Sikhs, Chinese, Jews, Bengalis, gypsies – and they all vied with each other for 'ethnic handouts' and 'ethnic positions' and set themselves against each other, politicking for 'ethnic power'.

But, curiously enough, where this credo of ethnic need first arose was not in the ante-chambers of socialist local authorities but in the liberal pages of Scarman's report on *The Brixton Disorders*. The evidence before Lord Scarman – the police force were battering down the homes of black people in Brixton with sledgehammers as he sat – pointed implacably to institutional and state racism. But, like so many adjudicators before him, so unquestioning was Lord Scarman's belief in the fairness of British institutions that he set his face resolutely against any criticism of them. Instead, he leant over backwards – and you need such a mixed metaphor to convey the contortions of his lordship's position – to restore the balance of justice against 'racial disadvantage', by means of 'positive action' in terms of 'ethnic need'. The idea was to help racial or ethnic minorities overcome their specific disadvantages so as to bring them up to the same level as the rest of society – and then leave them, like everyone else, to the vagaries of market forces.

But, in absolving the state and its institutions of racism, the burden of 'racial disadvantage' was passed on to the minorities themselves – as though it were they who were wanting in something. An infliction had become an affliction, a disadvantage a disability – and passed under the rubric of 'ethnic need'. The remedy, therefore, was to be sought in ethnic programmes and ethnic policy, not in dismantling racist structures and outlawing racism.

It was, at best, a *laissez-faire* view of racism which brooked no state intervention, least of all in its own affairs and institutions, except in the lesser matters of administration such as recruitment and training, say, of police officers.

But for left-wing councils, casting around for anti-racist policies in the wake of the inner-city 'riots' of 1981, Scarman was a godsend. 'Positive action' and 'ethnic need', besides,

148

seemed to have a socialist ring to them – holding out the prospect of socialist planning without detracting from the morality of socialist caring. Having themselves failed to incorporate or relate to the struggles of the black working class in the post-war years and see how they advanced the struggle of the class as a whole, the white Left had no socialist frame of reference to fight racism and, by default, turned to Scarman. Fighting racism the way that blacks had fought it, besides, looked like bucking the system, whereas upholding 'ethnicism' was a safe bet.

In the process, the fight was taken off the streets and out of the communities and into the town halls – to be played out in committees and cabals. And racism itself became personalised into individuals, white individuals in power, in the institutions of the local state. Scarman, in denying the existence of institutional racism, had shifted its centre of gravity to the individual. The town-hall socialists however, applying a corrective to Scarman, kept institutional racism but changed its definition to mean 'prejudice plus power' – that is, personal prejudice plus the power a white official possesses to translate that prejudice into (racist) practice. So all you had to do was to make him or her aware of his or her racism – through RAT (Racism Awareness Training) classes – and prejudice, discrimination, would go out of power and make things fairer for blacks. Power, that is, was a matter of interpersonal relationships, and by changing individuals you changed the relationships that determined the power structures. Conversely, and this was not so much in the original RAT writ as in its codicil, if black people were to challenge such power effectively, they should become aware of who they were and what they could do – find out what their real identity was in terms of race, class, gender and raise their particular blend of consciousness.

The workings of RAT – born in a military base in Florida, reared at the University of Oklahoma by Judy Katz (see her *White awareness handbook for anti-racism training*) and officially held up in Britain a year before the 1981 disturbances by the

Race Relations Adviser to the Home Office – and its subsequent spread all over Britain have been examined elsewhere.[2] What is important to note here, however, is the imputation of guilt that underlined its philosophy and informed its every practice. White people, RAT held, were by virtue of their history and upbringing guilty of racism. And, even when they fought their racism, they were still no more than anti-racist racists – because racism was immanent in the white psyche, part of its collective unconscious – in the blood perhaps? – or it was original sin. The argument bordered on the genetic and blended the religious with the sociobiological.

But even after RAT was killed off by black activists and buried – with a memorial service held appropriately enough at the GLC in its dying days – it got reincarnated as ART, Anti-Racist Training, and continued to purvey guilt under other guises.

And it is that sense of guilt, of personal guilt, which marked the events at Brent and at Burnage – the one inflicted by the authorities, the other self-inflicted.

But then guilt itself has begun to replace shame as a moral value in society at large. Guilt, as Helen Merrell Lynd[3] has pointed out, closes one down on oneself, internalises one's inadequacies, breeds a sense of helplessness. Above all, it tries to live up to the standards set out by others for one. Shame, on the other hand, sets one's own standards for oneself, opens one out to one's own possibilities and those of others. To be guilty of racism is to have transgressed someone else's standards, to be ashamed of it is to fail one's own.

Shame, however, has gone out of Thatcherite Britain – the shame of being a racist, of being a capitalist, of getting power, making money, regardless of all else, everyone else. We have been taken over by the morality of grocer capitalism, merchant capitalism, buy and sell capitalism where profit is only tempered by Calvinist moralism – and it is the same set of values that has trickled down into the race relations industry.

150

Of course, there is a morality involved in the fight against racism, but it refers not to the morality of individuals but to the morality of social justice. It is the prosperous, sanctimonious Right that prescribes morals to people and, from the height of its smug conceit, ordains how people should think and behave. It is a moralism that reflects a mean, narrow, closed-down, ungenerous view of life – one that does not take risks with people, with human relationships, enlarge human creativity, 'exhaust', in Pindar's phrase, 'the realm of the possible'. It seeks, instead, to gather up all the infinite variety of human experience and force it into the ungiving mould of its own righteousness. And it does it in the name of the individual, as though the individual grows in solitary confinement, removed from the collective good, in competition with everyone, trying to do the other in, instead of raising the other up and oneself with it.

The Left's mistake was to accept this spurious equation of individual growth with individualism and confuse personal moralism with socialist morality – both (individualism and moralism) potent ingredients in the witches' brew of right-wing fundamentalism.

It is such a fundamentalism that informs certain aspects of the proposed Education Bill – in particular, its National Curriculum which not only narrows the focus of the subjects that it prescribes as core, such as History, to a one-dimensional nationalist perspective but actively discourages at the same time the study of international subjects such as Peace Studies or Black Studies. Children are not to be put at risk to the world outside, opened out to the experience of other races and peoples, or encouraged to look at themselves and their histories from the vantage point of such experience. On the contrary, they are not even to be taught to relate healthily to the different experiences and cultures of the fellow students around them through an education in other cultures and in the racism of their own – which renders those other cultures inferior. Instead, they are, if the New Right continues to have its say, to be afforded a 'colour-blind', conflict-free education in a world replete with colour and conflict.

References

1. *Manchester Evening News* (25 April 1988).
2. See 'RAT and the degradation of black struggle', p. 77 of this volume.
3. Helen Merrell Lynd, *On shame and the search for identity* (New York, 1981).

9

Racism 1992

There is a new racism emerging from the interstices of the old
– less visible, more virulent, open to fascism and European – a
racism directed against the migrants, refugees and asylum-
seekers displaced from their own countries by the depredations of international capital. Indeed, it is capital's need to
break its national fetters and become European – to compete
with American and Japanese capital, not least in the exploitation of the Third World – that has led to the growing influx
of migrants into Europe. On the face of it, Europe does not
want them, it would like to give full rein to capital without
incurring its consequences: Third World immigrants create
social and political problems. And yet, it is their labour, cheap
and captive, that fuels vast areas of an ever-expanding service
sector and makes their privatisation profitable. The problem
as before is how to make economic gain without incurring
social cost or political dislocation. And the answer as before is
to let an unfettered racism, a racism open to market forces,
exercise (an informal) internal control while at the same time
imposing soft-option regulations on the intake of refugees,
preferably on humanitarian grounds as bespeaks European
culture and mores.

The development of such a Pan-European racism is already

present in Britain alongside the old British variety. But Britain, unlike the rest of Europe, has relied so much and so long on (imported) colonial labour and has been so slow to grasp the nettle of the technological revolution that the change-over to the European mode has been slow and halting. Even so, the Immigration Act of 1971 had already heralded Britain's entry into Europe two years later by putting an end to all primary or settler immigration from the 'New Commonwealth' and opting, instead, for the *Gastarbeiter* labour of Europe. Commonwealth citizens were henceforth on a par with aliens. Other restrictions followed, making it virtually impossible for those already settled here to bring their fiancés and dependants over. Deportations were made easier and Mrs Thatcher assured the nation that she at least would not let it be 'rather swamped by people with a different culture'.

For a while it looked as though the Powellite project of 'induced repatriation' might take off.[1] But the campaigns of blacks against unjust immigration laws and quickfire deportations, proclaiming that they were 'Here to stay, Here to fight', and the rebellions of young blacks against an increasingly racist and repressive system, put paid to such a hope or programme. And it was left to the Nationality Act of 1981 to 'regularise' the nationality of Britain's black population, citizenise them, in preparation for a Europe *sans frontières*.

That Labour's concept of that citizenship allowed black people to move up the class ladder without forgoing their cultures (in a sort of pluralist capitalism) while the Tory version required that they become truly British to get anywhere in Thatcherite Britain ('Labour says you're black, we say you're British' their election slogan ran) is worth noting only in passing. The point, however, is that in the Nationality Act of 1981 (which Labour framed and the Tories passed) both parties agreed to abandon the ancient right of birth on British soil (*jus soli*) as the basis of citizenship and located it instead in descent, patriality (*jus sanguinis*) – with the corollary, of course, that those who had already acquired British

154

citizenship by virtue of settlement here could hand down such citizenship to their descendants.

British citizenship, henceforth, could not automatically devolve on Commonwealth citizens (including those settled here since the 1971 Immigration Act came into force in 1973), on British overseas citizens or citizens of British dependent territories, excepting Gibraltar (because it is in Europe!) and, since 1983, the Falklands (because it is British!!).

The purpose of the Nationality Act, in effect, was not just to tidy up the citizenship mess left by successive immigration acts but to rid Britain of its remaining obligations of Empire and bring it into line with Europe.

Similarly, the visa restrictions imposed on certain black Commonwealth countries in 1985 and 1986, the fines made against airlines bringing in passengers without the required documents in the Carriers' Liability Act of 1987, and the provisions of the 1988 Immigration Act criminalising over-stayers and making deportations even more summary, have more to do with the new Third World immigrants and refugees coming into Europe than with the blacks already settled in Britain – and with defining, in the run-up to 1992, exactly who is a citizen and who has a right to work.

The problem for an open Europe, in other words, is how to close it against immigrants and refugees from the Third World. But not so that their labour is entirely lost. For it is they who do the low-skilled, menial, dangerous and dirty jobs in silicon-age capitalism – as their counterparts did a generation ago in the reconstruction of post-war Europe. Except that, now, such work – temporary, flexible and casual – is the very basis on which post-industrial society is run. And not just in the service sector, which is more readily perceived, but also, less visibly, in manufacturing and the distributive trades and, in some parts of Europe, in agriculture.

The number of such immigrants might be higher in mainland Europe than in Britain, but here, too, the hotel and catering workers, the contract cleaners in hospitals, airports, and so on, the security guards in the private security firms, petrol-pump attendants, domestics, fast-food assistants, hospital auxiliaries and porters and so many others come increasingly from Colombia, Chile, Turkey, Sudan, Sri Lanka, Eritrea, Iran. And they enter not so much as migrant labour, tied to a work permit and hence to a specific job (such as the 14,000 Filipinos recruited in the 1970s into the hotel and catering industry and as domestic servants), but as refugees and asylum-seekers, fleeing the economic mayhem and political terror in their countries. With no rights of settlement, rarely the right to work, no right to housing or to medical care, and under the constant threat of deportation, the new migrants are forced to accept wages and conditions which no indigenous worker, black or white, would accept. They have no pension rights, no social security, the employers do not have to insure them – they are illicit, illegal, replaceable.

All of which makes feasible the privatisation of key areas of the state's service sector, makes viable government policies to return the mentally sick and the old to 'community care' and further enhances the yuppie culture with servants and slaves.

In manufacturing, revolutionary changes in the production process have led to the use of an increasingly flexible work-force, divided into a functionally flexible 'core group' which can adjust to changes in technology, and a numerically flexible 'peripheral group' which can be adjusted to changes in the market and is, therefore, temporary, part-time, *ad-hoc*, casual. And who better to fit that bill than the peripatetic migrant or refugee?

In the retail sector, too, migrant labour has become absolutely crucial. The computerisation of distribution and sales has allowed big stores like Marks & Spencer to do away with warehousing and middlemen. Instead, they have at their bidding a number of small manufacturers and suppliers whose contracts (and therefore livelihood) depend upon their ability to change production according to the demands and vagaries of the market. They must be able, as in the garments

156

industry for instance, to switch lines at a moment's notice from one fast-fashion to another, discard a pattern today, produce from a new one tomorrow. And that demands a completely flexible workforce which can be taken on or laid off at will, which will be prepared to work long and unsocial hours to fulfil a particular contract. Increasingly, that work-force comes not only from Asian women working in the home but also from the ununionised, illegal Third World migrants working in the sweatshops.

In some countries of Europe like Italy, the agricultural sector is becoming dependent upon the super-exploitation of peripatetic Third World workers. The chic grape-picking holiday in France, once popular with students, has given way to a more systematised use of cheap labour. Agricultural migrant workers travel from harvest to harvest, as each crop demands to be picked at a definite time. By definition the work is intense and short-term and the rates of pay (for piece-work, always) abysmal. Recent reports in Italian newspapers have put the pay of immigrant tomato pickers in southern Italy at 40p for 35 kilos and, in Caserta, Ghanaians looking after cattle were said to be earning £11 for a twelve-hour day.[2]

And between 'jobs' the Third World worker ekes out a living on the pavements and beaches of Europe. He might sell newspapers in Vienna, 'Lacoste' jumpers in Lisbon, sun-glasses or African jewellery on the Costa del Sol, entertain tourists outside the Pompidou Centre. But wherever he is (and it is invariably a he), he is still unfree – dependent upon a supplier for his goods, open to the harassment of police identity-checks, facing the racist hostility of local traders.

Little has been written about the life and conditions of these workers in Britain – where the tradition of investigative jour-nalism has been choked off by the paparazzi – and even less is known about the crucial role they play in modern capitalism. But in Germany, Günter Wallraff, a writer and journalist, lived in the guise of an illegal Turkish worker, 'Ali', and exposed the plight of the 'lowest of the low' and the racism that keeps them that way in a riveting book, *Ganz Unten* (now published in English by Methuen).[3] The book, which sold millions of copies both in Germany and France, earned the opprobrium of, and lawsuits from, many of the largest German multinationals. For, in revealing the unacceptable face of the Turk, Wallraff also revealed the unacceptable face of post-industrial capitalism. After a pitiless stint in fast-foods at McDonald's, Ali makes for the factories and building sites where he unblocks lavatories ankle-deep in piss and covered in racist graffiti; removes sludge from pipes atop tall buildings in 17 degrees of frost; shovels and inhales coke dust hour after hour below ground level; crawls into a pig-iron ferry to clear a blockage with pneumatic tools and no mask. Wallraff's revelations, of how pharmaceutical industries are only too ready to use illegal Third World immigrants as guinea-pigs in their experiments with new drugs (for commercial rather than medical purposes) and of the cynical way in which sub-contractors are prepared to hire out 'temporary' Turks to clean up nuclear power plants so that they return home before the radiation takes effect, testify to the fact that the Turk is literally regarded as sub-human and, therefore, disposable (the word is Wallraff's).

But the racism that defines the Third World immigrant as inferior and locks him permanently into an underclass is also that which hides from the public gaze the murkier doings of industry. And contracting out the shit work allows management to avert its face from its own doings and come up smelling of roses. That also saves it from the legal consequences of employing unregistered, uninsured workers and transgressing safety regulations – for these are the responsibility of the sub-contractor. The law does not want to know either: the labour is alien, foreign and therefore rightless. Nor does the government, which wants the work – cheap, unorganised, invisible – but not the workers.

A whole system of exploitation is thus erected on the back of Third World workers, but racism keeps it from the light of

158

day – and racism and institutional sclerosis put it beyond the unions' purview. And the workers themselves are prevented by the constantly changing, *ad hoc* nature of their work from organising on their own behalf. Seldom are the same workers allowed to do the same job or work in the same place for too long – and often they do not speak the same language or connect culturally. And because many are illegal or seeking asylum and are fearful of being sent back to the authoritarian regimes they escaped from they become capital's captive labour *par excellence*.

But it is capital, multinational capital, that throws them up on Europe's shores in the first place. Requiring regimes that are hospitable to their investment, provide markets for their goods, yield labour for the activities, multinational corporations predicate the dictatorships that imperialism sets up for them. Trade no longer follows the flag, the flag follows trade. All sorts of trade: the trade in armaments which foments local wars, the trade in tourism which makes hotels out of fishermen's homes and peasants' huts and bids the people eat cake, the agribusiness trade which, as in Sri Lanka, is turning ricefields into pineapple plantations as once it turned them into tea, the trade in debt which keeps the Third World for ever on its knees and feathers the bed of international finance – and the trade in peoples which follows as a consequence of these.

The fascist dictatorships and the authoritarian democracies that Western powers set up in the Third World countries in their own economic and political interests are also those that provide the West with the flexible labour force it needs to run post-industrial society. Racism is the control mechanism that keeps that labour force within social and political bounds.

We are moving from an ethnocentric racism to a Eurocentric racism, from the different racisms of the different member states to a common, market racism, without losing out on the institutional differentials which are necessary to manage the insurgent black population within each nation-state. Citizenship may open Europe's borders to blacks and allow them free movement, but racism which cannot tell one black from another, a citizen from an immigrant, an immigrant from a refugee – and classes all Third World peoples as immigrants and refugees and all immigrants and refugees as terrorists and drug-dealers – is going to make such movement fraught and fancy.

References

1. See A. Sivanandan, 'From immigration control to "induced repatriation"' in *A different hunger* (London, 1982).

2. Cited in Marco Martiniello, 'Racism and immigration in Italy' (unpublished paper September 1988).

3. G. Wallraff, *Lowest of the low* (London, 1988).

Socialism and Imperialism

If colonialism and racism were inseparable at an earlier time, today's racism belongs to a new phase of imperialist development. And, despite the apparent co-option of the Third World into a world system, imperialism still wreaks havoc on Third World peoples, their livelihoods and their cultures. 'Warren and the Third World' mounts a critique of a school of thought which holds that imperialism as a vehicle for capitalist development and bourgeois democracy is not in itself without benefit to the Third World.

'New circuits of imperialism' enlarges on that critique to show how the technological revolution has enabled capital to deepen further and to extend the exploitation of Third World countries while pretending to implicate them in the trajectory of its own growth – leading to the demise of bourgeois democracy (if any) and the rise of parliamentary authoritarianism and/or dictatorships. Yet the technology that enhances capitalist depredation is also that which makes possible the inauguration of a new liberatory socialism.

10

Warren and the Third World*

Imperialism, says Warren is good for us – us denizens of the Third World, that is – because it is the vehicle, the agent, the harbinger of capitalism. And capitalism, we have on Marx's authority, raises the level of our productive forces and raises us from misery and tyranny and the dark night of our souls.** More, it creates a real proletariat who can make a real revolution, not the sort of half-arsed working class you get in the Third World these days, a working class sold on bourgeois nationalism and electing to fight 'external alleged enemies' instead of their own ruling class – thereby inveigling Western Marxists into confusing 'the socialist working-class movement in the industrialized capitalist countries' with 'the intrinsically bourgeois' nationalist anti-imperialist movement of the Third World.

And if there is any lingering doubt that imperialism is good for us, Warren is quick to assure that it is nevertheless temporary – for, whatever Lenin may think, imperialism declines as capitalism advances. Once, that is, imperialism has

* A review of Bill Warren's *Imperialism: pioneer of capitalism* (London, 1980).
** Marx also warned against 'transforming my historical sketch of the genesis of capitalism in Western Europe into an historico-philosophic theory of the general path of development prescribed by fate to all nations ...'[1]

delivered itself of capital and set it on its way, it goes away and dies, letting a thousand capitalisms bloom – interdependently – ever after. Imperialism's task in fact is almost over, for we are already in 'an era of declining imperialism and advancing capitalism'. Capitalism, quite clearly, is the highest stage of imperialism.

Imperialism, in other words, creates its own contradiction in creating Third World capitalism, and capitalism creates its own contradiction in creating the working class that is destined to overthrow it. The result: socialism.

Without imperialism, then, there is no capitalism (for the Third World); without capitalism, no socialism. So if we want socialism, we had better embrace imperialism.

That in essence is what Warren says to me – shorn of his Marxist pretensions, his self-selective statistics, his calling to witness of reactionary writers (from Ram Mohan Roy and Ahluwalia to Gann and Duignan) and his much-vaunted iconoclasm (as though to break icons is in itself a revolutionary act). Perhaps there are other things he says which are significant, such as the cock-up that Lenin made about imperialism to give imperialism a bad name and the moralism of the 'development of under-development' theorists that led them to throw away the capitalist baby with the imperialist bath-water. But these discoveries, momentous though they may be for the Marxist playboys of the Western world, have no bearing on the lives of Third World peoples for whom imperialism is, first and last, the palpable experience of foreign domination.

It is there in the rice they do not grow (let them eat wheat, says Warren – on PL 480?), in the land they no longer own (but that transforms agriculture and makes for wage-labour), in the shanties they live in (capitalism's 'informal sector'), in the wages they cannot live on (poverty for some now means prosperity for all later: no exploitation, no capitalism), in the jobs they do not have (exaggerated), in the fuel and clothing beyond their reach (they have access to 'durable consumer goods' instead – 'such as bicycles, sewing machines, motorbikes, radios and even television sets and refrigerators' – which 'significantly enhance the quality of life of poor households'). It erodes their culture and humiliates them into political subjugation. And their hatred of it is a visceral hatred, individual and collective, transgressing class and invoking popular national resistance.

It is the racial arrogance of Western 'Marxists' like Warren that interprets nationalism as the continuing ploy of a venal bourgeoisie and not the resistance of a people to unceasing oppression. The bourgeoisie did not create nationalism; imperialism did that. What the bourgeoisie did was to put it to its own uses, often under the rubric of socialism. But such uses have proved to be short-lived — for imperialism, in its Warrenite mission of advancing capitalism, was quick to cast the bourgeoisie in a collaborationist role and alienate it from the people — to install its own polities and regimes. So that, even as Warren was writing, nationalism in the Third World was increasingly taking the form of mass movements directed against its own ruling class and its imperial masters.

Warren's failure to understand the dynamics of Third World nationalism is further compounded by his inability to distinguish between reactionary (bourgeois) nationalism and the revolutionary nationalism that combusted the revolutions of Ho and Fidel and Cabral and Mao.

It may be that such revolutions do not achieve for their societies the level of the productive forces that Warren's capitalism could have assured them and therein provide 'a bridge to socialism'. But what imperialism brings into question is not the level of the productive forces but the ownership of the means of production — and what socialism offers is that such ownership shall accrue to the benefit of all the people and wipe out poverty, inequality and injustice. Socialism, for 'the damned of the earth', is not just an economic project coming after capitalism, but an ideology of human worth whose time has come. And they at least — the workers and peasants of the Third World — are having a bash at socialism while Warren's appointed agents of revolution lie in Rip-van-Winkle sleep in the snug arms of capital.

Equally spurious is Warren's claim that capitalism in the Third World is economically, politically and culturally progressive in the way that Western capitalism is. That capitalism is an advance on pre-capitalist modes is not in dispute – any more than that the feudal mode is more progressive than the slavery mode. But Warren's measurements of capitalist progress in the Third World are not just platitudinous; they are also unilinear and one-dimensional – comparing not whole modes but the individual dimensions of each mode: the economic with the economic (unequal exchange is better than no exchange at all), the political with the political (bourgeois democracy is better than pre-capitalist tyranny), the cultural with the cultural (individuality and rationality are better than the herd instinct and superstition). Why not compare instead the economic, political and cultural to each other at once? Where in colonial capitalism, for instance, was there even a suggestion of political democracy except at its end? When did the colonies ever enjoy 'the moral and cultural standards' of capitalism: 'equality, justice, generosity, independence of spirit and mind, the spirit of inquiry and adventure, opposition to cruelty, not to mention political democracy'? And in the neo-colonial (or post-independent if Warren prefers it) era, why has all the GNP that, on Warren's showing, the Third World has amassed led not to greater political freedom for the masses but to less, not to a culture of equality, justice, generosity, and so on but to inequality, injustice, covetousness? And most so in those 'newly industrialising' countries – South Korea, Taiwan, Singapore, Brazil – where GNP is at its highest?

Quite clearly capitalism's economic project in the Third World has not generated the political freedom and 'the moral and cultural standards' that it did in the West.* The econ-

* Or it could be argued that all that a stunted economy would allow was a stunted political system and a stunted culture. But this is to go over ground that Warren has rejected.

omic, political and cultural dimensions of capital have not kept pace with each other, do not have the symbiotic relationship that reinforces the capitalist mode and allows it to regenerate itself despite periodical crises (not least, by benefit of imperialism). On the contrary, they are in contradiction – precisely because Third World capitalism did not grow out of its own momentum, was not organic to its societies. Imperialism may have pioneered peripheral capitalism, but it neither declines nor allows capitalism to take indigenous root, as Warren suggests. If it did either of these, it would not be necessary to harness economic progress/exploitation to political authoritarianism sustained by imperialist intervention.

To put it differently, the holistic view that Warren has of capitalism is applicable, if at all, to the West, where capitalism had its roots, evolved out of its own internal dynamic and was able to ameliorate the excesses of economic exploitation with political placebos and cultural anodynes. The political system mediated the economic system and culture legitimated it, keeping class struggle within manageable proportions. Force, if used at all, was a last resort. In the periphery, on the other hand, force in all its guises has been the first resort, the *sine qua non* of capitalist exploitation – requiring the political system to be placed outside and above the economic, to act as a cohesive (and coercive) force maintaining the economic order of things. So that the resistance to economic exploitation has also become a resistance to political hegemony, initially expressed in nationalist and cultural terms. Hence the revolutions in these countries are not necessarily class, socialist, revolutions – they do not begin as such anyway. They are not even nationalist revolutions as we know them. They are mass movements with national and revolutionary components – sometimes religious, sometimes secular, often both, but always against the repressive political state and its imperial backers.[2]

References

1. Marx to the Editorial Board of Otechestvenniye Zapiski in *Marx and Engels, selected correspondence* (Moscow, 1975).

2. See A. Sivanandan, 'Imperialism and disorganic development in the silicon age' in *A different hunger* (London, 1982).

11

New Circuits of Imperialism

Imperialism is still the highest stage of capitalism – only, the circuits of imperialism have changed with the changes wrought in capital by the revolution in the production process. The magnitude of that revolution, as fundamental as that of the Industrial Revolution, and as comprehensive and cumulative, can only be quantified when it finally comes to rest. But even its initial tremors, like those of the Industrial Revolution, have challenged the social order, shifted the gravitational pull of employment from one sector (industrial this time) to another (the service sector) and pointed to the end of the existing polity (today, the nation-state) as a viable economic unit. And it has jolted the 'socialist' states of the Soviet Union and China into modernising their economies, into putting economics back in command. What beggars comparison, however, is that where once steam and subsequently electricity replaced muscle power, today microelectronics, in Sir Ieuan Maddock's grand metaphor, replaces the brain.[1] Hitherto it has largely been the energy component of labour that was being replaced, today it is more the skill component. The 'dead labour' that goes into computers is not so much labour by hand as labour by brain.

And Prometheus is unbound again. Capital is freed from

the exigencies of labour. Not only can it do with less labour now – but also with less variety of labour, with the unskilled or semi-skilled at one end of the production process and the highly skilled at the other. The skills have been taken into the machines, leaving it to the unskilled to operate them and the highly skilled to programme them. Different skills, besides, can be combined and fed into the same computer – as in the diagnostic machines used in medicine. Different crafts can be merged as in the newspaper industry, where the arts of the compositor, the typesetter and the printer have been collapsed into a VDU and computer – thereby also reducing the space required to house them from a factory floor to a desktop. Faced with labour 'troubles', TV companies are resorting to news-gathering equipment which can combine the functions of sound, lighting and camera into one unit, and so do away with 'the crew system'.

The heavy labour-intensive industries of the period of industrial capitalism – iron, steel, shipbuilding – are dead or dying or have passed on to the 'newly industrialising countries' of the Third World where labour is still cheap and plentiful or could be made to be so. Coal is a-dying. Industries, that is, which employed thousands of workers on the factory floor and in the pits and bound them in communities of resistance to capital are gone or going from the centre – and traditional labour organisations rendered ineffectual and effete.

Even in those industries that are left behind, such as shipbuilding, computer-aided design (CAD) and computer-aided manufacture (CAM) have taken over a considerable part of the work of construction. Some of the construction, in fact, takes place not in the dock but in the factory. At the Harland and Wolff shipyard various parts of the ship are preconstructed before being welded together in the dock. In coal-mining face-workers' skills are now being built into machines and the supervision of these machines then transmitted to the surface via MINOS (mine operating system) and MIDAS (machine information display and automation system). And in the car industry robots are taking over much of the assembly-

170

line work of factory production. In Japan robots make robots.

The factories themselves can now be broken down into smaller units and scattered all over the world – in global assembly lines – stretching (in the microelectronics industry, for instance) from Silicon Valley in California or Silicon Glen in Scotland to the Export Processing Zones (EPZs) of Taiwan, Singapore, Malaysia and Sri Lanka. Or, in the car industry, different parts of a single motor can be made in different factories spread over Europe across the Atlantic through to the Pacific before being assembled and reassembled and preassembled in any given city of the world. 'The Ford Fiesta assembled at Dagenham', wrote Robin Murray in 1987, 'used transmissions from Bordeaux, road wheels from Genk, body panels from Spain and suspension components from West Germany.'[2] And Mitsubishi cars assembled as Lancers in Thailand, with transmissions from the Philippines, doors from Malaysia and sundry other parts from Indonesia, are rebadged as Dodge and Plymouth Colts for delivery to Chrysler in Canada.[3]

The growing use of flexible manufacturing (FMS), whereby plants can be oriented from one type of product to another without retooling, allows capital to gear production to the needs of the market. In Pirelli's new electric-wire factory in Wales, for instance, FMS has enabled production to be switched from one type of wire to another or one colour casing to another within minutes.[4] And the introduction of FMS in Boeing's Renton plant in Seattle has enabled it to turn out a 737 every one and a half days.[5]

Changes in the production process, that is, have freed industrial capital (industrial, banking, they are all one now*

---

* 'Some large MNCs develop and control their own transnational banking networks ... There are large Swiss banks which are subsidiaries of US MNCs (Dow Banking, Bank Firestone, Bankinvest, Transinfer Bank, Philip Brothers) ... The Schnieder group has shares in Belgian, West German and Italian banks and its own bank, BUE, has subsidiaries in Switzerland, Luxembourg and the USA ... Dow Chemical has a network of eight banks covering nine countries.'[6]

except in the way they are deployed) from spatial strictures, given it mobility of plant and flexibility of production, enabling it to move the factory to the market, custom-build the product for the consumer or, as in the garment industry, come back to its home base when the design, layout and cutting techniques have become incorporated into a computer and do not need the cheap labour of the periphery any more. *Machina volente*, capital can take up its factory and walk any time labour gives it trouble or proves costly. Ford has recently moved its Sierra plant out of Dagenham, with its culture of trade union militancy, to the folding colliery town of 'quiet, conservative, Catholic' Genk to produce twice the number of cars with less than a fourth the number of shop stewards and twice the number of robots.[7] And in the Midlands Asian garment-makers have combined new manufacturing techniques with cheap Asian female labour to undercut garment imports from Asia.

Hierarchies of production

It is not enough to understand these changes in terms of the globalisation of production and the new international division of labour any more without also examining the hierarchies of production in which these are set – with the developed countries (DCs) holding on to the new high-technology industries while 'devolving' the older industries of steel manufacture, ship-building and the like to the newly industrialising countries (NICs) and relegating light industries (textiles, toys, footwear) and the unskilled, 'back-end' work of assembling and testing chips to the underdeveloped countries proper (UDCs).* It is not, of course, a fixed watertight division: there is constant movement and overlap, especially as between the DCs and the NICs, in terms of the commodities produced and, to that extent, of their respective functions. But the gap between them never closes. Today's NICs do not become

172

tomorrow's DCs – and if they do, it will be only because the DCs have moved on to higher things, become HDCs (highly developed countries) – and the chances of the UDCs becoming NICs are even more remote. A country or two might escape its particular category – especially those that are into an industry as escalating as electronics – but the category itself cannot move out of its appointed station in the hierarchy of capital. If there is movement, it is no more than the movement of a conveyor belt that runs on fixed stations. It is the belt that moves, not the stations; if they did, the whole system would collapse. There cannot, in other words, be a world of classless capitalism, where all the nations are equally capitalist.

'Unrealistic aspirations'...

Countries like South Korea and Taiwan, for instance – even after long years of proving themselves relatively stable, reliable, hospitable (to American capital) and cast in America's image – have not been able to break out of the impasse of low and medium technology because of American and Japanese refusal to forgo technological superiority and/or market control. South Korea, the more advanced of the two countries, has been into wafer fabrication,** the 'front end' of the industry, for some time, but the memory chips it produces do not have the range or the market that the Japanese have – and

---

* These countries have been underdeveloped, in Walter Rodney's use of the term, by Europe and the USA, and to describe them as less developed countries (LDCs) is to overlook the responsibility for underdevelopment and to obscure the difference between them and the NICs – a distinction which is necessary not for taxonomic purposes but for evolving correct strategies of struggle. I have, however, left out the oil-producing NICs and those UDCs not central to my argument here.

** Wafer-fabrication or 'fab' is the etch-printing of integrated circuits (ICs) on to a wafer of silicon.

173

South Korea is not going to be given them because of 'intellectual property problems, trade barriers and a reluctance to talk about exchanging ideas, not to mention technology'.[8] Similarly, America has refused to countenance South Korea's ambitions to take off into the aerospace industry and has suggested it sticks to making components instead.[9]

Taiwan set up a whole science park seven years ago to woo 'high-tech' entrepreneurs into helping it 'leapfrog' from a low- to a medium- and hi-tech economy'. But, despite enticing seventy-three research-based companies (most of them in electronics, most of them American) into the park and 'allaying the fears of US companies about having their designs or technology, or both, being ripped off' by bringing in a 'US semiconductor industry veteran' to run the company, Taiwan seems to have leapfrogged into making chips 'imitating animal sounds – barks, bleats, miaows and roars – in toys.'[10]

Singapore, after twenty years of assembling and testing chips in the 'back end' of the industry (and twenty years is a long time in electronics), has just about made it into wafer fabrication – as has Hong Kong. But they are both alleged to lack the expertise and the market to inveigle sizeable foreign investment on which to take off.

Brazil and India are the other two NICs that are said to be headed for the big time – because of their export capacity in heavy industry such as iron, steel, shipbuilding and machine tools. But Brazil is strangled by debt ($115 billion) and inflation (934 per cent),[11] while India, though comparatively debt-free and in advance of other NICs in terms of traditional industry, is still to enter the silicon age.

And Mexico, though it has shown sustained growth over the past thirty years, seems to have owed much of its success to the discovery of oil, on the one hand, and its border economy (based on in-bond assembly plants, *maquiladoras*, literally 'golden mills'), on the other – neither of which can be counted on for permanent prosperity, one being subject to the vagaries of nature, the other to the vagaries of American car production. For although the *maquiladoras* – an EPZ by any other name ... – also host the manufacture of various electronic goods such as TVs and air-conditioners, their real importance is that, by providing access to a cheap offshore labour reserve in-shore ('just 1,546 miles from Detroit'), they help maintain the competitive edge of the American car industry. 'The bottom line is this', declared Rex Maingot of American Industries Inc. to a conference of business executives at Expo Maquila '86, 'your cost per Mexican worker is 69 cents an hour versus at least $9 an hour in the States – a saving of $15,000 a year per worker. You can see how down here a GM car can be made competitive with the Japanese.'[12] And judging from Mexico's slow death by debt ($104 billion) and negative growth (−0.5 per cent in 1988),[13] it is more likely that the country, instead of ascending to the DCs, is sinking into the UDCs.

... and realistic development

But 'unrealistic aspirations' apart, the DCs do not mind the NICs excelling them in yesterday's industries. Brazil, Mexico, South Korea and Taiwan have all become major exporters of steel in the last fifteen years and Brazil today is the third largest in the world. Over half the EEC's iron-ore needs, besides, is met by Brazil – at 'banana prices', it might be added. South Korea has recently overtaken Japan as the foremost shipbuilding nation, with Taiwan following close behind. Mexico, Brazil, Korea, Singapore, Hong Kong, Taiwan are all manufacturers and exporters of electrical goods and transport equipment. And almost all the NICs have taken off, and are able to fall back on, textile and garment manufacture – a fact curiously reminiscent of Britain's own take-off into the Industrial Revolution on cotton.

'In 1960', comments Nigel Harris, 'the old-established core of the world system in North America and Western Europe produced 71 per cent of the world's products and 78 per cent of manufacturing output. Twenty-one years later, those respective shares had fallen to 60 and 59 per cent. The shares of the United States and Britain – 49 and 53 per cent in 1960 – were by 1981 down to 35 and 33 per cent.' The World Bank, he concludes, 'estimates that the trend will reduce the share of Western Europe and North America in manufacturing to under half by 1990.'[14]

Judged on the basis of industrialisation, the NICs of Latin America and South East Asia have doubtless leapt into the twentieth century in a bound. But to argue that they are in competition with the DCs is to overlook the fact that the DCs, having entered into a whole new ball game, have willingly ceded their old ballpark to the NICs.

Judged on the basis of their export capacity in manufactured goods, the NICs could even be seen as 'fast closing the gap with the more developed countries'.[15] The point, however, is that the DCs have moved into a whole new era, a whole new realm of production – with electronics and lasers and biogenetics and nuclear power, and synthetic 'raw' materials replacing cotton and steel and copper – and the gap between them (the DCs) and the NICs has become epochal.

Judged on the basis of their GDPs,* the NICs, of South East Asia in particular, may be seen as displaying accelerated growth. But how has that growth benefited the mass of people? Where has it lifted them from the morass of poverty and hunger and hopelessness in which previous centuries of subjugation had sunk them? Where (with apologies to Eliot) is the development we have lost in growth?

---

* Between 1973 and 1984 the annual growth rate of GDP for South Korea, for instance, was 7.2 per cent, Taiwan 8.5 per cent, Hong Kong 9.1 per cent, Singapore 8.2 per cent.[16]

Debt and dependency

The path of capitalist 'development' bring us 'nearer to death ... no nearer to God'. Because it is a dependent capitalist development – a development that subjects itself to the demands of metropolitan capital, the exigencies of metropolitan need. It is tied development – tied to the purse-strings of the multinational corporations, the transnational banks and, in the final analysis, to the directions and directives of the International Monetary Fund and the World Bank. So that even when it advances in its own cause, it is led into advances for the few at the expense of the many. It is a development that creates a species of mutant capitalism that has to consume its own environment to survive.

Brazil's rapid industrialisation owes not a little to what Peter Evans calls the 'triple alliance' of multinational capital, state capital and 'elite local capital',[17] but it is also to the same combination of forces that it owes its people's poverty, its ecological devastation and its slow death by debt (at \$115 billion, the highest in the world). A case in point is the proposed construction of the Kararao hydroelectric dam in the Amazon, which, while providing badly needed power to run the industries that will provide the exports to pay off debt, will also mean the wholesale destruction of the country's rainforests and the annihilation of its Indian peoples.

Already vast areas of Amazonia have been ravaged and moonscaped by the search for gold (Brazil is the fourth largest producer), the mining of iron ore (on which the EEC and Japan rely for their steel) and the cutting down of trees that have taken 500 years to grow (to provide hardwood for the First World). South Africa's ConsGold, Britain's Rio Tinto Zinc and a number of Japanese and American corporations are involved in the mining projects (which also extend to bauxite and manganese) along with local big-time capitalists, small-time land speculators and sundry parasites such as moneylenders and *garimpeiros* (gold-diggers). And the

Brazilian government, having got into debt to get into development, can only get out of debt by getting further into 'development'. But that 'development' – in the Xingu river dam – has
now come up against the united resistance of the Indian
peoples across Brazil and into North America, the green
movement and, strangely enough, the World Bank (ostensibly
in the interests of ecology, but probably in the hope that the
plans of the Indians and the environmentalists to raise funds
to buy off the Brazilian government and pull it out of debt will
also help keep the Bank from throwing good money after
bad*).[19]

Mexico's industrialisation, like Brazil's, also took off on the
basis of alliances between foreign and local capital (state and
private). By 1980, the amount of foreign capital (mostly American) invested in the country (mostly in manufacture) totalled
$27 billion. Foreign companies were said to control over half
the output of private mining ... 84 per cent of the rubber
industry, 80 per cent of tobacco, 67 per cent of chemicals, 62
per cent of machinery and 79 per cent of electrical equipment.'[20] And although the country's emergence as an oil
producer should have kept it economically afloat, it only
served to drown it in debt – since most of the money borrowed
to develop the oil industry ended up in the Swiss bank
accounts of corrupt officials and (allegedly) ex-President
Lopez-Portillo,[21] while most of the oil revenue went into the
coffers of the right-wing Oil Workers' Union and its leader,
Joaquin Hernandez Galicia.** And Mexico has had to borrow
again to recover from its debt crisis.

In South East Asia industrialisation was (with the obvious
exception of Hong Kong) fostered and fashioned by the state
before being 'handed over' to private capital. The state

* Brazil has also put itself outside the 'good boy' rules of the World Bank by
refusing to sign the nuclear non-proliferation treaty.[18]
** Joaquin Hernandez Galicia and fifty-one other union officials were put
under arrest by the new President Carlos Salinas de Gortari in January this
year.[22]

occupied 'the commanding heights' of the economy, controlling the banking system, public spending, investment – and the labour market. And it provided the infrastructure and climate that would attract foreign capital. It was the sort of combination of central planning and robber-baron enterprise* that seemed particularly suited to the specifically export-oriented industrialisation of the South East Asian NICs.

Today there is hardly an industry (and a lot of them are in electronics) in these countries which is not a joint venture with multinationals or is not controlled by them. To a certain extent, this is predicated by the nature of the electronics industry itself – with its convergences, integrations and mergers – but it largely stems from metropolitan capital's need to keep both the technology and the markets within its own domain. And the only way that NICs can keep on 'growing' is by toeing the MNC line. Hyundai's repeated attempts to produce more sophisticated memory chips, for instance, were able to take off only on the basis of a joint venture with Texas Instruments.[23] Over half the companies in Taiwan's science-based industrial park are either subsidiaries of US companies ('such as the telecoms giant AT&T, the semi-conductor equipment manufacturer Varian and the disk-drive maker Priam') or joint ventures.[24] The first wafer-fabrication plant to be set up in Singapore five years ago was SGS-Thomson Microelectronics, a private joint venture between Italian and French conglomerates.[25] Hong Kong is all joint venture.

There is nothing independent about these countries. There is no autonomous growth, no development that speaks to the needs of the people. But then, export-oriented industrialisation is metropolitan-governed industrialisation. Domestic

---

* The phrase derives from ex-President J.R. Jayewardene's invitation to foreign capital – 'let the robber barons come' – when he opened the first EPZ in Sri Lanka.

capital is constrained by metropolitan capital, is servile to metropolitan capital. It owns but does not control, it produces but cannot sell; both production and market are in the gift of the centre.*

Whereas the NICs of Latin America have been tied to dependency through debt, the NICs of South East Asia accept dependency as a 'mode' of production, a way of life.

Hierarchies of labour

The trajectory of the UDCs is different and is set not so much by capital's design for production as by its drive for accumulation. We are dealing here with the crude, nasty end of capital, not with the refined, urbane aspect of its NIC adventures. It is not here in the UDCs to woo lesser capital but to gobble up resources. If capital inveigles the NICs into the deathly embrace of its own purpose, it lays waste the UDCs, with all its pristine voracity.

And what changes in the production process have done is to deliver these countries up to such exploitation in different and more absolutist ways than before – not least in the labour-intensive 'back end' of the electronics industry itself. Capital does not have to import cheap labour any more, with all its attendant social cost. It can move instead to the captive labour pools of the Third World and from one pool to another, choosing its locale of exploitation, its place of greatest profit, grading it according to the task in hand – which itself is a variable given the exponential changes in the electronics industry and the market-bound fate of an ever depressing light industry (the only industries that the UDCs can claim as their own).

* There are no mother countries any more, only mother multinationals. Which is partly the reason why South East Asian multinationals are beginning to emerge – but even these are tied to the 'mother multinationals'.

Thus there is a hierarchy of labour stretching from the centre to the outer periphery, not as between the highly skilled and the unskilled only but as among the unskilled themselves – so that the arduous, toxic work of bonding, for instance, tiny, hair-thin wires to circuit boards on wafers of silicon is done by the unskilled female labour of South East Asia, while the cleaner, safer, more straightforward task of operating the machinery into which the integrated circuits go is done by the deskilled workers at the centre. Capital is still dependent on exploiting workers for its profit, only now the brunt of that exploitation has shifted to the underdeveloped countries of the Third World, and the increasing intensity of exploitation there more than compensates for its comparative loss at the centre. Only the blind chauvinism of Eurocentric Marxism which mistakes its working class for the whole working class could bid the class farewell.

To put it differently, the technological revolution has allowed capital to shift the burden of extracting surplus value from the workers at the centre to the workers at the (outer) periphery. And that surplus value is not relative, as at the centre, but absolute. Capital does not need to pay peripheral labour a living wage to reproduce itself: it does not need labour on a long-term basis when technology is all the time catching up to replace it and, unlike at the centre, there is no social wage below which labour cannot fall, and what there is is readily abrogated by the government to let foreign capital in. And, in any case, there are enough cheaper and captive labour reserves in the periphery for capital to move around in, discarding each when done.[26]

And the governments of the UDCs, desperate not for development as such but to end the unemployment that threatens their regimes, enter into a Dutch auction with each other, offering the multinational corporations cheaper and cheaper labour, deunionised labour, captive labour, female labour and child labour – by removing whatever labour laws, whatever trade union rights have been gained in the past from at least

181

that part of the country, the EPZ, which foreign capital chooses for its own.* These are the only terms on which capital will come in and, once it is allowed in, it makes other demands – infrastructural demands, to begin with, such as unencumbered land, electric power. And if the power generated is insufficient to work its factories and/or takes away from the power available to the civilian population, it will dam up the rivers for you and develop hydroelectric schemes – and lend you the money to do it with, treat you to foreign experts (who know everything about damming up rivers but damn all about your country) – and irrigation schemes to open out your dry zones to landless peasants. And before you know where you are, it has taken over your land for agribusiness, to grow sugar-cane and pineapple where once you grew rice, and transformed the ordinary fare of the people, the fish from the seas and the fruit from the trees, into tourist delicacies to be fed into the maws of the Hiltons, the Intercontinentals and the Holiday Inns. In the meantime, you are in hock to the gills, everything you own is in pawn: your land, labour, raw materials, mineral reserves, the lot.

This is not a fanciful scenario, but one that obtains in Sri Lanka today. Admittedly, Sri Lanka – despite its previously high literacy rate (83 per cent), previously free education and health service and previously high turnout at general elections (70–80 per cent) (previously meaning before the World Bank got to it) – is somewhere near the bottom of the UDC table.** But even countries at the top, like Malaysia and Thailand, have scarcely graduated out of labour-intensive semiconductor assembly and light industry. Malaysia's plan to lift off into heavy industry with car manufacture and iron and steel production has since had to be 'rationalised' due to 'the

* The Dominican republic has put La Romana Zone under the control of foreign capital for thirty years.[27]
** With all that, Sri Lanka is still ahead of a number of even more underdeveloped countries in South Asia, Africa and the Caribbean – which are, however, not germane to my argument here.

prevailing weak financial position of local assemblers as well as the declining market for motor vehicles.'[28] And its attempts to move up into wafer-fabrication from integrated circuit assembly – which it is being priced out of by Thailand's cheaper labour force – have been 'hobbled by infrastructural constraints'.[29] The government is now falling back on traditional manufacture in palm oil, rubber, tin, and so on, and even in these has had to renege on its *bumiputra* (Malayanisation, literally 'sons of the soil') policies and permit foreign ownership and investment.[30]

Thailand has also got an edge (not only on Malaysia but other South East Asian countries) in the matter of joint venture car assembly and export, but it is currently being challenged by the Philippines' Car Development Programme, an all-Japanese affair. Indonesia is now catching up with Malaysia and Thailand (but, being rich in oil, has fallen into debt!).[31]

All these countries are, of course, involved in the 'back end' of the electronics industry and in garments manufacture to one extent or another, but Thailand now leads the way in agribusiness and food-processing. Pineapple and tomato plantations and 'agro-food' industries (such as animal feed for chickens for export) have taken over from 'traditional' agriculture; tuna and shrimp farming have become big business, and processed meats (such as sausage and ham) are being redirected from local consumption to export markets. For the Thai middle class there is instant noodles, frozen meatballs, processed dim sums and Indonesian satays 'on tap'. And all this with the help of agribusiness and food-processing conglomerates from the USA, Japan, Europe and even Taiwan. Dole has the largest pineapple plantation and canning operation in the country. Mitsubishi is involved in pineapple canning and prawn farming. Oscar Meyer has joint ventures in processed meats. Arbor Acres Farm Inc. has been a long time in the business of breeding and feeding and freezing chickens for export.

Thailand is today the world's largest exporter of canned pineapple and tuna – and frozen food, it is estimated, will soon be a multi-billion dollar export earner. In the meantime, Thailand imports food.[32]

So far from these countries resolving their unemployment problems and rising to the status of NICs, their more likely course seems to be a gradual slide into stunted growth and a different pattern of unemployment – with more and more small farmers becoming seasonal wage-labourers in commercial agriculture, more and more rural workers being thrown up into the 'informal economy' of the cities and more and more women being mobilised into short-life electronic assembly work and abandoned.[33] But the drive for export-oriented growth and the competition of other UDCs implicates these governments even further in the designs of multinational capital, the strictures of the IMF and the strategies of the World Bank – till their (the governments') interests are no longer the interests of their people but of metropolitan capital, of which they are now the servitors. And what keeps them there is American imperialism.

To come at it from the opposite direction, what keeps Third World labour cheap and captive for industrial conglomerates and enables land to be taken away from the peasants and handed over to agribusiness and the mineral resources to mining companies and brings whole countries within the economic jurisdiction of the agents of multinational capital, the IMF and World Bank, is the installation and maintenance of authoritarian Third World regimes by Western powers.

Setting up the new order

Trade no longer follows the flag; the flag follows trade. Capital has broken its national bounds, technology allows it, and governments must follow in capital's wake to set up the political and social orders within which it can safely and profitably operate – if need be with force, but with culture first.

Today that culture is transmitted not through education or through a genteel propaganda of superiority (British Council style) but subliminally, subcutaneously: in the food you eat, the clothes you wear, the music you hear, the television you watch, the newspapers you read. You do not eat a hamburger, the universal 'food', without taking in the American way of life with it:* you do not watch television (and it is mostly American in the Third World) without accepting the American world view; you do not listen to pop music – your pop, their pop, it's all pap – without losing your ability to hear other voices, your ability to reflect, weigh, meditate; you do not read the newspapers without losing your sense of truth.

Fast food for the culture of cooking, ready-made clichés for the act of thinking, style for content, sound in place of music, noise in place of sound, reading shorn of reflection, an easy superficiality for uneasy depth, sentimentality passed off as love, individual greed in place of collective good – corporate American culture is a surrogate for culture. It dwarfs the mind, limits horizons, warps the imagination, impoverishes passion – consider the impact of Murdoch culture (his nationality is irrelevant) on a country like Sri Lanka, which is still to recover from the cultural imperialism of another occupation – and smoothes the way for American hegemony.**

And tourism is not just a vehicle of that culture, but its vanguard: a defoliant that destroys the native culture as it

---

* 'Fast foods are becoming a way of life', acclaimed *Business Week*, as McDonalds' 'Americanisation of the Japanese ... reached a new peak', and *Advertising Age* confirmed that fast food 'is the food of the jeans generation, the new people who are looking to a common culture. South East Asians a generation ago thrived on Coca-Colanisation. Now their children are in the middle of a hamburger happening.'[34]

** The destabilisation of Unesco through the withdrawal of American (and British) financial support is an appreciation by the multinational culture industry that M'Bow's attempts to promote Third World culture were undermining the industry's message and challenging its domination and profitability.

advances, clears the ground for corporate industry to replace it with theirs. Tourism is not travel: search, curiosity, attachment. Tourism is reified leisure designed to relieve you (for a time) of your reified life. So, what it carries with it is the desperate excesses of its own culture and what it adopts and fetishises is the creative aspects of the native culture. Sri Lanka's beaches, a few years ago, were recommended by a paedophilia group in Britain as a good tourist venue for procuring children. And India, which once had *sanyasis**/ galore, now has Swamis Inc. Tourism transforms personal relationships into commercial relationships, use value into exchange value, breaks down the last vestiges of communalism and replaces it not with bourgeois culture but with post-bourgeois nihilism.

But if culture fails to win subject peoples to their own subjugation under regimes ordained by imperialism, there is always force, war – not necessarily direct, though there is that, too, as in the invasion of Grenada, but indirect, through low-intensity warfare or conflict (LIC) aimed at subverting resistance and preventing revolutionary movements from coming into being. LIC, according to the US Joint Chiefs of Staff's declaration in 1985, is protracted war involving 'diplomatic, economic, and psycho-social pressures through terrorism and insurgency'[35] – which, spelt out, means 'insurgency and counter-insurgency operations, terrorism and counter-terrorism, surgical direct action military operations, psychological warfare, and even operations by conventional or general purpose forces'.[36] At one end of the spectrum, LIC is soft war, concealed war at the grass-roots level, a war of paralysis of the will to resist, but at the other it is hard war, using terrorism and counterinsurgency and armed force. PSYOP (psychological operations), for instance, was the 'primary component' of LIC in El Salvador for a while and combined propaganda based on Coca Cola

* People who have given up worldly things and chosen poverty as a way of life.

selling techniques with precise disinformation put out by an Institute for Popular Education set up by the CIA in the Ministry of Communications and Culture. 'Descending upon remote villages', reported Dan Siegel and Joy Hackel, 'with *mariachi* bands, multicolored leaflets, clowns and candies for children, and taped advertisements targeting their parents, the military engaged in a major public relations blitz across the country.' At the same time TV, radio and newspapers carried on a sustained campaign to 'undermine the image of the guerillas while enhancing that of the government'. And on the international front carefully doctored material was 'leaked' by the National Security Council to selected reporters 'to change the country's image abroad and persuade the US Congress to continue to supply aid'.*[37]

In Nicaragua the CIA PSYOP manual urged '"political proselytism" and civic-action operations working side-by-side with peasants ... building, fishing, repairing etc'. But this was to be coupled with 'the selective use of violence', whereby 'contra provocateurs "armed with clubs, iron rods, placards, and if possible small fire arms" would instigate mob riots in the cities'.[38]

Besides fomenting 'preventive counter-revolution' (the phrase is Marcuse's), LIC also aims at destabilising 'unfriendly' Third World regimes such as Mozambique, Angola and Nicaragua by providing 'diplomatic, military and economic support ... for an insurgent force seeking freedom from an adversary government'[39] – insurgent forces such as MNR, UNITA and the Contras. In the case of Nicaragua, however, LIC has also involved the sowing of mines in the country's harbours 'to disrupt the flow of shipping essential to Nicaraguan trade during the peak export period' (Oliver North in a 'top secret' memorandum)[40] and the destruction of its oil facilities – both operations conducted by a specially

---

* The media efforts to portray General Noriega of Panama as a drugs-dealer would also appear to be such a CIA/NSC-led disinformation campaign.

trained force of 'unilaterally controlled Latino assets' (UCLAs)*. But in 1983 the LIC merchants combined with the World Bank to stop Nicaragua getting a loan to build a fleet of fishing boats on the grounds that the oil that was necessary to operate the boats (a condition imposed by this non-political Bank specially for Nicaragua) had run out in the meantime – thanks to the setting fire of its oil tanks by 'unknown' raiders from a mother-ship off-shore.[41]

The fomentation of insurgencies and local wars also helps Western powers to sell even more arms to Third World countries – to fuel the wars that fuel the arms sales – and get them deeper and deeper into debt and dependency. 'Without these sales', commented Tom Gervasi, Director of the Center of Military Research, in a TV programme recently, 'the developing nations cannot maintain the industry, and unemployment and bankruptcy will follow.' Besides, 'in order to arm ourselves properly, we have got to arm the world; to get the price down to what we can afford, we must sell more.'[42]

Of course, the whole point of LIC, in the final analysis, is to provide multinationals with a climate hospitable to trade and investment – all sorts of trade and investment – or, as Colonel Motley put it in the *Military Review*, 'to influence politico-military outcomes in the resource-rich and strategically located Third World areas'.[43] In Latin America the desired 'politico-military outcomes' have led to a variety of military juntas, from the savage in Chile (where the monetarist theories of Friedman's 'Chicago boys' were first practised) to the confused in Bolivia. In South East Asia they have resulted in all sorts of authoritarian regimes, from the dictatorships of South Korea and (till recently) the Philippines to the parliamentary oligarchies of Singapore and Sri Lanka. The NICs, both of Latin America and South East Asia, seem, by and large, to have the outright dictatorships (mutants, perhaps, of

---

* We are in the rarefied world of military lingo here – in itself a sort of covert operation.

their own sociopolitical history), while the UDCs appear to sport varieties of parliamentary authoritarianism. Which would point to the theorem that the greater and/or faster the growth of Third World countries, the quicker their graduation into fully-fledged dictatorships. Or even that totalitarian regimes are as much the form of government 'tolerable' to silicon-age imperialism as mock-Westminster was to industrial colonialism. Except that in recent years the United States has shown a certain flexibility in changing dictatorships around to 'friendly democracies', as in the Philippines, or recycling them through democratic processes such as elections and referenda, as in Chile and Haiti, so as to keep US interests in place.

Casualties of imperialism

The economic depredations of multinational capital*, the political repression of the regimes that host it and the LIC waged by Western powers to keep these regimes *in situ* all combine to effect the brutal dislocation and displacement of people all over the Third World and force them to flee their countries. Whether as economic refugees or as political asylum-seekers is no matter – for, however their arrival at the centre may be categorised, their ejection from their countries is, as I have shown, both economic and political at once. To distinguish between them is not just wilfully to misunderstand the machinations of imperialism today, but to pretend that the struggle against imperialism is not also here, at the centre, or has nothing to do with workers' struggles here.

For, apart from everything else, these – the refugees, migrants and asylum-seekers, the flotsam and jetsam of latter-day imperialism – are the new underclass of silicon-age capitalism. It is they who perform the arduous, unskilled, dirty

---

* And I have not even touched on its ecological depredations here – but see *Race & Class*, January–March 1989.

jobs in the ever-expanding service sector, who constitute the casual, *ad hoc*, temporary workers in computerised manufacture, who provide agribusiness with manual farm labour. They are the invisible workers in the service industries, serving in the up-front kitchens at McDonald's, as porters and cleaners in hospitals and shops, as waiters and petrol-pump attendants, security guards and night watchmen, servants and slaves. They are the peripheral workers in manufacture, peripheral in the manufacturing sense, too, because modern production processes do not require a permanent workforce but a functionally flexible 'core group' which can adjust to changes in technology and a numerically flexible 'peripheral group' which can be adjusted to changes in the market. They are the sweatshop workers in the primitive putting-out system of the garment industry. They are tomato-pickers for agribusiness.[44] They are, in a word, the cheap and captive labour force – rightless, rootless, peripatetic and temporary, illegal even – without which post-industrial society cannot run.

Their condition has been graphically described in *Ganz Unten* (published recently in English as *Lowest of the low*[45]) by a German investigative journalist, Günter Wallraff, who in the guise of a Turkish labourer, Ali, lived through a year of a migrant worker's life. Like any migrant worker, Wallraff/Ali is hired and fired at will, sat upon and spat upon, used and abused, vilified, reified and thrown upon a heap (in Turkey for preference) when he is done with. At first he hires himself out – to all sorts of menial jobs in restaurants and building sites and construction works – but soon discovers that he can continue to work only if he comes under the aegis, the protection, of a sub-contractor who hires him out to a contractor who contracts to do the dirty work for reputable firms who do not want to know that they are doing it. That work ranges from clearing frozen sludge from massive pipes on high buildings in 17 degrees of frost and shovelling hot, grimy coke dust hour after hour below ground level to being hired out as a human guinea-pig to a pharmaceutical firm and cleaning out a

190

nuclear power station, the carcinogenic effects of which would show only after Ali has returned to Turkey (the condition on which he got the job in the first place).

The firms that get his work have no responsibility for him. For Ali is hired out to them by labour contractors who have obtained him as part of a labour gang from sub-contractors and sub-sub-contractors and so on down the line. And all that Ali gets is what is left of his wages when everybody above him has taken his cut. He has no national insurance, no pension rights, no right to health care and social security, no right to a fair wage – and if he baulks at it, he is handed over to the police and deported home to a worse fate. He is the apotheosis of captive labour, dispensable, disposable, yielding absolute surplus value – right here in the centre.

You do not have to go to Germany to find the Alis of this world, though. They are here in Britain, too, among the refugees from Colombia, Chile, Sri Lanka, Sudan, Eritrea, Iran, the Philippines, Ghana – from every part of the world where imperialism has set foot.

The moment of socialism

But if these are the new circuits of imperialism made possible by the revolution in the productive forces, it is that same revolution that allows us to break the circuit and move towards socialism. The liberation of the productive forces must mean the liberation of man- and womankind – all men and women in the Third World, the First, wherever – not the greater liberation of a few at a greater cost to the many. But to do that we have got to seize the technology, put ourselves in command of it, not let it run away with itself into capital's terrain.

It is inconceivable that when we can produce more food we should throw it away, that when we can run factories without debasing workers we should debase them, that when we have found the leisure to be more creative in we should turn

191

ourselves into mindless junkies, that when we have invented the ultimate weapon of destruction we should not live in peace, that when we have learnt to master nature we should not let nature put out its thousand blooms, that when we have reached the summit of individual freedom we should not be working for the collective good.

Socialism is a moral creed, a secular faith – tolerant, loving, creative, increasing all to increase the one. It is that morality, above all, that the movement of workers has garnered and fostered and kept alive all these generations to inform and fashion our societies when Prometheus had been unbound again. What we have learnt from the labour movement, what we must hold on to, are not the old ways of organisation, the old modes of thought, the old concepts of battle against capital, but the values and traditions that were hammered out on the smithy of those battles: loyalty, solidarity, camaraderie, unity, all the great and simple things that make us human.

That is the morality of socialism that the working-class movement, the peasants' movement, the women's, black and gay movements, the green and anti-nuclear movements – all the movements of liberation have sung out. Technology can now make it flesh, and we cannot let capital take it away from us.

We can now ordain our societies so that there is greater productivity with less labour, improved consumption for all and more time to be human in. When our problem is no longer the production of goods as such, we should be looking to their more equitable distribution; when large numbers of workers are no longer necessary for such production, we should be looking to the more equitable distribution of work. If the same number of goods can be produced by half the workforce, it follows that the whole workforce need work only half the time rather than leave the other half unemployed. Not because work itself is sacrosanct, but because the culture of self-esteem and worth erected on the notions of working and earning will be a long time a-dying. We can set the process in

192

motion, however, by providing everybody with a minimum wage whether he or she works or not – so assuring effective demand, on the one hand, and replacing the work ethic with the leisure ethic, on the other. But such leisure will be active, creative leisure – not reified or nuclearising of us, but growing, organic, connecting us to people again: old people, children, the sick and disabled, the oppressed and the exploited. And education will be geared not just to jobs but to using leisure intelligently and creatively, to working things out for ourselves – for the technology that does all the thinking for us in the machines we produce is also the technology that requires us to return to the basic principles that produce such thinking: it requires that we not only know that 2 and 2 make 4, but why. It enables us to return to fundamentals, to holistic thinking, to an authority over our own experience, and so removes us from our captive submission to the media, politicians, the video civilisation.

We have cultures of resistance to create, communities of resistance to build, a world to win. Now is the moment of socialism. And capital shall have no dominion.

References

1. Sir Ieuan Maddock, 'Beyond the Protestant ethic', *New Scientist* (23 November 1978).

2. Robin Murray, 'Ownership, control and the market', *New Left Review*, no. 164 (July–August 1987).

3. Paul Handley, 'Long road to success', *Far Eastern Economic Review* (28 January 1988).

4. Peter Large, 'Pirelli slips into total automation on its Welsh industrial Kibbutz', *Guardian* (4 August 1988).

5. Nick Garnett, 'The culture shock of automation', *Financial Times* (7 October 1988).

6. Wladimir Andreff, 'The international centralisation of capital and the re-ordering of world capitalism', *Capital and Class*, no. 22 (Spring 1984).

7. Charles Leadbeater, 'Dagenham's decline is Genk's gain', *Financial Times* (30 January 1989).

8. 'South Korea embarks on a mass memory test', *Far Eastern Economic Review* (18 August 1988).

9. John McBeth and Mark Clifford, 'Ambitious flight plans filed: South Korea wants to buy an aerospace industry', *Far Eastern Economic Review* (9 June 1988).

10. Bob Johnstone, 'Taiwan has designs on booming niche markets', *Far Eastern Economic Review* (18 August 1988).

11. *Latin American Monitor*, vol. 6, no. 1 (February 1989).

12. *Multinational Monitor*, vol. 8, no. 2 (February 1987).

13. *Latin American Monitor*, vol. 6, no. 1 (February 1989).

14. Nigel Harris, *The end of the Third World: newly industrialising countries and the decline of an ideology* (London, 1987).

15. Ibid.

16. Clive Hamilton, 'Can the rest of Asia emulate the NICs?', *Third World Quarterly*, vol. 9, no. 4 (October 1987).

17. Peter Evans, *Dependent development: the alliance of multinational, state and local capital in Brazil* (Princeton, NJ, 1979).

18. *Latin American Monitor*, vol. 6, no. 1 (February 1989).

19. Walter Schwarz, *Guardian* (13 February and 27 February 1989); Louise Byrne, *Observer* (26 February 1989), and *The World this Week*, Channel 4 TV (26 February 1989).

20. N. Harris, *The end of the Third World*.

21. Susan George, *A fate worse than debt* (London, 1988).

22. *Latin American Monitor*, vol. 6, no. 1 (February 1989).

23. 'South Korea embarks on a mass memory test'.

24. Bob Johnstone, 'Diverting the brain drain: Taiwan science park woos hi-tech entrepreneurs', *Far Eastern Economic Review* (28 January 1988).

25. Carl Goldstein, 'Government pushes Singapore into wafer fabrication', *Far Eastern Economic Review* (18 August 1988).

26. See A. Sivanandan, 'Imperialism and disorganic development in the silicon age' in *A Different Hunger* (London, 1982), and Swasti Mitter, *Common fate, common bond: women in the global economy* (London, 1986).

27. Global and Conceptual Studies Branch Division for Industrial Studies, *Restructuring world industry in a period of crisis – the role of innovation* (Vienna, 1981).

28. Nick Seaward, 'A rethink on rationalisation', *Far Eastern Economic Review* (24 March 1988).

29. Carl Goldstein, 'Malaysia's back-end boom', *Far Eastern Economic Review* (25 August 1988).

30. Nick Seaward, 'The race to stay ahead', *Far Eastern Economic Review* (8 October 1987); and Nick Seaward, 'A new pragmatism', *Far Eastern Economic Review* (21 January 1988).

31. Paul Handley, 'Long road to success', *Far Eastern Economic Review* (28 January 1988); and Michael Vatikiotis, 'The energy to change', *Far Eastern Economic Review* (21 January 1988).

32. Carl Goldstein, 'Asia's supermarket', *Far Eastern Economic Review* (29

December 1988); and Paisai Sricharatchanya, 'Not just chicken feed', *Far Eastern Economic Review* (3 March 1988).

33. Saskia Sassen, *The mobility of labor and capital* (Cambridge, 1988).

34. Quoted in Armand Mattelart, *Transnationals and the Third World* (South Hadley, MA, 1983).

35. Michael T. Klare, 'The interventionist impulse' in Michael T. Klare and Peter Kornbluh, *Low intensity warfare* (New York, 1988).

36. Lieutenant Colonel John M. Oseth, quoted in M.T. Klare, 'The interventionist impulse'.

37. Daniel Siegel and Joy Hackel, 'El Salvador: counterinsurgency revisited' in M.T. Klare and P. Kornbluh, *Low intensity warfare.*

38. Peter Kornbluh, 'Nicaragua: US proinsurgency warfare' in M.T. Klare and P. Kornbluh, *Low intensity warfare.*

39. *Joint Low-Intensity Conflict Project final report*, quoted in Michael T. Klare and Peter Kornbluh, 'The new interventionism', in M.T. Klare and P. Kornbluh, *Low intensity warfare.*

40. Quoted in P. Kornbluh, 'Nicaragua: US proinsurgency warfare'.

41 'The masters of war', *The Four Horsemen*, Central TV (9 April 1986).

42. Ibid.

43. Quoted in M.T. Klare and P. Kornbluh, 'The new interventionism.

44. See 'Racism 1992', p. 153 in this volume.

45. Günter Wallraff, *Lowest of the low* (London, 1988).

Race, Class and State
in Post-Colonial Societies

12

Sri Lanka: A Case Study

There have been no race riots in Sri Lanka since independence. What there has been is a series of increasingly virulent pogroms against the Tamil people by the Sinhala state, resulting in the degeneracy of Sinhala society and its rapid descent into barbarism. And all this has been achieved in the name of Sinhala civilisation and Buddhist enlightenment – within a matter of thirty-five years – by the concerted efforts of politicians, priests and private armies.

Colonial capitalism and nationalism

When the British left Ceylon in 1948, the lines of communal conflict had already been drawn. One hundred and fifty years of British rule had brought together three different social formations under one central administration for purposes of economic exploitation; but for purposes of political control, the colonial government had reinforced the communal divisions that ran like a seam around those social formations. It divided in order to rule what it integrated in order to exploit. And it raised a class of administrators, suckled on English language and English culture, to reconcile the contradictions.

199

But then, the type of capitalism that developed in Sri Lanka under the British could neither destroy the pre-capitalist modes of production nor develop a coherent capitalist system in which the economic base would determine (in the final analysis, of course) the political and ideological superstructure. Instead, it had a differential impact on the different social formations and made capitalism's uneven development more uneven still. And what it could not cohere through organic capitalist development, it unified through administrative diktat. In the event, the social formations of the Kandyan highlands, the maritime provinces and the Northern peninsula,* which had for centuries coexisted side by side, now began to vie with each other for the favours of the colonial state – or, rather, the dominant classes within these social formations began to do so.

The character of that class differed with each social formation. In the Kandyan social formation, dominated by the feudal mode of production and untouched by foreign conquest till the advent of the British in 1815, the dominant class was the feudal aristocracy. In the coastal areas, and more particularly the western littoral, which had been subjected to almost 300 years of Portuguese commerce and Dutch mercantile capitalism, a merchant class with private property in land had emerged. The barren North, though similarly subjected to Portuguese (and then Dutch) rule from the early seventeenth century, was inhospitable to all colonial enterprise except missionary. The dominant mode, though tribute-paying, was not strictly feudal: the land was owned outright by the highest caste, the *vellala*, and not feudated of the king.[1] And the highest caste also happened to be the most numerous (unlike in India). Hence, the landholdings were small – and further fragmented by the dowry system.

The population of the Kandyan kingdom was predomi-

---

* These formed three separate kingdoms – the Kandyan, Kotte and Jaffna – at the time of the first European intrusion by the Portuguese in 1505.

nantly Sinhala and Buddhist, though the king and the royal court were mostly Tamil. The maritime provinces had a mixture of 'races' (Arabs, Burghers,* Sinhalese, Tamils) and religions (Catholic, Protestant, Muslim, Buddhist, Hindu) but were largely Sinhalese and Buddhist. The Northern peninsula, though Christianised by Portuguese and Dutch missions, remained predominantly Hindu – and Tamil. The caste system was more rigid here than in the other two social formations, but was ameliorated by the comparatively smaller numbers of the lower castes (in relation to the *vellalas*).

Into these social formations colonial capitalism inserted the plantation 'mode' – as an enclave, within what was once the Kandyan kingdom, with its own imported, indentured, Indian Tamil labour force and a social order of its own, a colony within a colony – on common land on which the Sinhala peasants had once grazed their cattle, and on forest land which had freed them if need be from corvée labour through slash and burn cultivation. Waste lands, the British called them, without ownership or title, and, passing an Ordinance that decreed them property of the Crown (1840), gave them away to the British planter at the upset price of five shillings per acre.[2] Already in 1818, whole villages had been alienated to the Kandyan nobility as reward for their help in quelling the peasant rebellion of the previous year – thereby altering a service and tribute-paying relationship into one of landlord and tenant. A landed aristocracy had been born and, with it, a landless peasantry. It was left to the Waste Lands Ordinance of 1897 to dispossess them completely, but, rather than drift into the semi-slave conditions of plantation work, they remained on the land as agricultural labour.

By the end of the nineteenth century, the plantation 'mode' had begun to dominate the economy, subsume all other modes to its own uses, build an infrastrucure of railways and roads to take its produce to world markets, and develop a

---

* Descendants of mixed marriages between the Dutch and the Ceylonese.

mighty business of sorting and selling, clearing and forwarding, insuring and shipping – and a species of local sucker capitalists to go with it. And to that species were added the dominant classes of earlier social formations to form the genus 'comprador'.

Some of these, particularly in the South, now owned their own little coconut, coffee and rubber plantations and graphite mines, either settled on them by grateful Dutch and British administrators or bought outright from the ill-gotten gains of the arrack industry. And they could afford to finish off their sons' education in Oxford and Cambridge and, later, the LSE, the better to enable them to take their place beside the colonialists in running the country.

However, it was also from this area of the country, the longest exposed to foreign influence and domination, that a proletariat emerged from the ranks of a long dispossessed peasantry – to work in the docks and the railways and the roads, in the engineering works and the construction industry. But it was still a proletariat with one foot in the land – or an eye to the land that its wages could buy back. Only the Tamil worker imported from south India to do the more laborious work in the ports and on the roads constituted the classical urban proletariat of capitalism.

The Tamil North was infertile, barren, with no rivers, no forests, no mountains – nothing grew there except children. But if it was inhospitable to colonial enterprise, it was inviting of missionary zeal and education. The first was to close down its economic options, the second to open them up in the service of the Raj.* The industry of a people who had worked an ungiving land was now given over to education, and the government service, into which education could take them. Education was land. And so the *vellalas* sent their sons to school and into the colonial service and the professions – and those who did well rose in prestige and position and came to

---

* Tamils served the British in Malaya, Singapore, etc.

own land and property, in Colombo and other parts of the country where their services took them. They soon came to be known as the 'Colombo Tamils' and were to take their place beside their English-educated Sinhala counterparts in their common quest for political office.

Below them was another tier of government service, Tamils who had probably made it to 7th standard English or even the Junior Cambridge (failed) – and it was they who did the clerical work, the lesser accounts (later, of course, to become cashiers and *shroffs** in the *kachcheries*** and banks) or went about helping the British to open up railway stations and post offices in the malaria-infested interior. Forced to leave their families at home in Jaffna, they became a rootless migrant labour force with only their religion and their language and their culture to hold on to.

For the vast majority of the people in Jaffna Province, however, and especially for the low-caste folk, very little had changed. The *vellalas* still owned the fragmented land the lower castes worked for them for a pittance.

If the ruling classes of the old formations and the rising new bourgeoisie of the plantation economy were beginning to find their comprador niche in the colonial order – though not without combat – and therein discover a common purpose, there was little to unite the various sections of the working class. The plantation workers were segregated in a bantustan and separated by language, caste and creed – and, above all, the labour process – from the Sinhala peasantry around them and from the rest of the working class. Only on the docks and the railways and the roads did the Indian labourer work side by side with Sinhala labour. And as for the native Tamil labourer, he was virtually non-existent outside the Jaffna peninsula and the Eastern Province. The most frequent contact that the Sinhala worker had with the indigenous

* Chief cashiers.
** Town halls.

Tamil was in the latter's capacity as small shopkeeper or lesser bureaucrat. Only among the lower-middle class clerical workers was there a shared work experience among Sinhalese and Tamils – but their unity suffered from the handicaps of their class.

Neither a national bourgeoisie, then, nor a fully-fledged proletariat and only the most venal of petit-bourgeoisies – 'small landowners, artisans, craftsmen, small petty producers mainly rural-based ... educated in the indigenous languages' and 'a new group (mainly urban) of clerks, minor bureaucrats, shopkeepers and teachers generated by the needs of the plantation economy'[3] – that was the class character of Sri Lanka at the turn of the century, with the British plantocracy at the top and Indian merchant capitalists a tier below.

Colonial capitalism had bred neither a capitalist class that out of sheer economic compulsion was dying to break its colonial integument nor a proletariat that could see beyond race and religion to its own class interests. Power for the colonial bourgeoisie and the colonial proletariat lay not in economic hegemony or in class struggle, but in the trappings and appurtenances of the colonial state on the one hand and its handouts and favours on the other. The 'bourgeoisie' vied for a place in the colonial sun, the 'proletariat' for a space in bourgeois patronage. The path to economic power was through political power – politics was not, as in central capitalism, the handmaiden of economics – and political power was in the hands of the colonial state. State power was all.

For a moment, though, the nationalist and working-class agitations of the first quarter of the twentieth century looked as though they might take off into anti-colonial struggle. Elements of such a movement had already emerged in the last decades of the nineteenth century in the form of a broad-based religious revival – Buddhist, Hindu and Muslim – aimed at contesting Christian privilege and Christian culture. Led by the middle-class intelligentsia, it had found its immediate expression in a rash of anti-Christian publications, followed by the founding of Buddhist, Hindu and Muslim schools, and ending up in the pioneering strike of the printing workers in 1893, during which arose (and fell) the first trade union: that of the printers.* The reactionary excesses of this revival, however, had also resulted in the first religious riot – between Catholics and Buddhists in the north of Colombo.

It was this same spirit of religious revivalism that fired the bourgeois-led temperance movement of 1903–05 and, raging through the South in demonstrations, processions, publications, associations, singed the beard of government. More, it pointed the way to rebellion among ordinary working-class people and set the mood for the carters' strike of 1906.** The strike was remarkable in that it had all communities and creeds in its ranks and won the unstinting support of all the working people of Colombo, who egged the carters on to greater defiance of the police. And this in turn encouraged the temperance movement to spread itself further into the working population and the rural masses and become more self-consciously political. But the constitutional reform of 1910 confined the franchise to the Western educated elite and continued to keep the rising new bourgeoisie from power, precipitating its involvement in the railway strike of 1912. Though the strike itself was 'secular', relating to the cost of living and wages of railway workers, and included workers of all creeds and communities, the Sinhala strikers were not unaffected by the anti-Indian outpourings in the Sinhala press and the strident nationalism of the more aggressive leaders like Dharmapala, who now inveighed against Moors and Tamils (in addition to Europeans) as 'infidels of a degraded race'. Consequently, when the strike was bought off with a Commission and the Commission itself failed to grant any of the workers' demands, whether about pay, conditions of work, promotion or the use of Indian labour in preference to Sinhala, the

* Much of the information in this section is owed to Kumari Jayawardena's seminal and path-breaking work on the labour movement in Ceylon.[4]
** Bullock carts were essential for transporting plantation produce and exports and imports to and from Colombo harbour.

workers' simmering frustration and anger, made worse by the shortages of the 1914–18 war, burst out in physical violence against Moor traders and moneylenders. Anti-Muslim riots had already broken out in Kandy over a religious dispute the previous day and the railway workers in Colombo now found common cause with them.

The riots spread and the government, which had espoused the cause of the Muslims, overreacted, fearing that the whole thing was a Sinhala–German plot. Martial law was declared on 2 June 1915 and every white man, civilian and military, given permission to shoot and kill at will.* Punjab soldiers, mostly Muslim, were brought in to maintain law and order and the courts martial sentenced over fifty people to summary execution. Temperance leaders (even the most moderate, like D.S. Senanayake, the future prime minister) were imprisoned and railway workers who had revealed themselves as militants at the hearings of the Railway Commission exiled to the Eastern Province.

The bourgeois nationalist 'revolution' was dead – it had died of its own religious and communal contradictions: its inability to turn a religious crusade into a (secular) political campaign embracing all sects and/or a working-class movement embracing all races. The cultural resistance of the Sinhala Buddhists, in other words, did not – precisely because it was Sinhala and Buddhist – 'take on', as Cabral has it, 'new forms (political, economic, armed) in order fully to contest foreign domination'. And it remained confined to Sinhala Buddhism precisely because the 'bourgeoisie' that colonial capitalism created had vision of neither nation nor class.

This also applied to the Tamil 'bourgeoisie' who, raised on Western education and Western values, found a sinecure in government office and were loath to rock the colonial boat. There was the odd exception, though, like Arunachalam who even as Registrar-General took up the cause of his people,

* By a subsequent Act of Indemnity the 'shooters' were placed beyond the reach of the law.

206

Sinhalese and Tamil, Buddhist and Hindu, urban worker and estate labourer – and was to found not only the Ceylon National Congress as a vehicle for nationalist politics but a plethora of welfare organisations to serve the interests of the masses.* And for a while it looked as though, at the level of political bargaining with the colonial government at least, the Sinhala and Tamil bourgeoisies could come together – they had earlier 'elected' the Tamil Ramanathan to the 'educated seat' in the Legislative Council and he in turn championed the Sinhala cause in the riots of 1915.** But Governor Manning, who had formerly handled the Mahdi uprising in the Sudan and other such threats to British power, found even such a fragile unity of the Western-educated elite threatening to him and his government's position and set out to play the communal game.*** And the lick-spittle bourgeoisie took to it as to the manner born. Soon they were reviving their feudal feuds – with the effete up-country aristocracy demanding self-determination for the 'Kandyan race', the Tamils holding up their better (Western) education and their faithful government service for preferential treatment, and the low-country Sinhalese shrewdly building up their communal base among the rural elite of native physicians, village schoolmasters and Buddhist monks through Mahajana Sabhas (Peoples' Associations) cobbled together from the now defunct temperance organisations. (They were subsequently to provide the basis for Bandaranaike's Sinhala Maha Sabha and mark out his communal constituency.)†

* Arunachalam left Congress and politics when, after 1920, Congress moderates were inveigled into participating in the Legislative Council.
** Sinhala communalism at this time was directed against the Indian Tamils and not the 'indigenous'.
*** The Ceylonese 'seats' in the Legislative Council were directly apportioned on a communal basis and Governor Manning sought to reinforce this in perpetuity. 'In such a community as this', he wrote to the Colonial Office, 'there is naturally plenty of racial strife and jealousy and that will be of value in deciding the composition of the Council.'[5]
† The Tamil response to the Mahajana Sabhas was the Mahajana Sabhais!

But if the bourgeoisie had shot its radical bolt and settled for constitutional plea-bargaining through lobbies such as the Ceylon National Congress, the working-class movement benefited by the religious-nationalist demise to become more secularly working-class. And the fact that the reformists now sought their support in the rural elite and not among the urban workers left the latter free to pursue their own class interests. Hence, in the railway and dock strikes of 1920, the workers relied on their own resources and self-organisation to take on the employers and win.* And it was the self-assurance of the working class that determined the militancy of its subsequent leadership in the Ceylon Labour Union and A.E. Goonesinha and characterised the general strike of 1923 and the rash of strikes between 1927 and 1929 – creating in the process an urban working class united across caste and creed and community. More importantly, it was this working-class tail that now began to wag the nationalist dog and pitch Goonesinha (in his political persona) and his Young Lanka League into the more militant politics of *swaraj*. In this they were influenced by the nationalist movement in India – and that in turn augured well for the continuing unity between the urban proletariat and the plantation workers. Though Goonesinha himself had made no attempt to extend his trade union activities to the plantations, he was unstinting in his support of the struggles conducted first by Arunachalam (between 1913 and 1922) and then by Natesa Iyer, Indian member of the Legislative Council, to improve the wages and conditions of Indian estate labour. Natesa Iyer, in fact, was Goonesinha's lieutenant in the dock strike of 1927 and had prevailed upon blackleg labour imported from India to return home – and before that they had jointly edited a paper that was uncompromising in its demand for *swaraj*.

But Goonesinha was also influenced by the British trade

* The Ceylon Workers Welfare League, which was founded by Arunachalam and his Social Service League in 1919, and later blossomed into the Ceylon Workers' Federation, never took off into true unionism.

union movement and the way it articulated with the parliamentary politics of the British Labour Party and, on his return from the Commonwealth Labour Conference in London in 1928, founded the Ceylon Labour Party and the All-Ceylon Trades Union Congress. This was also the time that the Donoughmore Commission on constitutional reform, appointed by Colonial Secretary Lord Passfield (Sydney Webb), was advocating adult suffrage for Ceylon, despite the strident protests of the Ceylon National Congress – and Goonesinha saw the enfranchisement of the working class as his and, therefore, their path to power. He was, after all, the leader of both the trade union movement and the Labour Party, and no doubt his political interest could only serve the workers' economic interest. When, therefore, a deepening recession put the Sinhala urban workers at loggerheads with their Indian fellows, it was not working-class solidarity that claimed Goonesinha's attention but the need to win over the Sinhala majority to his 'parliamentary' cause. He did not, in other words, help the workers close ranks against the colonial employers as a national labour leader should have; instead, he used their Sinhala chauvinism to gain a ready-made electoral majority. And in his paper, *Viraya* (Hero!), he returned to the virulent communalism of the bourgeois nationalists before him and reinforced further the prejudices of the Sinhala working class. In 1931, he was elected to the solidly Sinhala seat of Colombo Central – and trade unions passed into the keeping of political parties.

The second nationalist 'revolution', based in the working class, was dead also.* It had died, like its bourgeois counter-

---

* Two more flutters of anti-colonial nationalism were to follow – the first, in 1931, when the Jaffna Youth Congress called for a boycott of the State Council elections because the Donoughmore Constitution had not awarded *swaraj*, and the second, in the years following, when anti-Poppy Day protests (the Surya Mal campaign) threatened to burgeon into a fully-fledged anti-British movement under the auspices of the newly-formed (Marxist) Lanka Sama Samaja Party (LSSP). But the first, remarkable though it was for its anti-caste, anti-communal stance, never got beyond the peninsula and the second got two of its leaders into the State Council where hardly a shot was fired.[6]

part, of its own communal contradictions. But, unlike the latter, those contradictions had been fomented by a leadership that saw in adult suffrage and territorial representation the built-in advantages of communalism. Equally, the minorities – and in particular the largest and most influential minority, the Tamils – were afraid that they would lose out on the privileges that the divisive politics of colonialism had awarded them beyond their electoral weight. The Kandyan nobility by now had merged its waning fortunes with the up and coming low-country Sinhala entrepreneur-politico and was more anxious about what it would lose through the enfranchisement of the plantation worker than about what it would gain by retaining its (nominated) communal seat in Council. But the signs were that a future Sinhala government would neuter the Indian vote.

The Donoughmore Commissioners had set their faces sternly against Manning's communal scheme of representation in the expectation that territorial electorates had a better chance of engendering a non-communal party system. But they had reckoned without the client bourgeoisie, to whom they must have been really alluding when they wrote that 'the conception of patriotism in Ceylon is as much racial as national'.[7] In the event, the Constitution of 1931 – after a brief spasm of Sinhala–Tamil collaboration in the Western reaches of the first State Council where Oxford and Cambridge vied only for debating honours – finally sealed up the communal lines of government that had been fostered by the British for over a century.* So that even when the semblance of a non-communal party system began to emerge with the founding of the LSSP in 1933, it was set in the matrix of bourgeois parliamentary politics (its leaders were from that class anyway) and destined, therefore, to end up in communalism albeit some twenty-five years later. By the time the Soulbury Commission,

---

* Representations right up to the 1920s had been on a communal basis and by nomination of the Governor.

210

in the wake of the war and India's successful independence struggle, came to serve up self-government to Ceylon on an Indian platter, an entrenched Pan-Sinhala ministry in the last State Council had pointed the way to political, and hence economic, domination.* All that was needed was a racist ideology to substantiate the one and facilitate the other – and that would be found through communalism.

Colonial capitalism had failed capitalism's first precept – to put economics in command. Instead, it had overlaid the economies of existing social formations to one degree or another with a plantation economy and held them down with a strong state and a mimic culture. What little capitalism escaped through the interstices of a metropolitan-oriented economy was invariably merchant capitalism. And merchant capital's path to power is through patronage. It has not the self-assurance, the audacity of industrial capital, to fashion its own political hegemony – or its style to fashion the culture that furnishes its *raison d'être*.

Everything about colonial capitalism is disorganic, fissiparous, uncreative. It articulates nothing. Even its contradictions do not allow of growth; they congeal instead into paradoxes, holding two dissimilar truths together – a mirage of progress and equally invidious.

Colonial capitalism creates nothing and destroys nothing.**

---

* The minorities led by G.G. Ponnambalam and his Tamil Congress had demanded a combined territorial and communal representation which could effect a fifty-fifty balance between the Sinhalese and the rest, but the Soulbury Commission could not go back on the Donoughmore Constitution and universal franchise.

** India, though cited as the archetypal example of the opposite view that capitalism in a colony is, in the final analysis, creative (or creative-destructive) was really the exception. India's burgeoning capitalism and its capitalist class were *suppressed* by the British. And it was the nationalist struggle of this suppressed Indian bourgeoisie – to whose assistance Gandhi's feudal genius brought the masses, armed with non-violence and the *charka* – that was the backbone of the independence movement. This is also why bourgeois democracy took natural root in India and not in Ceylon or any other British colony.

Instead, it distorts, disfigures, disorientates. It develops the productive forces only to stifle them in the service of the 'mother country'. It engenders new social relations and social classes only to suspend them between the past and the future: the bourgeois temperament remains feudal, the proletarian mind unreleased from the land. It creates a hybrid culture only to frustrate its finest flowering. It promotes liberal democracy only to pave the way to dictatorship. Colonial capitalism aborts capitalist development and leaves the dead foetus in the womb of the past.

From nationalism to communalism

The first act of an independent Ceylonese government under D.S. Senanayake and his United National Party (UNP) was to render plantation workers stateless on the ground that they could not provide legally valid documentation to show that they were citizens of Ceylon by registration or descent. The second (virtually) was to disfranchise them – on the ground that they were not Ceylon nationals! At one parliamentary stroke (more or less), the bourgeoisie had removed a tenth of the population and the whole of the plantation proletariat from effective participation in their and their country's affairs. Constituencies in which the plantation workers once had enough electoral clout to return their own representatives – or tilt the balance in favour of a workers' party like the LSSP* – now became rotten boroughs for one rotten section of the bourgeoisie or another. Whole constituencies in the hill country were denuded of voters – Talawakelle, for example, dropping from 19,298 to 2,912 – giving an extraordinary weightage to the Sinhala rural voter who, guided in his communal prejudices by the sanction of the law and the

---

* The LSSP's All Ceylon Estate Workers' Union had supported the plantation workers in their struggles and led the historic strikes on Mooloya and Wewessa estates in the 1930s.[8]

benefits of patronage, was, in Ludowyk's telling phrase, 'on his way to becoming the centre of gravity in the political world of Ceylon'.[9]

The Sinhala bourgeoisie was finding its political kingdom through the uses of communalism – and it was a measure of the degeneracy of the Tamil bourgeoisie as represented in G.G. Ponnambalam's Tamil Congress that it was prepared to betray the Indian Tamils to stay in power.* But its turn was still to come.

The portents were already there – in 1949 – when the government inaugurated an irrigation scheme in a predominantly Tamil area of the Eastern Province to settle Sinhala colonists. The idea ostensibly was to provide land for the landless Sinhala peasantry – but in the event, those chosen were the nominees of politicians in search of sure seats. State aid made that assurance doubly sure – the settler was both landowner and state-aided cultivator – and he, together with the casual labourer whom his patron had already recruited to the irrigation schemes, would have the run of the settlement. They would 'take care of business', turn into a private army if need be. Their allegiance was to their political patron, the patron's to the governing party, the party's to its (Sinhala) majority. Whether or not colonisation schemes helped the landless Sinhala peasant, they certainly altered the communal composition of constituencies so as to give the Sinhalese a majority. The Tamils were outvoted before they had even begun.

Bandaranaike read the electoral signs early on – and in 1951 left the UNP to form the Sri Lanka Freedom Party (SLFP) from the nucleus of his Sinhala Maha Sabha. He was a son and a nephew removed from the UNP line to the throne, anyway, and now was as good a time as any to make his populist move. As Minister for Local Government (1936–51) and

---

* There were two exceptions though: S.J.V. Chelvanayakam and C. Vanni-ansingham, who broke away from the Tamil Congress (TC) to form the Federal Party (FP).

through his work with the Mahajana Sabhas of the temperance era (from which his Sinhala Maha Sabha had sprung), he had found the pulse if not of the Sinhala masses, at least of their traditional leaders: the monk, the physician and the teacher – and in their future he saw his own.

But though Prime Minister D.S. Senanayake died the following year, Bandaranaike had to wait till 1956 – till, that is the old man's son and nephew had their whack at government – before he and his SLFP could make a serious bid for power. 1956 also happened to be the year of the Buddha Jayanti (the 2,500th anniversary of the Buddha's death), said to commemorate the 'unique threefold event' of the founding of Buddhism, the settlement of Ceylon and the origins of the Sinhala people. And Solomon West Ridgeway Dias Bandaranaike was not loath to present himself as champion of Sinhala Buddhism: the triangular relationship between king, *sangha* (the clergy) and the people of the ancient polity could not have been far from his mind. Sinhala, he declared, abandoning his previous stand for *swabasha* (use of both the vernacular languages), would be the official language and Buddhism the state religion. But the UNP had also latched on to the communalist game and, in the Dutch auction that followed, Bandaranaike committed his party to making Sinhala the official language within twenty-four fours of being elected. Even so, the coalition the SLFP had concocted could not have defeated the UNP so decisively but for the agreement of the Marxist parties not to contest the same seats* (on the ground that if the SLFP was not quite socialist, the UNP was certainly capitalist). One breakaway faction of the international Marxists in fact joined the SLFP coalition to form the future government (on the ground, one suspects, that it was all right to be nationalist at home, so long as you were internationalist

* The LSSP and the Communist Party (CP) stood for parity of language, but in their anxiety to be Left (class-wise), they ended up by being Right (race-wise). But, for all that, they were the only parties to put up Tamil candidates at all. The electorates were beginning to be communalised.

abroad). That this faction was led by Philip Gunawardena, the father of international Marxism (in Ceylon, that is), served only to show the way to future Trotskyite strategy.

The first act of the 'people's government' was to take away the language rights of a fifth of the people – with a Bill that decreed that Sinhala was to replace English as the sole official language of the country. The philosophy behind the Official Language Act was to give the common man and woman a voice in their country's affairs. It was intolerable that only the 5 per cent (both Sinhalese and Tamil) who spoke English should run the government or reap the benefits of office – and it was absurd that 95 per cent of the population should conduct their official dealings through interpreters who translated their native tongues back into a foreign language in order to be (officially) understood. But it was equally intolerable – and unjust – that the Act, in giving voice to the Sinhala masses, should have shut out that of the Tamils. (The LSSP and CP, having avoided the language issue at the election, fought valiantly now for parity – but who was going to believe them?)

In protest, the Federal Party staged a Gandhian *satyagraha* opposite the Houses of Parliament – and a Sinhala mob egged on by Bandaranaike's coalition partners beat them up. The violence spread to other parts of Colombo and sparked off a conflagration in Gal Oya Valley in which over 150 Tamils were killed by Sinhala 'settlers'. It was no longer the Tamil vote or Tamil land that was endangered by colonisation schemes, but Tamil lives.

At its convention a few months later, the Federal Party, to which more and more Tamils had been driven by Sinhala separatism, called for a federal constitution, equal status for Tamil as an official language, the repeal of the citizenship laws and an end to the colonisation of Tamil areas. If the government did not meet its conditions within a year, it threatened mass civil disobedience.

In July 1957, the Prime Minister conceded the justice of the Tamil case and entered into a pact with Chelvanayakam, the

Federal Party leader, to provide legislation that would grant regional autonomy, recognise Tamil as 'the language of administration of the Northern and Eastern Provinces', and end Sinhala colonisation of Tamil areas. But no sooner was the Bandaranaike–Chelvanayakam Pact concluded than the communalist forces that Bandaranaike himself had nurtured began a violent campaign against it. Only this time, they were led by the UNP Shadow Minister of Finance, J.R. Jayewardene, who headed a 'pilgrimage' of *bhikkus* (monks) and thugs to the Tooth Temple in Kandy to save the Sinhala Buddhist polity – and was waylaid by an opposing gang of thugs some miles from Colombo.*

The goondas had been given their head. It only needed government sanction before they cut loose. And that came when, in retaliation for the obliteration of Sinhala number plates on state-owned buses in the North, the goondas in Colombo were allowed by an unseeing police to deface Tamil businesses and homes and harass Tamil passersby. Their depredations spread to other parts of the country, sanctioned now by priests and political bosses. It was all '*appey anduwa*' (our government) now.

The Prime Minister prevaricated over the promised legislation. The UNP, protesting against the division of the country, pushed division further. The Eksath Bhikku Peramuna (United Front of Monks) threatened non-violence if the pact was not abrogated. On the morning of 9 April 1958, 200 *bhikkus* and hundreds more of their assorted cohorts laid siege to the Prime Minister's residence. By afternoon he capitulated: the Pact was revoked.

The *bhikkus* had arrived on the political stage, with the goon squads in close attendance. There was very little to choose

* This was led by another Bandaranayake (MP) who, after various sojourns in various parties of various hues, was to end up an intrepid communalist (irrespective of party). It was a journey that was to be traversed by a whole host of MPs, both Left and Right, according to the vicissitudes of the parliamentary game.

216

between them anyway. The days when the *sangha* had stood for learning and scholarship had faded under the impact of colonial neglect and Christian endeavour. The *pirivennas* (universities) which turned out educated priests and princes alike had fallen into desuetude. The secular learning that was a necessary part of a *samanera*'s (novice's) apprenticeship had become secondary to ritual and the preaching of *banna* and the recital of the *gatha* in Pali, a language as dead as Latin, reified ritual. And the *samanera* himself came to be seen as a necessary aid to clerical celibacy. The Buddhist *bhikku* of the classical era, sworn to abstinence and poverty, freed of greed, had, with rare exception, been succeeded by worldly monks who used their traditional position (restored to them by Bandaranaike) to become wielders of patronage and purveyors of power. Some of them were rich and powerful in their own right – and the prince of them all was the incumbent of the ancient temple of Kelaniya Buddharakkita Thero, whose taste in liquor and women was legend throughout the land. Even the Catholic church at its most corrupt could scarcely have done better – except that it was then at the end of its power; the Buddhist clerics were at the (second) beginning of theirs.

Every move that Bandaranaike now made to make amends for his betrayal of the Pact – such as a Bill on the reasonable use of Tamil – was blocked by priests and politicians and the Sinhala press and the mass hysteria they whipped up in the country. The Sinhala language, they warned, was in danger of extinction – and with it the Sinhala people. Where else in the world was Sinhala spoken but in Ceylon? The Tamils at least could look across the Palk Strait to the 40 million Tamils in Tamil Nadu for the preservation of their language and culture.* Their allegiance, in any case, was not to Lanka but

* 'Danger of South Indian domination was the product of Sinhalese fears of Tamil reactions to the suppression of their language by a Sinhala-only policy.'[10] Ludowyk was writing in 1966, but the attitude of the Sri Lanka government to India after the pogroms of 1983 vindicates his analysis – except that, since then, 'Sinhalese fears' have been honed into a fine ideology of 'Indian expansionism'.

India. Ceylon was for the Sinhalese – and Sinhala should prevail over every other language 'from Point Pedro to Dondra Head'.

The Marxist parties were no help to Bandaranaike either. They were more intent on 'embarrassing the government' with strikes than on helping it find a solution to the language question – apart from reiterating their 'principled stand' for parity in parliament. But all they discovered in the course of the strikes was that they were losing their troops to communalism.

The country was fast dividing into two separate communities. Even the veneer of class politics that had, at independence, separated the Right (the UNP) from the Left (LSSP) was beginning to wear thin under the impact of SLFP communalism – not that communalism mattered *per se* (as yet) but it was a sure passport to power. What was learnt from the disfranchisement of the Indian Tamils could be put to use to emasculate the 'native Tamils'. But Bandaranaike's ride to power on the back of communal politics, and his inability to climb off once he got there, proved that communalism was a one-way ticket – to communalism. That had not deterred either the Right or the Left, though, from being pulled, in varying degrees and at varying pace, into the 'middle-path' of Sinhala Buddhism. The pampered Tamil middle class, having first played along with the Sinhala bourgeoisie, had been forced into fighting Sinhala communalism with Tamil communalism (albeit non-violently).

The 'Marxist' parties, having thrown themselves wholeheartedly into parliamentary politics from their inception – the leader of the Opposition, Dr N.M. Perera, was also leader of the LSSP – were incapable of fighting the vital issues of class and race outside parliament without having an eye to the vote at the same time. When they failed to defeat the Bill disfranchising the plantation workers in the House, they neither brought out their unions in support of their fellow workers nor continued to further the Indian workers' cause in the country at large. Similarly, they were prepared to fight Bandaranaike's 'Sinhala only' Bill in parliament (having first put him there) but failed to fight it outside, either with their trade union power or with their not inconsiderable support among the Sinhala and Tamil intelligentsia. The only extra-parliamentary struggle they had waged was in the *hartal* of 1953, when they 'led' the spontaneous uprisings of the masses against rising food prices and the cessation of rice subsidies. But though the government fled to the safety of a ship in harbour, from where to conduct its affairs, the 'Marxists' turned tail at the last moment and left the workers stranded. Now, against the rising tide of communalism, all they could do was to advance the cause of parity in a bourgeois parliament or retreat to the comfort of Marxist dogma and dismiss communalism as a capitalist red herring spoiling the spoor of class struggle.

There was no one to speak up for the Tamils except the Tamils. And no Tamil party spoke to their interest like the Federal Party. But the Federalists had failed to deliver on the Bandaranaike–Chelvanayakam Pact. It was imperative, therefore, that their convention in May 1958 should resurrect the strategy of mass disobedience, the threat of which had brought Bandaranaike to the negotiating table in the first place.

But as they set out for the convention in Vavuniya in the Northern Province, the goon squads, under instructions from their political bosses, were getting ready to waylay them at Polonnaruwa. Their instructions at this stage, according to Tarzie Vittachi's painfully objective report of the events, were to 'stone buses and trains, hoot and generally signify "disapprobation"'.[11] But this was the same assortment of casual labourers and squatters from the irrigation and land development schemes in Polonnaruwa area who, a year earlier, had driven Tamil workers from the land allotted to them under a compensation scheme. They had called themselves the Sinhala Hamudawa then (the Sinhala army), and, led by a monk, had set out to stem a Tamil 'invasion' of their traditional homelands. Another invading horde of Tamils, it was now put about, was converging from Trincomalee and Batticaloa on the ancient capital of Polonnaruwa – and the Sinhala Hamudawa girded for battle, derailing and smashing up trains in the hunt for Tamils. And when that yielded little, they rampaged through the town 'raping, looting and beating up Tamil labourers and officers'. In the days following, the atrocities began to mount in number and intensity and spread rapidly to other parts of the country. In Batticaloa, Tamil fishermen retaliated by burning the huts of their Sinhalese fellows and driving them out into a hostile sea. In Colombo and the South, Tamil businesses and properties were looted and set on fire – and Tamil passengers in cars and buses, identified by their inability to read Sinhala or recite a Buddhist *gatha* (hymn), taken out and murdered. In Ratmalana, opposite the bus terminal, a game of Tamil-burning had developed, where one man would chase the victim with a can of petrol and douse him, while another flicked a lighted match at him. And yet the government said and did nothing.

When the Prime Minister finally came on the radio – four days after the 'riots' began – ostensibly to heal the communal breach, he pointed to the unexplained death of a Sinhala businessman and ex-mayor (of Nuwara Eliya) in the Tamil District of Batticaloa on 25 May as the cause of 'the various acts of violence and lawlessness' that had begun three days earlier! The death of one Sinhalese man seemed to weigh more heavily on the Prime Minister's conscience than the hundreds of Tamils burnt, mutilated, raped and hacked to death. Only the previous night, Tamil labourers and their families on the government farms at Polonnaruwa and Hingurakgoda had been simultaneously massacred. At Polonnaruwa, they had fled into the sugar-cane bushes of their own planting, only to be burnt out of hiding and bludgeoned to death. At Hingurakgoda, forty families were systematically slaughtered. Only the initiative, courage and innate humanity of the government agent of the District and his police officers and constables (all Sinhala) prevented the spread of mass murder. No such roll-call of honour was conceivable twenty-five years later.

The Prime Minister's broadcast served only to incense the Sinhalese further and trigger off a spate of rumours about Tamil atrocities – which in turn justified the killing of more Tamils. Finally, on 27 May, the Governor-General, Sir Oliver Goonetilleke, declared a State of Emergency and brought out the troops.* The riots continued in parts of Colombo despite the curfew and reached Jaffna the following day – when reports of an attack on a Hindu temple in the South and the burning of its priest led to a revenge attack on a Buddhist temple in Jaffna town and the vandalisation, the following day, of a resplendent Buddhist shrine on the offshore island of Nainativu. 'No attempt was made to do bodily harm to the Sinhalese', comments Vittachi. But 'they were told to leave their homes and their shops ... and then their goods were dragged out on to the road and heaped up and burnt.' That, at least, the 'local leaders' felt was owed to 'their brothers and sisters in the South'.[13]

And there were 12,000 of them in the refugee camps in Colombo alone, who were eventually sent off to Jaffna by ship, because the roads and railways were still unsafe. And that led a racist Sinhala MP to make the unintentional prophecy that it was the government that was dividing the country by sending the Tamils back to the North and East. But the government put it all down to a Muscovite plot – and placed the Tamil leaders in detention.

With the Emergency to keep Sinhala mobs at bay and detention to keep Federalists out of Tamil reach, Bandaranaike returned to his 'middle path' and brought in an Act which gave him, as Prime Minister, the right to effect regulations for the reasonable use of Tamil – and then proceeded to

* 'The Prime Minister had decided to allow the Governor-General to take the spotlight so that he could also take the rap.'[12]

do nothing. A year later, he was shot dead by a *bhikku* – at the instigation of the Rev Buddharakkita Thero, the sybarite high priest of the Kelaniya temple and secretary of the Eksath Bhikku Peramuna.

From communalism to racism

Communalism had grown out of a soured nationalism which, having failed to wrest power from the British through an anti-colonial struggle uniting the various communities, turned them (the communities) to wresting it from each other when it was thrown to them like a bone. The trappings of bourgeois democracy had decreed that that power should reside in the majority. Such a majority was already waiting in the wings. All it needed was the sanction of government and the blessing of religion to define it as Sinhala and Buddhist. And those it had found by 1958. What Sinhala communalism was still to find, though, before it took on the dimensions of racism, was its institutionalisation in the apparatuses – legislative, executive and judicial – of the state. And that was to come in the 'reign' of the two SLFP governments, 1960–65 and 1970–77, and more particularly in the second, which was a coalition of the SLFP, LSSP and CP known as the United Front. But in between, both the UNP and the SLFP (and its allies), depending on which party was in opposition at the time, kept up a barrage of Sinhala Buddhist propaganda to bring down the other's government, and 'communalised' the electorate in the process.

The response of the Federal Party (and the tainted Tamil Congress) to the growing state racism – right up to 1972 when a new constitution put paid to their middle-class hopes of being accommodated as equals within a Sinhala polity – was to run from one party to another with parliamentary power deals, 'committing' *satyagraha* when repulsed.

In March 1960, the Federal Party tried to make a deal with a hung UNP government to keep it in power, but the FP's

222

demands were too close to the Bandaranaike-Chelvanayakam Pact for UNP comfort. The FP then hawked its fifteen MPs to the SLFP, to bring down the UNP government, for the same price, and was accepted. But when the SLFP was returned to office in the July election with a big enough majority to form its own government, it reneged on its agreement with the FP. At that point, the FP went into *satyagraha* – which on this occasion was widespread enough to paralyse the administration in the Tamil districts. The government sent in the troops and, when the FP retaliated with its own postal service and stamps, subjected Jaffna to its first reign of army brutality.

The parliamentary power game was over, certainly as far as the SLFP was concerned. The UNP, runners-up as always in the communal stakes, might still need to make overtures to the FP to form a government, but the SLFP had drawn the LSSP and CP closer to its bosom with its mock socialist policies. Bandaranaike had already nationalised transport and the handling of cargo in the docks. His widow took over petrol stations, mission schools, one bank (the Bank of Ceylon) and insurance. This, and the offer of three ministries in her cabinet (albeit in the dying days of her government), endeared her to the revolutionary Marxists of the LSSP who promptly abandoned 'parity' for power. (The CP, even without the blandishments of power, had given up its 'principled stand' on parity of status for the two languages two years earlier, in 1962.)

Virtually the first act of the SLFP–LSSP coalition was to formulate a plan to repatriate the (disfranchised) plantation workers. For sixteen years they had remained stateless and voteless, but so long as India had refused to have them 'back', they could at least stay on in the country of their birth. But now a tidy agreement had been planned between the two governments (in the 'Sirimavo–Shastri Pact') to repatriate the many by giving citizenship to the few.* And the 'Marxists',

* Under this agreement, 525,000 plantation workers were to be repatriated to India and 300,000 given Ceylonese citizenship over a period of fifteen years.

who had once found their way to State Council and parliament through the votes of the plantation workers, were now a party to their evacuation. The LSSP even agreed to Mrs Bandaranaike putting them, when citizenised (plus those who were already citizens), on a separate (communal) electoral register.* If Mrs Bandaranaike could not get the urban working class on her side, she could at least get its leaders to do her bidding.

It was little wonder, then, that when the next government – a UNP concoction of several parties including the FP, the TC and Philip Gunawardene (ex-Marxist, ex-SLFP minister) – announced the introduction of regulations for 'the reasonable use of Tamil', based on Bandaranaike's Tamil Language Act of 1958, the SLFP should get its new-found partners, the LSSP and CP, to join its viciously communal anti-government demonstrations by bringing out their unions on strike.

The communalisation of the Sinhala working class was wellnigh complete. A few unions still remained untainted by the communal leadership of the Marxist Left – such as the Ceylon Mercantile Union under Bala Tampoe and those within the Ceylon Trade Union Federation under Sanmugathasan. But they were both Tamils and, though politically active in their different parties, were careful not to intrude 'the national question' into trade union politics.** All that remained now was for the LSSP and CP to help formulate policies that would be repressive of the Tamil people and of the working class alike. And that was to come with their ascent to power with the SLFP in the United Front (UF) government of 1970–77.

---

* As a consequence, the Ceylon Workers Congress, the most powerful trade union among the plantation workers, led by S. Thondaman, went over to the UNP for the first time since 1947, and a UNP government repudiated the policy of a special register a couple of years later.
** Sanmugathasan, in fact, had remained in the CP when the party betrayed its stand on parity (1962) – and it was only over the Sino-Soviet rift in 1963 that he broke away to form the pro-Chinese Ceylon Communist Party (CCP), taking the CTUF with him. And at that point, the CP mounted a scurrilous communal campaign against him to woo back the rank and file.

But by now, the economy was in a sorry mess. Successive governments had squandered whatever sterling assets had accrued to them during the war years. Foreign exchange earnings from tea, rubber and coconut, which constituted 90 per cent of the country's exports, had fallen with the fall in world prices. Two-thirds of those earnings went on imports of essential foodstuffs. And neither the UNP's agricultural policies, from colonisation schemes to 'green revolution' (1965–70), nor the SLFP's import-substitution and nationalisation schemes had produced either self-sufficiency in food or industrial take-off. Instead, the former had made for few rural capitalists and a number of small peasant cultivators and the latter for a new *mudalali* (entrepreneur) class and an expanding public sector. Both sets of policies favoured the Sinhala Buddhists in the rural areas, but left out of the reckoning their children who, raised on free education and populist rhetoric, demanded jobs and socialism.* And when the UF government failed to produce on the one and reneged on the other, the Sinhala youth rose up in armed rebellion. They had organised themselves secretly into a close-knit revolutionary party, Janatha Vimukthi Peramuna (JVP, the People's Liberation Front), five years earlier, and it now needed the concerted efforts of several governments to help the UF put down the insurrection. When it finally succeeded, it did so with ruthless efficiency, wiping out some 8,000 youths** without socialist qualm or populist tear, and detaining 14,000 more.

---

* Over 14 per cent of the population (of 12 million) were unemployed. Of these, over 70 per cent were in the rural areas and aged 19–25, nearly all of them educated to secondary school level.

** This is the figure given in *Nouvel Observateur* (23 May 1971) by René Dumont, who was in Ceylon during the insurrection. Others have put it higher, but exact figures are hard to come by as the UF government's Emergency Regulations of March 1971 authorised police officers 'to take all such measures as may be necessary for the taking possession and burial or cremation of any dead body' without having to account in any way before the law. It was a regulation that was to be renewed by President Jayewardene in 1983.[14]

The insurrection occurred in April 1971, but for the rest of its term of office, which the UF, with 125 out of 151 seats in parliament, extended with impunity to 1977, the government governed under emergency regulations – curbing civil rights, inhibiting judicial independence, muzzling the press, banning strikes in essential services (which covered everything from the manufacture of ice to the supply of water) and prohibiting political activity. And it used these regulations to put Tamil student militants in detention, where some of them came into contact with JVP detainees for the first time. (The JVP, based in the Sinhala Buddhist heartland, had not addressed itself to the 'Tamil question' except to point to the threat of 'Indian expansionism' with which they sometimes identified the estate workers.)

In 1972, the government introduced a new constitution making the National State Assembly 'the supreme instrument of state power' (legislative, executive, judicial), and registering Sri Lanka as a Buddhist state with Sinhala as its official language.*

A Press Bill followed, bringing the 'capitalist press' under government control.** Since Radio Ceylon was already a state corporation, the national media were now virtually in government hands. As for local government elections, they just dropped out of sight.

While the UF government was putting its political house in order, its Finance Minister, Dr N.M. Perera, was running back and forth between Colombo and Washington trying to get the IMF to give him a socialist loan or two. Nationalisation

---

* The chief architect of this constitution was another 'revolutionary Marxist', Dr Colvin R. de Silva (who appears later in these pages in the guise of the Minister of Plantation Industries).
** This was directed at Associated Newspapers, whose owners had for decades virtually told the nation what to think and how to vote – and had earlier mounted a filthy campaign against Mrs Bandaranaike personally at the elections. Government control was, among other things, short-sighted, as it was bound to serve the interests of the UNP, the press's class allies, when the government changed.

226

was proving to be costly and import-substitution looked as though it still needed foreign assistance – by way of machinery and plant and some raw material even. But these were schemes which, apart from being 'socialist' and, more importantly, seen to be such, were helping to create a truly indigenous class of capitalists to serve the country and a fine upstanding state bureaucracy to serve the people. And, of course, you could not have the one without the other. To do business you needed quotas, licences, permits, bank credit (that is why they nationalised the banks) – and that is where state patronage came in, and the state bureaucracy to channel that patronage. And the bureaucrats themselves were state appointees. But that is what planning is all about. And planning is socialism.

If this Trotskyite version of socialism brought a blush to Muscovite cheeks, it also gratified the populism of the SLFP – for a while. For the expanding public sector had opened up avenues of employment for the Sinhala rural youth from whose ranks the JVP insurgents had sprung. But to make sure that they could find room at the top, the government introduced standardisation schemes in education, whereby weightage was to be given to rural youth as against their urban counterparts – a sort of positive discrimination/affirmative action for the disadvantaged. That at least was the ostensible purpose behind district-wise standardisation, and since urban schools had better equipment, science facilities, teachers, and so on, it appeared to be a justifiable one and not aimed specifically at Tamils in Jaffna schools.* But prompted by Sinhala Buddhist agitation and JVP insurgency, the government also introduced a media-wise standardisation scheme which was a method of adjusting examination marks between the two language media so that those sitting in the Sinhala medium needed fewer marks to get into university than those sitting in the Tamil medium.

---

* But, since districts included towns, this weightage system did not act in favour of the rural areas either.[15]

The effect on the Tamils was momentous. Standardisation wiped out at a stroke the meagre opportunities that education had held out for the up-country Tamils, and for the Tamils in the North and East it put paid to all ambition and hope. Already their language had been taken from them, and with that their access to government jobs. And then this government had narrowed it further with a chit system which gave jobs only to political appointees; but then, there was no public sector development at all in the North and East. Trade, too, had gone into Sinhala hands with the government's entry into the import and retail business. But the Tamils had continued through education to make it to the professions. Now that also was taken from them. Language and learning – these were their land, their livelihood, their legacy, their sense of civilisation. They had not built great tanks and irrigation schemes or even managed to industrialise their homelands, but they had written poems, played plays and sung such songs – literature was their art form, and music. Language had lent itself to the first, the harshness of work to the second. And now it was all taken from them, and had made a bleak land bleaker still.

In January 1974, the Tamils held a congress in Jaffna to celebrate their Tamil language and Tamil culture. Tamil poets, philosophers, scholars and artists came from all over the Tamil-speaking world to be present at the occasion. Mrs Bandaranaike opposed the idea of the conference but could not in the glare of publicity forbid it. But Mayor Duraiyappah, the SLFP's Tamil stooge, got the message and cleared out of town, leaving the police a free hand. And on the last day of the conference, with the conference spilling over from Veerasingham Hall on to the esplanade outside to make itself available to the thousands assembled there, the police on the pretext of an unwarranted public meeting charged into the crowd with tear gas and baton, bringing down the electric pylons and killing nine people in the process.

The youth were stunned. The government held out no comforting hand or apology. The Tamil United Front – a

228

consortium of Tamil bourgeois parties (the FP, the TC and the CWC)* – provoked into unity by the Sinhala Buddhist constitution of 1972, indulged in its customary rhetoric and did nothing. And the youth took it upon themselves to take on the Sinhala state. A series of bank robberies followed and as the police, put beyond the reach of law by emergency law, stepped up their operations, the youth organised themselves into the Tamil New Tigers (TNT) and elected to shoot down the arrogant and strutting symbol of Sinhala state power in Jaffna, Alfred Duraiyappah. It was a slap in the face for the government, which promptly arrested and detained and tortured over a hundred young people at random and then proceeded to erect a statue to Duraiyappah in the heart of Jaffna town. (The imperial lesson had not been unlearnt even by the Marxists in the government.)

The state repression that followed Duraiyappah's killing drove the burgeoning movement underground, where it began to ponder the tenets and practice of Marxism. Already, the activities of Sanmugathasan's CCP in leading the depressed castes' temple entry movement in Jaffna in the latter part of the 1960s were fresh in their minds, and from their teachers they had learnt of the Jaffna Youth League and the once progressive policies of the LSSP and CP. But they were also immersed in the nationalist rhetoric of the FP and the TC who, like their Sinhala counterparts, kept harking back to a glorious past when the Tamils had their own kingdom. It was a powerful argument for a people bereft of dignity and belonging and particularly for the young who, in addition, were bereft of a future – and met at the same time the Marxist requirements for nationhood. The Marxists themselves – those outside parliament, that is – had substituted

---

* The Tamil leaders of these parties were plantation owners and employers of Indian Tamil estate workers. 'G.G. Ponnambalam (TC) was the owner of Sri Niwasa estate at Waga, S.J.V. Chelvanayakam (FP) was the owner of an estate in Maskeliya and Thondaman (CWC) was the owner of Wavenden estate in Pusellawa and Medegoda estate in Dolosbage.'[16]

rote learning for concrete investigation and shoved it all back to the Tamil youth for resolution under the rubric of the national question. And this uneasy mating of bourgeois historicism with historical materialism has continued to plague the theory and practice of Tamil revolutionaries even today.

Meanwhile, in 1975, the government socialists (there used to be government Christians under the British) achieved the summit of their nationalisation policies by taking over the plantations (which were losing money anyway) and paying compensation to their foreign owners. Three years earlier, the government had taken over private landholdings in excess of twenty-five acres (paddy) and fifty (other produce). Some of the land so recaptured was alienated to the Sinhala peasantry (Mrs Bandaranaike was reversing the betrayal of her Radala forefathers when they sold out the Kandyan people to the British, taking some of their common land as payment). Other land was turned over to co-operatives under the aegis of MPs. Together, these measures dispossessed a whole host of plantation workers of their livelihood and reduced them to destitution and death on the roads of Nawalapitiya and Gampola and Hatton.*

But even as the UF reached its socialist summit, its constituent parts fell to bickering over who should take the credit for the ascent, the LSSP or the SLFP, and whose constituency should benefit by it – and Mrs Bandaranaike promptly settled the argument by dismissing the LSSP from the coalition. The CP followed somewhat (a year and a half, in fact) later – and parliament was dissolved soon afterwards.

In July 1977, the UNP swept into power, with 140 out of 168 seats. The LSSP and CP won not one, the SLFP eight. The Tamil United Liberation Front, who had added Liberation (TULF) to Unity (TUF) in its 1976 Conference in order to keep up with 'the boys' and now stood for the separate state

---

* The Minister of Plantation Industries was the Trotskyite Colvin R. de Silva, the constitution-maker of 1972.

of Eelam, won eighteen seats and became the main opposition party – and its leader, Amirthalingam became the official leader of the alternative government of the Sinhala state!

State capitalism was over, but it had left in its wake a detritus of broken promises, half-baked industrial schemes, bits and pieces of land reform, rising prices, debt and corruption. And it had created a Sinhala Buddhist state-class, institutionalised (and constitutionalised) racism and re-created the culture of racial superiority. The Tamils were a people apart, Jaffna another country, without benefit of employment or education or economic advancement, separate – except for central control. And even that control was no longer through representative local government (local elections had ceased in 1971) but through appointees of the state and its police force and, occasionally, the army. The army was by now almost all Sinhalese (it boasted a whole regiment of them called Sinha Regiment), though the navy and the air force still had a sprinkling of Tamils, mostly in the upper echelons, and the police was fast becoming a force of Sinhalese only, but again with willing Tamils in the higher ranks. It would not be long before there was one government (civil) for the Sinhalese and another (military) for the Tamils.

In education, the state's policy of separate development created not only a Sinhala 'stream' and a Tamil 'stream' (so that nation shall not speak unto nation!) and made the one superior to the other through 'standardisation',* but also carried on the theme of Arya-Sinhala racial superiority into Sinhala textbooks. Tamils (let alone other communities) seldom appeared in these books and when they did it was as invaders or immigrants. In the meticulous phraseology of the Council for Communal Harmony through the Media (CCHM), 'not only do the Sinhala readers continue to main-

* Sri Lanka must be the only country in the world where such affirmative action is used to safeguard the interests of the majority on the ground that they are a minority – in the world. But, then, so are the Chinese.

tain their monocultural character in these grades [3–9]; they also project an image of a Sinhala Buddhist identity which is defined fundamentally through opposition to and struggle against Tamil invaders in past history'. By contrast, the Tamil readers issued by the same government department were all multicultural in their content and contained 'material presenting relations of friendship between Tamil children on the one hand and both Sinhala and Muslim children on the other'.[17] Whatever the racist thinking behind this policy – and the readers, published under the last government, continue to be reprinted under this – it should certainly help produce a generation of small-minded, insular Sinhala nazis.

If this is one waste of human potential, there is yet another in the plantation areas, where institutionalised racism first raised its head and now thrives on 'benign neglect' – with no schools worth speaking of, no books, no equipment, not enough teachers. 'What goes by the name of the *Maha Vidyalaya* (high school) at Welimada', mourns Gnanamuttu, 'consists of two half-walled buildings. The senior section of the school ... is a few feet below the main road. It has to compete with a bi-weekly fair with its dust, its noise and its smells. The junior section with its half-walls [is] dangerously near the river, which in January 1975 invaded the school and carried away its furniture'.[18]

If the culture of racism was being bred in the schools, it was disseminated through the Sinhala media and reproduced in the singularly Sinhala Buddhist activities of the Ministry of Culture. The 'independent' press, still (by and large) anti-SLFP and anti-Left, was confidently Sinhala Buddhist rather than overtly racist, but the North and the East of the country might just as well not have existed for all the coverage they got in these papers. The state-controlled radio was rarely impartial in its reporting of events (in the Sinhala medium) and its interpretation of events, if not the reports themselves, often diverged as between the Sinhala and English programmes. The Sinhala music it broadcast was, perhaps inevitably, (given

the 'culture' of the times) narrowly nationalist: where Soma-
pala and Chitra once sang meaningless love lyrics, Nanda
Malini Gokula's mellifluous voice now conveyed the message
of the Lion Race in the nursery songs that a mother sang to
her child as she put him to sleep.

The Ministry of Cultural Affairs, for its part, saw Sri
Lankan culture as wholly Sinhala Buddhist. And nowhere was
this clearer than in the plethora of art exhibitions, music
festivals, folk dance and drama that it assembled for the Non-
Aligned Conference in 1976. Or look at the *Sri Lanka Year Book*
for, say, 1975, under Fine Arts and Cultural Activities and see
whether you can find one mention of Tamil art or craft, never
mind 'culture'.

It was, however, in the 'commanding heights of the
economy' that state racism held sway. Between them,
nationalisation and import-substitution and government
control of the import-export business had 'corporatised' and
bureaucratised virtually every avenue of economic activity.
And since state corporations were invariably situated in
Sinhala areas for the benefit of Sinhala voters, and appoint-
ments both to them and to the state bureaucracy were made
on the basis of political patronage, Tamils could rarely find
employment in the public sector. If they tried their hand at
trade, their path was blocked not only by the need to get
quotas, permits and licences, which were generally available
only to political favourites, but also by government co-operatives which now handled almost all of the import and retail
business, from rice and flour to toothbrushes and toys, both in
the villages and in the towns. If they tried industry, hopefully
under the aegis of the government's protectionist policies, they
found they had little or no access to credit facilities. 'The local
credit market', as Newton Gunasinghe has pointed out in his
brilliant essay on the economics of racism (though he does not
call it that), was 'dominated by the two state banks. The direc-
tors of these were also persons appointed on the basis of political patronage and were closely linked to the political parties

in power. Given this situation, the same conditions that applied to the issuance of quotas, permits and licences applied to the granting of bank credit. Here too, Sinhala entrepreneurs linked to the ruling political party stood to gain, whereas Tamil entrepreneurs, especially the middle-level ones who enjoyed no upper-class social status and lacked political patronage, did not enjoy any specific advantage.'[19] And even those Tamils who did manage, by virtue of their class, to enjoy political patronage – and they were never more than a handful – seldom extended their enterprise to the Tamil areas.

If colonial capitalism had failed to penetrate the North and East, neither state capitalism nor the private enterprise that grew in its shadow made any impact on them either. But then, the driving force of underdeveloped state capitalism is not economic but political and ideological. The politics is the politics of achieving and keeping power, the ideology that of reinforcing and substantiating that politics. The vehicle for the first is (initially) social democracy, the basis for the second the culture of a soured nationalism which failed to take on colonial capitalism and therein find its progressive dynamic. Where that culture is not homogeneous (what culture is?) and falls neatly into communal categories, themselves the result of differential social formations, it is these categories that are exploited to achieve political power. The process of maintaining – and reproducing – that power, however, wins for one community economic (and political) dominance over all others and alters the relationship between them from the horizontal to the vertical, in a hierarchy of power. When that hierarchy then becomes institutionalised in the apparatuses of the state, accepted by civil society and authenticated by ideologies of racial superiority and/or historical primacy, communalism takes on the dimensions and class connotations of racism.[20]

To put it differently, communalism implies a parallel relationship between (communal) groups, antagonistic perhaps but not necessarily unequal; racism connotes a hierarchical relationship of power, institutionalised in the state apparatus. Communal violence, therefore, refers to that which occurs between (communal) groups, not to that inflicted on one group by the state, representing another. Hence, the use of the term (communal) 'riots', when what is meant – or should be – is state pogroms.* This is not just a euphemism but a violent distortion of the truth – which further adds to the pretended innocence of the state. Communalism is an 'afraid' word.

Communalism is also a portmanteau word: it takes in all the dirty linen of religion, language, culture, 'ethnicity'. And it is a flat word, one-dimensional – gives no idea of the dynamics of relationships within a community or between communities.

Above all, communalism, like ethnicity, is a pluralist word in a class world. They both describe, but do not tell – are historicist rather than historical. Worse, they pretend that society is all vertical; differentiated by 'ethnic' or communal groups and not by class, or, if by class, only as a sub-division of ethnicity or at best 'linked' to it. And this is not just a distortion of reality, but an acceptance of it – a prelude either to side-tracking it into 'group conflict' or abstracting it into 'the national question'.

Communal categories belong to the period of colonial capitalism, when they were disinterred from their social formations to serve British rule. They came to maturity in the decades before independence in what Bipan Chandra has called a 'vicarious nationalism'[21] – which, in the years following, impregnated the body politic, to give birth to state racism.** And it is that racism which is today growing into fascism.

---

* The Centre for Society and Religion, which prides itself on its work for social justice, but retreats into pietism on race matters, calls them 'communal disturbances'. Others, mainly academics (both Tamil and Sinhala), talk of 'inter-ethnic hostility', 'ethnic disharmony', etc.
** Its bastard child was already in existence in the plantations.

From racism to fascism

The UNP came to power in 1977 with the best of capitalist intentions – or so it seemed from their manifesto. They were going to get rid of all that stuffy state corporation business and let the clean air of free enterprise blow through their open economy. They were going to do away with racism and corruption because these things fouled up the capitalist works. They would restore the rule of law, the independence of the judiciary, the freedom of the press. they would not only maintain existing welfare programmes such as subsidised food and free educational and medical services – for that, after all, was the tradition of the country – but even increase the weekly rice ration. They understood that the demand of the 'Tamil-speaking people' for a separate state arose from 'the lack of a solution to their problems' and promised an early all-party conference that would 'take all possible steps to remedy the grievances in such fields as (1) Education (2) Colonisation (3) Use of Tamil language (4) Employment in the Public and semi-Public Corporations'. They aimed, above all, to create a 'just and free society' through righteous (*dharmista*) government.[22]

Within two weeks of taking office, the *dharmista* government stood by and watched while its police burnt down the Jaffna market – because they had been refused free entry into the city's carnival! Police arrogance and brutality had become the norm in Jaffna under the UF government, but the UNP's readiness to turn a blind eye to police conduct now boosted their confidence. As the anti-Tamil violence, fired by rumour, was taken up by Sinhala mobs and spread to other parts of the country, the police not only did nothing but helped fuel the rumours. The government contented itself with clapping on curfews which were broken – under police supervision. The Prime Minister, J.R. Jayewardene, refused to declare a state of emergency because it was 'contrary to democratic principles' – and for two weeks a reign of terror was unleashed on the

236

Tamils. They were beaten, maimed, stabbed and killed in their hundreds, their children terrorised, their shops and houses looted and burnt. In Colombo alone, over 35,000 refugees were crowded into six schools with bad sanitation, little food and less medical help – and threats of being bombed out of the camps as well – before being packed off, finally, to Jaffna by train and ship and plane.

But it was the plantation workers who suffered most. Their line-rooms were burnt, their possessions looted, the men beaten, the women gang-raped. And they ended up in transit camps. Transit to where, though? Jaffna? But Jaffna was not their home.[23]

This was the first time that the 'plantation Tamils' had been subjected to mob violence, but then they had already been violated by successive governments for thirty years and left prey to attack. Sinhala Buddhist ideology had long held them responsible for taking Sinhala land, but another strand had been added to it in recent years which held them responsible for taking Sinhala jobs – and the originator of this thinking had now arrived in the inner ranks of the cabinet.

This was the first time, too, that the police force so openly connived at assault and arson and looting, but they had been given a free hand against the JVP in 1971 and against the Tamils ever since – with guarantee of absolution. The UNP could do no less.*

It was a bad start for Jayewardene capitalism, but the IMF and World Bank rallied to his side – in exchange for devaluation, 'rationalisation' of food subsidies and cuts in the welfare programmes. A Western aid consortium followed with added help to establish a Free Trade Zone (FTZ) and develop Colombo as a commercial and tourist centre. But the project

---

* Five years later, with proceedings still pending in the courts, the UNP passed an Act indemnifying ministers, public officers, members of the security forces and members acting under their authority in respect of acts committed during the communal disturbances of August 1977 'with a view to restoring law and order'.[24]

above all which, according to the Finance Minister, had won the unequivocal support of the IMF and World Bank and 'captured the imagination of the Aid-Group countries' was the harnessing of the waters of the Mahaveli River to generate hydroelectric power and open out land in the Dry Zone. And it was not difficult to see why: if investors in the FTZ needed power, it would not be long before agribusiness needed land – and the day of the FTZs was fast receding, anyway.

But whatever the specific needs of the various projects, the overall requirement was 'political stability'. That stability was assured in September 1978 by a new constitution (pushed through parliament in three weeks) which concentrated exec-utive power in the hands of a President (elected directly), weakened parliament by making it responsible to him or her but not vice versa, and ushered in proportional representation as the basis for all future elections – thereby ensuring that no other party could ever again find the two-thirds majority necessary to play around with the constitution as the UNP could. And if investors needed further reassurance, Article 157 stipulated that no future government could revoke or alter any treaty or agreement entered into – on the basis of a two-thirds majority in parliament – with a foreign state or 'its nationals ... corporations, companies and other associations' for the 'promotion and protection of their investments'.

But all these constitutional provisos could not safeguard, let alone attract, foreign investment if it was constantly being threatened by labour problems and civil strife. The unions could be brought into line with an Essential Services Act (like that of the UF), and their membership, in any case, was moving from the ranks of the defeated parties to the UNP's union, the Jathika Sevaka Sangamaya (JSS), under Mathew, the Minister of Industries. As for the left-wing disorder of the JVP, their fangs had been drawn by the release of their leaders from jail and into electoral politics.[25] But there was still 'the Tamil problem'. The pogroms of 1977 and the detentions and torture that followed had served only to increase the militancy

238

of the Tamil youth and their uncompromising commitment to fight the Sinhala state. Only a few months earlier, they had killed the notorious torturer and traitor, Inspector Bastiampillai, and set up the Liberation Tigers of Tamil Eelam (LTTE). The President had proscribed them, but now he was holding out a palliative by offering in the constitution the status of a national language for Tamil. And though that status was not quite defined, he hoped perhaps that it would count as a step in the right direction and a sign of his resolve to tackle the 'Tamil question'.*

But the President reckoned without the racists in his government who kept up a constant barrage of anti-Tamil propaganda within parliament and without. Mathew, the Minister of Industries, made a dramatic 'exposure' in the House of the way Tamil examiners were cheating in the marking of A-level Tamil-medium papers to the detriment of Sinhala students. The charge was never investigated officially, (despite demands by the university teachers, both Sinhala and Tamil), but Mathew had found another platform – and a privileged one at that – to broadcast his poisonous views. And if that was not enough, he made use of the government press to publish and distribute free of charge a book of his accusations with a preface by a *bhikku* in Sinhala and English. De Alwis, the Minister of State, sang the praises of the priests who had set out once again from their *viharas* and their temples to save Buddhism from the marauding Tamils. 'But for the venerable monks', he pointed out, 'there would be no Sinhala race ... no Buddhism ... no culture known as the culture of Sri Lanka.'[26]

The government-controlled press picked up the racist themes and launched its own campaigns against the Tamils, highlighting racially inflammatory stories and giving different

---

* With the inauguration of the new constitution, the President raised Thondaman, the leader of the plantation workers and president of their biggest union, the CWC, to cabinet rank. Another (UNP) Tamil, Devanayagam, was already Minister of Justice!

versions of events in the different language papers. Anything that happened in the North, from bank robbery to common assault, was described as terrorism. There was no news of Jaffna except sensational news – no ordinary people there leading ordinary lives – and a culture was growing up in the South which viewed all Tamils, including the TULF!, as terrorists. And again, it was Mathew and his cohorts who, having helped orchestrate the definition, now provided the solution: 'Terrorists have to be killed because they are terrorists. They are like mad dogs and no better than that.'[27]

The government was setting itself up for an armed confrontation with the Tamil youth. And when, in July 1979, a Tamil police inspector was shot dead in Jaffna, the President clamped down a state of emergency in Jaffna District and sent in Sinhala troops, under Brigadier Weeratunga, with orders to wipe out terrorism within six months. The combined police and army operations, under emergency laws and then under an even more horrendous Prevention of Terrorism Act* (which combined the worst features of both the British and South African Acts), resulted in the mutilation and murder of three youths, the disappearance of three others,** the detention and torture of several people and the terrorisation of the whole population.[28]

At the end of the six months, the spectre of terrorism that Mathew and Co. had summoned up and the President had sent troops to 'wipe out' had been made flesh by the army – and provoked the counter-violence of the Tamil youth. From now on, it was war against the state and its occupying army. If the UF's economic policies had made the Tamils a separate people, the UNP's political tactics were making them a separate nation.

---

* The Minister of Justice, under whom the Act was passed, was Devenayagam, a Tamil.
** These were youths who were arrested by the police on 14 July (before Brigadier Weeratunga arrived in Jaffna). The bodies of two of them were found mutilated, one died later in hospital and the bodies of three others were never found.

It was a politics, however, that ran against the grain of an open economy which, of nature, lets a thousand capitalist flowers bloom. The top-level entrepreneurs (Sinhala and Tamil), as Newton Gunasinghe points out, could now unfold into their next phase of expansion and make it to the export markets through joint ventures with foreign capital.[29] But the middle entrepreneurs, who had thrived in the hothouse of state protection to produce their import-substitution goods, were pushed out into the cold by foreign imports. The effect of liberalising trade, however, and setting it free of government co-operatives was to give the middle-level Tamil entrepreneurs, who had not been cosseted by the state, an edge over their Sinhala counterparts.*

Jobs, too, were becoming less difficult for Tamils to get with the growth of trade and commerce, tourism and the service sector – areas in which proficiency in the Sinhala language was not particularly advantageous. For the poorer classes, both Sinhala and Tamil, migration to the oil-rich Middle East was opening up a veritable eldorado of instant riches and consumer culture.

But none of these developments went to the North and East. If it was indeed capitalism that was flourishing in the rest of the country, it was making no headway in the Tamil areas. The Tamil youth were still trapped in a racist educational system and denied economic mobility. Tamil land in the North, where it was not being state-settled by Sinhala colonists, was not going to be irrigated by the Mahaveli project either. The small market-gardener in Jaffna who produced cash crops like onions and chillies and potatoes was hit by the imports of these commodities from India and Pakistan. Tamil industry did not have government blessing or blandishment to inveigle foreign capital. The Trincomalee port in the East

---

* It was no accident, therefore, that Tamil businesses in Colombo were marked out for attack by the planners of the July 1983 pogroms (see various articles in *Race & Class*, vol. XXVI, no. 1, 1984).

might still gain some attention from imperial interests but, for that very reason, would remain an exclusive concern of the Sinhala state. Whatever tourist industry there was on the east coast – and the Tourist Board which gave out the licences was run by De Alwis – was in Sinhala hands. And even where the Mahaveli might still reach out to the predominantly Tamil district of Batticaloa, Sinhala colonists would be brought in to reap its benefits.

What underdeveloped capitalism could not develop, state racism had to contain. And when the resistance to that racism reached, of necessity, the proportions of armed struggle, the containment policies of the state would seek a military solution.

That, however, was not going to guarantee the political stability that Jayewardene had promised the IMF and World Bank. And now that he, deft wielder of carrot and stick that he thought he was, had done his stick bit by sending in the army 'to wipe out the menace of terrorism in six months', he would do the thing with the carrot by offering the Tamils a chance to run their own local affairs through the District Development Councils (DDCs).*

The TULF was prepared to go along with the President and participate in the elections to the DDCs in the North and East in June 1981, but the Tigers,** whose number and variety had grown through state repression, denounced them and the TULF. Since 1979, the war between the Sinhala state and the Tamil youth had escalated. Armed with guns they had taken from the enemy and moving about on bicycles through *olungais* (labyrinthine lanes) that ran into other *olungais*, losing the

---

* DDCs were introduced by the Jayewardene government as a form of local administration with central (ministerial) control.
** The Liberation Tigers of Tamil Eelam, who grew out of the Tamil New Tigers (TNT), were the first group to take up armed struggle. Other groups have sprung up since then but, whatever their temporary differences, they all are, as far as the Tamil people are concerned, their common liberators. And it is in that generic sense that the term is used here.

242

pursuing police or army and their cumbrous vehicles in the process,* they had become adept at bank raid and ambushes and, in March 1981, had pulled off a daring robbery of the state bank in Neervelli (Jaffna). The arrests, detentions and tortures that followed have been recorded elsewhere in *Race & Class* and by Amnesty International, but the effect of them was to turn the North into a cauldron of resistance.

Despite that, however, the President decided to go ahead with the elections to the DDCs. It was no longer a matter of 'concessions' but of will: he was determined to show the Tamils that not everyone wanted Eelam, even if he had to force them to vote. Accordingly, he put up UNP candidates and sent in a special contingent of police to supervise the elections – followed by ministers Mathew and Dissanayake. A (Tamil) UNP candidate was assassinated, a policeman killed and the police and the army went on the rampage – burning, looting and killing – burning down this time the Jaffna Library as well and its monumental collection of books and manuscripts. Unable to wipe out a people, they were driven to destroy their heritage.** The barbarians had arrived – under one guise or another.

The elections still went ahead, but not all the rigging and the tampering could yield up one UNP seat in the North. The TULF won them all. And the government brought in a motion of no confidence in the TULF leader – on the grounds that he had slandered Sri Lanka abroad – and slandered the Tamil people instead in the House and in the press, inciting violence against the Tamils in the South and East and, once

---

* The government was at one stage to propose the banning of bicycles in Jaffna.[30]
** 'In the entire catalogue of carnage, arson, pillage and murder', wrote Ian Goonetileke, the doyen of Sri Lankan librarians and bibliophiles, 'the complete destruction by an act of calculated and cold-blooded incendiarism of the splendid Jaffna Public Library is the most wounding to the sensibility of our brethren in the North, and must outrage the human feelings of every person in the land, whatever his political, racial or religious persuasion.'[31]

more, on the plantations. But this time, the attacks on the estate workers, carried out by private armies – in government buses – had all the hallmarks of politicians in high places. And so horrendous was the mayhem and the murder visited on these defenceless people that it even moved the President to cry out, 'what sort of animals are these?'[32] But a few months later, the army was moving into the estate workers' squatter settlements in Vavuniya, where they had been driven by previous pogroms, and taking away for questioning the Gandhiyam volunteers who had helped them resettle – on the pretext that they (the volunteers) were 'terrorists'.* Once again, the most abysmally poor and exploited section of the Tamil people had been chosen for a dry run for the planning of pogroms yet to come.

Jayewardene was caught up in the vortex of his own manipulations, an uncertain accomplice now of the forces he himself had unleashed. Neither the imperatives of a capitalist economy which required the dismantling of institutional racism nor the concentration of political power in one party and one man which made that dismantling possible had guided government policies. But then, the very forces that brought the government to power and gave it such a massive majority were also those that kept the government from according the Tamil people their basic rights. Those forces were now represented in the cabinet itself and given access to state power. The Minister of Industry and Scientific Affairs, the Minister of Lands and Mahaveli Development and the Minister of State were all self-avowed Sinhala supremacists, and the first two had a close working relationship with the Buddhist clergy who, like the Associated Newspapers of an earlier period, were now become king-makers.

The contradictions between the economics of capitalism and the politics of racism were thus epitomised within the

* Gandhiyam was a charity set up in 1976 by Tamils as a community and social service. It mainly helped settle plantation Tamil refugees who fled from the hill country in 1977 and 1981.

cabinet itself – and pointed the way to the authoritarian state. Already in the various confrontations that the government had had with the unions, the UNP's JSS had been used, either as an unofficial army of thugs or as an official government union, to beat up or counter-demonstrate against the striking workers. In July 1980, a general strike brought about by soaring inflation, rising food prices, welfare cuts and repressive trade union legislation, such as the Essential Services Act, had been crushed by the JSS at the cost of a worker's life and followed up by the government's sacking of some 80,000 workers. Protests and demonstrations by university students had been settled with summary violence and the same goon squads had disrupted public meetings that had anything to say against the government.

Now, with the economy in a mess and the aid-givers worried about 'political stability', the government decided to kowtow to the IMF further. The FTZ had not been a success: Sri Lanka had clearly come in at the fag-end of the multina-tionals' 'putting-out' system in the microelectronics and garment industries.* Joint venture investments outside the FTZ had served more to open up the domestic market for foreign investors than the foreign market for domestic entre-preneurs. The Mahaveli project was becoming increasingly costly and the funds for its various sub-projects not readily available. But it still held out the one real attraction – for agribusiness. The Minister of Lands had made no bones about it when he announced in March 1981 the government's intention 'to ask for all forms of agricultural and agro-based industrial investment', and pointed to Guthries' proposed lease of 28,000 acres for palm oil production.** This would,

---

* Technologies in both these fields had advanced so much and so fast that it was becoming more profitable to bring them back home or use the already well-tried assembly lines abroad. The main attraction that Sri Lanka's FTZ offered was its export quota in the garment industry – to those countries like Hong Kong, Korea and Singapore which had used up their export quotas.
** Whether this particular project came off in the end is uncertain, but others are certainly in the pipeline.

however, take the government away from its stated plans for immediate self-sufficiency in food and add to the disgruntlement of the peasantry. There was also the possibility of leasing out Trincomalee as a naval base to the USA – and the Reagan administration was certainly keen to firm up its hold in the Indian Ocean – but this again has not found favour with the public.

Clearly what was required for economic advancement and the political stability it called for was stronger and longer government. And since the President's stock, the President felt, was higher in the country than his government's, he brought forward the elections to the Presidency to October 1982 by amending the constitution, and won – thanks to the self-annihilating policies of the opposition (from the SLFP to the LSSP and JVP!) who all put up candidates.

The prolongation of parliament was another matter, but there was always the four-fifths majority in the House to amend the constitution yet again and bring in a referendum in lieu of elections to justify the government staying in power. It was essentially a vote asking the voters to give up their right to vote. But this time it was not so much the internecine politics of the opposition that gave the government a victory, but its use of intimidation, impersonation, forgeries, theft (of ballot boxes), assault and every known violation of electoral practice and principle (and some purely Sri Lankan). It was a method of electioneering that had been perfected and legitimated in the Tamil North – but had passed the Sinhala voters by.

Political violence had become an accepted method of government and a culture of violence had now settled on the land. And with it, hand in hand, went a culture of open economy consumerism, Middle East bonanzas and tourist titillations, of greed and selfishness and dog-eat-dog relationships – all of which were paraded and perpetuated by an arse-licking government press. There was no public debate or discussion which did not break into altercation or fisticuffs, no protest or demonstration which was not set upon by hooligans and thugs. Women were not beyond assault, whether they were workers in the garment industries at Ekala or ex-MPs leading a march of women on International Women's Day. And it did not matter that they might be elderly: that respect for the old, which Sri Lankan culture once boasted, was gone. Instead, policemen who carried out such violence were rewarded with promotion and judges who found against them intimidated by goons brought in on government buses to flaunt their thuggery before their justices' homes.

Eminent scholars who voiced their opinions of dissent in public were set upon and beaten – while piddly little sociologists who descended into the lurid investigation of sexual manners or historians who cobbled together books from other people's books or researchers in institutions that produced great tomes of meaningless abstraction which left them safe continued to make it into the upper echelons of academia. The universities themselves had ceased to be places of learning and become the seed-beds of reactionary excellence – and provided the climate for the racial violence that erupted in the Peradeniya University in May 1983, when Sinhala students assaulted and chased Tamil students out of the campus, or a few weeks later in the Colombo Medical Hostel, when Tamil students were again harassed and beaten up.*

Real learning was scorned and learned men, doyens of Buddhist education who once upheld the great Buddhist heritage of scholarship and truth, had fallen prey to government propaganda and preferments.

And Buddhism itself had ceased to be the great philosophy of *ahimsa* and become the tool of a venal clergy in search of secular power. The influence they once had over the minds and mores of people through their own self-abnegating and disciplined conduct of life, gentle and humane, guiding by precept and example, had in the course of three decades of

* For the substantiation of all these, see the courageous reports in the *Saturday Review, Lanka Guardian* and Civil Rights Movement documents.

virulent nationalism been exchanged for financial and political influence – till they were no more than fascist thugs in saffron robes recruiting private armies for primitive politicians, settling Sinhala settlers on Tamil land, pushing the Trojan horse of Buddhist shrines into the North and East, deciding government policy even before it is made – not king-makers any more but kings.

If the police and the army ran the North and the East, the *bhikkus* and the thugs provided law and order in the South.

The pogroms that followed in July and August 1983,[33] heralded by countless acts of brutality, torture and murder in Jaffna and Vavuniya and Trincomalee and culminating in the merciless state-sponsored killing of helpless Tamils in jail, had for their context and their climate the policies of an authoritarian state, the spurious culture of imported capitalism, the degeneracy of the Sinhala intelligentsia and the decadence of Sinhala Buddhist society – all of them the product, one way or another, of soured nationalism married to imperial capital, leading to dictatorship. But then, it is a pattern, with variations, that has been set in country after Third World country wherever the IMF and World Bank have set foot.

Against that mounting dictatorship stands only the armed resistance of the Tamil freedom-fighters – and whatever the goal in view, their immediate and inevitable task is to continue their unrelenting war against the fascist state, providing in the process the opportunity for the Sinhala people to mount their own resistance to the racism that corrodes their society and the fascism that thrives on it. Tamil liberation is the easier won through the weakening of the Sinhala state from within, socialism the surer achieved through struggles not narrowly nationalist. There is no socialism after liberation; socialism is the process through which liberation is won.

References

1. Michael Banks, 'Caste in Jaffna' in E.R. Leach (ed.), *Aspects of caste in South India, Ceylon and North West Pakistan* (Cambridge, 1969).

2. E.F.C. Ludowyk, *The modern history of Ceylon* (London, 1966).

3. See Kumari Jayawardena, 'Class formation and communalism', *Race & Class*, vol. XXVI, no. 1 (1984).

4. Kumari Jayawardena, *The rise of the labour movement in Ceylon* (Durham, NC, 1972).

5. Ibid.

6. Kumari Jayawardena, 'The origins of the left movement in Sri Lanka', *Modern Ceylon Studies*, vol. 2, no. 2 (July 1971).

7. J. Russell, *Communal politics under the Donoughmore Constitution 1931–1947* (Dehiwala, Sri Lanka, 1982).

8. G.J. Lerski, *Origins of Trotskyism in Ceylon* (Stanford, CA, 1968).

9. E.F.C. Ludowyk, *Modern history*.

10. Ibid.

11. Tarzie Vittachi, *Emergency '58* (London, 1958).

12. Ibid.

13. Ibid.

14. For an acute, but in hindsight optimistic, analysis of the JVP insurrection, see Fred Halliday, 'The Ceylonese insurrection', *New Left Review*, no. 69 (September–October 1971).

15. C.R. De Silva, 'Weightage in university admissions: standardisation and district quotas in Sri Lanka (Ceylon)', University of Ceylon, Ceylon Studies seminar 1875 series no. 2 (March 1975).

16. S. Ponnambalam, *Sri Lanka: The Tamil liberation struggle*, (London, 1983).

17. Council for Communal Harmony Through the Media, 'How schoolbooks foster communalism' (Colombo).

18. G.A. Gnanamuttu, *Education and the Indian plantation worker in Sri Lanka* (Colombo, 1977).

19. N. Gunasinghe, 'The open economy and its impact on ethnic relations in Sri Lanka', *Lanka Guardian*, vol. 6, no. 17 (1 January 1984); vol. 6, no. 18 (15 January 1984); vol. 6, no. 19 (1 February 1984).

20. See various essays in A. Sivanandan, *A different hunger: writings on black resistance* (London, 1982).

21. Bipan Chandra, 'Historians of modern India and communalism' in Romila Thapar, Harbans Mukhia and Bipan Chandra, *Communalism and the writing of Indian history* (New Delhi, 1969).

22. UNP Manifesto, 1977.

23. A. Sivanandan, 'Report from Sri Lanka, August 1977', *Race & Class*, vol. 19, no. 2 (Autumn 1977).

24. Cited in the *Report of an Amnesty International mission to Sri Lanka, 1982* (London, 1983).

25. For its increasingly racist line, see D.J., 'J.V.P takes "Masala Vadai" line, rejects devolution', *Lanka Guardian*, vol. 7, no. 3 (1 June 1984).

26. *Parliamentary Debates*, vol. 3 (2) no. 6, cols 1237–38.

27. *Parliamentary Debates*, 3 (2) no. 6, col. 1494.

28. For details, see Nancy Murray, 'The state against the Tamils' in 'Sri Lanka: racism and the authoritarian state', special issue of *Race & Class*, vol. 31, no. 4 (Summer 1984); MIRJE, *Emergency '79* (Kandy, 1980); *Report of an Amnesty International mission, 1982.*

29. N. Gunasinghe, 'The open economy'.

30. *Saturday Review* (25 June 1983).

31. See 'Sri Lanka: racism and the authoritarian state'.

32. In a letter to Father Paul Caspersz, President of MIRJE, in *Days of terror* (Colombo, 1981).

33. See 'Sri Lanka: racism and the authoritarian state', for details and analysis.